REVOLUTIONARY TURNS

Revolutionary *T U R N S*

Religion and America's Founding Era

★

Edited by Katherine Carté

University of Virginia Press
Charlottesville and London

The University of Virginia Press is situated on the traditional lands of the Monacan Nation, and the Commonwealth of Virginia was and is home to many other Indigenous people. We pay our respect to all of them, past and present. We also honor the enslaved African and African American people who built the University of Virginia, and we recognize their descendants. We commit to fostering voices from these communities through our publications and to deepening our collective understanding of their histories and contributions.

University of Virginia Press

Printed in the United States of America on acid-free paper

First published 2026

1 3 5 7 9 8 6 4 2

ISBN 978-0-8139-5558-2 (hardback)
ISBN 978-0-8139-5559-9 (paperback)
ISBN 978-0-8139-5560-5 (ebook)

Library of Congress Cataloging-in-Publication Data is available for this title.

Cover art: Christ Church, Philadelphia, engraved by J. P. Malcolm, 1814.
(Library of Congress Prints and Photographs Division,
Washington, DC, LC-DIG-pga-11623)
Cover design: Lindsay Starr

For Jon Butler, Mark Noll, and Amanda Porterfield
From whom we have learned so much

CONTENTS

Acknowledgments ix

Introduction: A Historiographical Reassessment of Religion and the American Revolution 1

Religious Ritual and Public Polarization in the American Revolution 33
SPENCER W. MCBRIDE

Thomas Barton's Crisis of Conscience: Community, Salvation, and Oaths of Allegiance on the Pennsylvania Frontier 48
PETER W. WALKER

"Singing Psalms, We Went in Amongst Them": Native Christianity, Relationships, and Continuity Across the Revolutionary War Period 67
JESSICA LAUREN NELSON

"No Rabbi in All of America": How the Revolution Remade the Synagogue 88
ADAM JORTNER

Disrupting Religion: Universalist Print Networks and the American Revolution 109
MICHAEL BAYSA

"Just Rights and Equal Laws": Disestablishment and the Memory of the Revolution 131
ALYSSA PENICK

"That Liberty, Wherewith God Has So Strangely Made Them Free": Methodist Expansion and Division in the Revolutionary Atlantic World 151
CHRISTOPHER CANNON JONES

The Rise and Fall of Evangelical Abolition in the Age of Revolution 173
Peter Y. Choi

"Every House a Church and State": Piety, Authority, and the Problem of Family Governance in the Early Republic 199
Shelby M. Balik

The Religious Appropriation of Revolutionary Rhetoric in the Early Republic 219
Seth Perry

List of Contributors 239

Index 243

ACKNOWLEDGMENTS

This volume is the result of the Sons of the American Revolution's ongoing commitment to encouraging strong and independent scholarship on the American Revolution and the origins of the United States. I would like to thank that organization and especially the indefatigable Joe Dooley for their support, both moral and financial. The SAR's efforts have become a cornerstone of new scholarship for historians of the Founding Era.

The 2021 SAR Annual Conference on the American Revolution was made possible by the generous support of the following: the Mount Vernon Ladies' Association; the George Washington Endowment Fund of the National Society of the SAR; the George Knight—Kenneth C. Patty Memorial Trust Fund of the Virginia Society of the SAR; the California Society SAR Ladies Auxiliary; the Missouri Society SAR Auxiliary; Powell Enterprises; the WinSet Group LLC; Warren and Nancy Alter; Abraham R. Byrd III, MD; Rt. Rev. and Mrs. Louis V. Carlson Jr.; Ernest B. Coggins Jr.; Col. Peter M. Davenport, US Army (ret.); James and Un Hui Yi Fosdyck; Mr. and Mrs. John H. Franklin Jr.; Joseph R. Godfrey, PhD; M. Kent and Lisa S. Gregory; Mr. and Mrs. Philip L. Hinshaw; James T. and Dianne D. Jones; the Kircher family; Tyler Parliman; Lanny and Ann Patten; Samuel C. Powell, PhD; Brian and Diane Stephens; Larry and Barbara Stevens; Col. Ernest L. Sutton, MD, US Army (ret.); Edward W. Ward; Timothy E. Ward; Davis Lee Wright; and, the George Mason Chapter and the George Washington Chapter, both of the Virginia Society SAR. Thanks are also due to the History Department and the Center for Presidential History at Southern Methodist University for help with publishing and indexing costs.

Sincere thanks are due to this volume's contributors for their thoughtful efforts and their deep engagement both with one another and with this volume. They made the discussions we shared in Providence, Rhode Island, in June 2021 a true joy. John Fea provided a stimulating and generative lecture to frame our discussions. Thanks are also owed to three wonderful (then) graduate students from Southern Methodist University's history PhD program, Camille Davis, Ashton Reynolds, and Christopher Walton. My ever-patient writing group, Mary Kupiek Cayton,

Elesha Coffman, Nicole Kirk, Jennifer Wiley Legath, Rachel Linsdey, Tisa Wenger, and Rachel Wheeler, offered numerous and generous readings of the volume's introduction over multiple iterations. I am grateful for the care and attention taken by the anonymous readers selected by the University of Virginia Press. They made the project much stronger. Nadine Zimmerli is an extraordinary editor; it is a privilege to work with her. Finally, I would like to thank my family, Jeffrey, Marshall, and Elaine Engel, each of whom sustains me in their own way.

INTRODUCTION

A Historiographical Reassessment of Religion and the American Revolution

★

RELIGION AND the American Revolution is a topic with a lot of baggage. Public audiences have deep investments, and so too do scholars of the period. Is the United States a Christian nation, a nation "founded on" religious freedom, or both, or neither? For many citizens, the "proper" answers to such questions ought to dictate matters of policy, not to mention school curricula. If the "founders" believed religion was important, it ought to remain important in the republic they shaped. Conversely, if freedom of religion—or even a wall of separation between church and state—is a primary "lesson" of the founding era, then it should guide contemporary civic life. In other words, historical interpretation undergirds attitudes on public policy.

For these reasons, questions about religion and the American Revolution persistently remain in the public eye when the topic of religion is under examination. For example, in October 2022 a Pew Research study found that 45 percent of American adults believed the United States should be a Christian nation; 51 percent did not think so. Asked whether the United States "is now" a Christian nation, 64 percent said no, while 33 percent replied in the affirmative. Finally, 60 percent thought the "founders of America originally intended for the U.S. to be a 'Christian nation.'" The more detailed breakdown of these answers by Pew unsurprisingly suggests wide variation by religious group, age, and political affiliation, but those differences of opinion should not obscure the researchers' basic assumption, that the place of religion in American life is intrinsically linked to a historical starting point in the era of the Revolution.[1]

The Pew study's sequential questions about what the nation's "founders" *intended*, what the present is, and what its ideal "should" be are important. In the first question, the imprecise term *founders* invokes national political leaders from the final decades of the eighteenth century, as well as the rebelling, fighting, and state-building they undertook. The survey's question presumes that with regard to issues of religion George Washington, John Adams, Thomas Jefferson, Benjamin Franklin, James Madison, and their fellow revolutionaries set the country's trajectory. With that image in mind, respondents then decided whether their present matched that past image and what the nation's relationship to Christianity "should" be (or become). The survey was, in other words, a referendum on whether the country's history with regard to religion had moved toward or away from an imagined origin point, as well as whether that trajectory was desirable. While it is important to note that the Pew study's authors found little consensus on what the term *Christian nation* connoted (a major concern of historical scholars), for the public at large discussions about religion in the nation's founding era appear inextricably linked to political worries about the present and future of the nation.

The political weight created by such anxieties both informs and creates problems for historians writing about the founding period. Historians cry foul at what they see as reductionism or as ahistorical formulations, insisting that the past was complicated, contingent, and messy. For academics, the Revolutionary era remains pivotal but nonetheless subject to banal realities: it grew directly out of the era that preceded it, nobody agreed on everything, powerful people wielded force in distinct and identifiable ways, both winners and losers mattered. Unfortunately, however, the answers generated by this sort of historical investigation are rarely soothing to those who are concerned about the place of religion in the founding period because they believe that it set the stage for the present.

At its best, historical writing bridges the gap between public conversations and scholarly preoccupations by answering current questions through an informed look at the past. The essays contained in this volume strive to meet this standard, but not by attempting to directly define the religious nature of the American Revolution or the nation that emerged from it by asking the kinds of questions raised in the Pew study. Instead, they ask questions about the many different roles religion played in the colonial state, about the role of political events in religious life, about the experiences of minority religious groups in an environment dominated by white Protestants, and about how Americans used their faiths to interpret the challenges and transformations of a difficult period in our history. All these questions remain a part of American civic life in one form or another, but each has *many* answers rather than a single one, dependent on the context in which it is asked. The contributors to this volume collectively argue that religion was an essential aspect of life in the Revolutionary era, but their findings suggest that its consequences and lessons cannot be reduced to simple answers to Pew's question "Do you think the founders of America originally intended the U.S. to be a Christian nation?"

As they tell a complex tale, the essays in this volume nonetheless agree on some key points. Most importantly, they agree that religion was not a driving cause of the American Revolution. In his pivotal 1990 survey of American religion before the Civil War, *Awash in a Sea of Faith*, Jon Butler wrote that "at its heart, the Revolution was a profoundly secular event."[2] He then elaborated and clarified: "The causes that brought [the Revolution] into being and the ideologies that shaped it placed religious concerns more at its margins than at its center."[3] More than thirty years later, the authors included in this volume still agree with Butler. The reasons why Americans joined together to resist parliamentary and then royal authority, first through political means (including civil disobedience) and then through military force, were not principally religious. Moreover, the central chain of events—from the Stamp Act to the Tea Party, Lexington and Concord through the Declaration of Independence, the grueling years of war, the failure of the Articles of Confederation, and the formation of the US Constitution—is best explained through political, military, and economic lenses.

Seeing the Revolution as secular in this way should not be taken to minimize the importance of religion (in its many forms) to the era of the American Revolution, however, or its importance to the people who lived through it. It should also not be taken as an a priori verdict on the question whether or how the United States was founded as a Christian nation or as a simple negation of religion's role in the past. Quite the opposite. The essays collected here find that religion functioned in pivotal ways to shape the experiences of Americans during the Revolutionary era, not least as a tool of statecraft wielded by those with influence. Americans—of many faiths and backgrounds—drew on religion to form the post-Revolutionary world and to understand that world. The legal transitions in religious establishment that occurred during the late eighteenth century were significant and grew out of the traumas of the war. The American Revolution was not a religious event, but the Revolution had significant consequences for religious lives.

Before turning to the specific contributions of the essays that follow, it is useful to delve a bit more deeply into where the anxiety around the subject of religion and the American Revolution originated and how Protestant piety became a metric for gauging the nation's political health. A good place to start is with Jedidiah Morse—a prominent geographer, historian, and minister of the early republic—and his role in the Bavarian Illuminati panic of the 1790s.[4] The Illuminati were a dreaded but largely fictional group of powerful European atheists who Morse, his fellow New England minister Timothy Dwight, and some in the early republic's Federalist Party feared were conspiring to undermine Christian institutions, as evidenced both by the dangerous turn of the French Revolution and also by a perceived decline in respect for traditional clerical authority in the United States. On a 1799 fast day called by President John Adams because of the Illuminati threat, Morse preached that the nation's "dangers are of two kinds, those which affect our religion, and those which affect our government." The two were, he explained, "so closely allied that they cannot, with propriety, be separated." In these words, he crystalized a powerful formulation for many concerned with the fate of the United States: was its "religion" safe enough to protect its freedoms and its existence as an independent nation?[5]

The Illuminati panic gave Morse and his peers the space to articulate fears that had been growing over the preceding decade, fears that the United States, precluded by its Constitution from establishing a national church, would fail to maintain the characteristics necessary for a virtuous citizenry. In 1798, President Adams wrote to a group of Massachusetts militia officers that he was worried about what might happen if the citizens of the United States were swept away by the political fervor and antipathies that characterized the French Revolution. "We have no Government armed with Power capable of contending with human Passions unbridled by morality and Religion," he mused. The "[US] Constitution was made only for a moral and religious People. It is wholly inadequate to the government of any other."[6] Two years earlier, in his Farewell Address, President George Washington had voiced similar trepidations: "Let us with caution indulge the supposition that morality can be maintained without religion. Whatever may be conceded to the influence of refined education on minds of peculiar structure, reason and experience both forbid us to expect that national morality can prevail in exclusion of religious principle."[7] Morse made the point even more explicit in his 1799 sermon: "Whenever the pillars of Christianity shall be overthrown, our present republican forms of government, and all the blessings which flow from them, must fall with them."[8] Morse and his fellow Federalist leaders feared that without *enough* religion, the country could not "keep" its republic, to use Benjamin Franklin's famous turn of phrase.[9]

In the early American republic, fears about the religious health of the United States—about there being enough religion—were widespread among its Federalist elites, and they were directly linked to fears of irreligion and skepticism.[10] Morse was a leader among those who attempted to organize an effective response. He worked tirelessly with his peers to build what the historian David Sehat has called the "moral establishment," a dense network of overlapping voluntary associations, public-private partnerships, and legislative initiatives that "upheld the moral ideals of Christianity in the name of the public good."[11] He was also a historian, and he participated in the rapid expansion of the early republic's "history culture."[12] He joined groups like the American Antiquarian Society and the Massachusetts Historical Society, and he wrote histories of America and of the Revolution geared to students.

In 1815, Morse wrote John Adams asking the esteemed former president for his memories of the founding era. The first response he received began with a recital of the many histories that were then already being written, followed by the assertion that "an History of military Operations from April 19th. 1775 to the 3d of September 1783 is not an History of the American Revolution." Instead, Adams offered Morse what may be perhaps the most famous single line summary of the conflict: "The Revolution was in the Minds and Hearts of the People, and in the Union of the Colonies, both of which were Substantially effected before Hostilities commenced."[13]

Morse was not satisfied with Adams's answer, although he would ultimately reprint it in his 1824 *Annals of the American Revolution; or, A record of the causes and events which produced, and terminated in the establishment and independence of the American Republic.*[14] Nine years earlier, however, when he first received Adams's letter, Morse wrote back to the former president explaining that the number of works on the Revolution did not daunt him, as he planned to write a "history of the interpositions of divine Providence in behalf of our country," with a "more *religious* cast than other histories."[15] In response to this second missive, Adams produced a new narrative of the origins of the American Revolution, one that combined the rise of religious diversity in the United States with an eye backward to a supposed English religious tyranny. "At this day," Adams wrote, "when we see Methodistical Bishops, Bishops of the Church of England, & Bishops, Archbishops, & Jesuits of the Church of Rome, with indifference;" he could not but wonder who would "beleive [*sic*], that the apprehension of Episcopacy, contributed 50 years ago, as much as any other cause, to arouse the attention, not only of the enquiring mind but of the common people? And urge them to close thinking on the Constitutional Authority of Parliament over the Colonies? This nevertheless, was a fact, as certain as any in the history of North America."[16] Morse printed this statement ascribing religious origins to the colonies' rift with Parliament in his 1824 history. It provided a providential cast to the writing, and it made concrete and authoritative Morse's effort to integrate the religiosity of Americans with their Revolution.

It is important not to overstate Morse's individual significance for the creation of the history (and mythology) of the American Revolution's religious story. He was one of many people, often rooted in New England and within the more traditional denominations of Congregationalism and Presbyterianism, who sought to build the young United States as a Christian republic through writing, voluntary societies, and political action. Although they represented only one strand of American religious life, their efforts were broadly consequential. The institutions and publications of the early republic's moral establishment imbued the United States' Protestant citizenry with a sense of their own providential importance. Yet that confident and culturally powerful posture contained within it a rigid tension born of the lasting fear that if the nation became less religious—less moral—the very project of the republic would fail.

In the centuries since, Americans have gradually expanded their conception of who counts as a moral American citizen, but they have retained a sense that those who "founded" the nation were unified in their Protestant Christianity. That opinion still echoes in one of American civil religion's most famous quips, President-elect Dwight D. Eisenhower's 1952 statement that "our form of Government has no sense unless it is founded in a deeply felt religious faith, and I don't care what it is." Eisenhower then added, "With us of course it is the Judeo-Christian concept, but it must be a religion that [*sic*] all men are created equal." Smoothly bringing together the ideas of shared religion and the national founding, Eisenhower reassured his listeners by gesturing to religion's place in unifying and building the United States, in a manner not so very different from the task Morse set for Adams in 1815.[17]

THESE POLITICAL versions of religion and the American Revolution, espoused more than a century apart by Morse and Eisenhower, relied on the idea that religion was central to the American Revolution and the project of the United States. Much academic work on the subject has reinforced that premise. In the 1840s, Robert Baird penned a widely influential history of American religion. A Protestant clergyman and activist both in the United States and in Europe, he believed his native land had a special place among the nations. Subtitled "An Account of the Origin, Progress, Relation to the State, and Present Condition of the Evangelical Churches in the United States," Baird's history posited that the country had a united Protestant past and spirit. Perhaps surprising to modern audiences, Baird described the colonial period as one of long religious decline (except for the Great Awakening), but he maintained faith in the special providence that guided Americans. He wrote that despite the "period of 168 years" in which colonial religion had experienced "decline, and even deadness," he felt "very certain that a minute examination of the history of the American Protestant churches would show" that the American religious spirit exceeded that of any other place. Indeed, God "did not abandon us forever," and despite chastisement, he "remembered the covenant which he made with our fathers." Baird thus had a negative view of the progress of religion in America but a positive view of the essential relationship between the American people and divine power.[18]

A similar dichotomy between worldly events (what Butler would later call "secular") and a providential narrative for Americans continued in Baird's discussion of the Revolution. He stressed that the era had been "unfavorable" for religion and that "effects of war on the churches of all communions were extensively and variously disastrous." To this he added, "To say nothing of the distraction of the mind from the subject of salvation, [the war's] more palpable influences were seen and felt everywhere."[19] But if churches struggled, Americans were united, according to Baird. He noted the number of clergymen who served as patriot chaplains, and he quoted a Revolutionary clergyman to argue that the "whole population, from New-England to Georgia, is of one mind, and determined to risk life and all things in defence of liberty. The few who think differently are not permitted to utter their sentiment."[20] In a time of turmoil American unity was paramount.

From the war, Baird turned to disestablishment and the separation of church and state. He stressed the significance of legal disestablishment for the churches. In this, as in the rest of his text, he balanced careful historical detail with a strong sense of the importance of Protestant Christianity to the government and the union. Indeed, his tone conveys the same need for a Protestant citizenry to support the republic that Morse, Adams, and Washington had expressed a half century earlier. Baird quoted Justice Joseph Story to make his point: "It yet remains a problem to be solved in human affairs, whether any free government can be permanent where the public worship of God, and the support of religion, constitute no part of the policy or duty of the State in any assignable shape."[21] Baird chronicled the historical reality of disestablishment, but like his predecessors, he measured his anxiety about the nation's survival against what he perceived as its unified, Protestant religiosity.

Baird's central concern was the history of American churches, not the history of the United States or the American Revolution, but his work remains important to this discussion because the historiography—of religion and the American Revolution—sits at the meeting point between the two. Insofar as historians of religion have tended to dominate the study of that subject, their intellectual habits, conflating "religion" with Protestant churches, for example, have tended to dominate the field, even as the providentialism of writers like Morse and Baird has been replaced by academic professionalism.

The issues Baird raised—colonial religiosity, American unity, and disestablishment as a key part of the Revolution—have remained key subjects in the study of religion and the American Revolution. Much time, for example, has been spent asking whether (or how much) "Patriots" relied on their religious beliefs when they chose to rebel, or in what ways religion inflected the "liberty" Baird said they shared, or the religious freedom they legally enshrined later. If religion was crucial in those moments, was Protestantism somehow intrinsic to the national project? In the second half of the twentieth century, a heyday for scholarship on the topic and an era in which public Christianity experienced a resurgence, many of the most well known scholars of religion and the American Revolution answered these questions in the affirmative, even if in a qualified way. This fact in no small measure accounts for the ongoing belief among public audiences that religion *mattered* in the nation's founding.

While some Cold War scholars, including Edmund Morgan, offered readers fairly neat connections between seventeenth-century Puritans and the Revolution, the most prominent arguments for religion's importance to the Revolution depended on the Protestant revivals of the mid-eighteenth century.[22] These arguments usually did not engage the events of the Revolution directly but rather used the Great Awakening to argue for an American population that was resistant to hierarchical authority and willing to act on ideological grounds because it was more than usually committed to ideas. For example, Alan Heimert's 1966 tome, *Religion and the American Mind,* asserted that the Great Awakening of the 1730s and 1740s brought Americans together to unite against the threat of tyranny. Although his methods drew fire, Heimert's essential insights were refined and redeployed by subsequent scholars, including Patricia Bonomi, Rhys Isaac, and Harry Stout. Their work reinforced the importance of the midcentury revivals to the narrative of the Revolution, if ambiguously so in terms of direct causality.[23]

Even historians of the Revolution who did not usually focus on religion pondered these questions. In 1983 John Murrin wondered if the Revolution could have been won, or would have happened at all, without the Great Awakening. He posited that "possibly" evangelicals "provide[d] the resiliency and stamina to endure a struggle that the less righteous would have abandoned."[24] A sense of the Great Awakening as an essential precursor to the Revolution persisted. As Thomas Kidd wrote in his 2010 survey of religion and the Revolution, the "legacy of revivalism was one element of the religious zeal furthering the controversy with Britain."[25]

A second strand of historiography linking religion to Americans' reasons for resisting the British Parliament wove John Adams's insight about episcopal controversy into the intellectual origins of the American Revolution. Carl Bridenbaugh's *Mitre and Sceptre,* published in 1962, explored colonial panic over the potential creation of an Anglican bishop and its role in galvanizing anti-Parliament sentiment.[26] Five years later, Bernard Bailyn furthered observed of anti-ecclesiastical movements in Virginia that "anti-establishment sentiment and constitutional arguments against Parliamentary power were intimately mingled from the very earliest pre-Revolutionary years." For Bailyn, the revolutionary energy religious issues brought had its real payoff in disestablishment, but along the way vigorous campaigns for greater religious freedom, often mounted by minority religious groups within the colonies, built powerful sentiment behind the Revolutionary cause.[27] In the decades after Bailyn's influential publication, historians of religion, most notably Nathan Hatch and Ruth Bloch, helped buttress the argument that theological beliefs, particularly in the form of millennialism, had tended to push Americans toward revolution. Similarly, historians of political thought emphasized the differences between American Revolutionary thought, which they linked to British dissenting traditions, and American loyalism, which they tied closely to a conservative, hierarchical Anglicanism.[28]

The topic of religion and the American Revolution, in these ideologically framed forms, took on particular prominence in the wider historiography of the American Revolution during the 1980s and 1990s. This shift was part of a field-wide turn toward investigating the political ideology of the 1760s and 1770s as a proxy for much of the Revolutionary conflict. When the colonists had enough political unity to agree to military resistance to Britain, this line of argument suggested, the major work of the Revolution was done. Insofar as it is easy to subsume theology into ideology, religious topics had a direct claim to significance in this paradigm. Such arguments drew much of their force from the premise that average colonists paid attention to religious matters even when they did not read political pamphlets or attend demonstrations. As Gordon Wood asserted in 1997, "Despite the growth of Enlightenment among elites in eighteenth-century America, Protestantism in one form or another still remained the principal means by which most common people ordered and explained the world and made it meaningful."[29] In other words, religion provided historians a solution for the problem of how elite ideas might have influenced the masses. The ubiquitous sermon served as unifying patriotic glue. Although scholars like Wood, and Murrin a decade earlier, carefully observed how problematic direct links between religion and revolution were to prove, they nonetheless gave readers a comfortable sense that normative Protestantism did essential national work. Perhaps it was not so very far from Baird's formulation after all.

The idea of a religiously unified American population always had its critics, of course. Even a cursory read of religious sources from the 1760s and 1770s finds schism and conflict in religious communities. Even for historians like Bailyn and Bonomi, politico-religious unity derived, counterintuitively, from collective experience with religious conflict. Their arguments thus require the reader to see religious communities as both the source and the resolution of division. Arguably the most lasting study to follow this line of argument, Rhys Isaac's 1982 Pulitzer Prize–winning *Transformation of Virginia,* put this dilemma at its center. Isaac deftly situated religious conflict in the late colonial religion as a cause of the social changes necessary for revolution, but he also left it as merely adjacent to the Revolution's main events. He then brought religious revolution and political revolution back together to explain Virginia's disestablishment process. As Isaac wrote, "The social implications of the two revolutionary processes ["the gentry-led patriot movement" and the "evangelical movement"] and the transformations of community ethos that, in combination, they worked, became clear in a struggle that ensued over the terms of a religious settlement."[30] Unity between religious factions, then, was not necessary before or during the revolution against Britain; rather it mattered at its end, when wide swaths of previously contending Americans would join together to support disestablishment. Disestablishment, rather than political independence or nation building, provided the Revolution's climax. A shared faith in religious freedom, rather than Jedidiah Morse's piety, became the guiding spirit of liberty in the United States, according to Isaac.

The dismantling of religious establishments is easier to demonstrate than the role of religion in the coming of the Revolution. The former definitely happened; the latter is at most a proposed influence on a wider event. Indeed, like Isaac's work, surveys of religion and the Revolution generally conclude (and sometimes culminate) with disestablishment in one form or another. Much of that scholarship has focused on Virginia because of its prominent struggle over the meaning and limits of religious liberty in the 1780s and because the "founding fathers" Thomas Jefferson and James Madison were involved.[31] Less triumphantly, another line of work follows New England, where establishments lasted much longer. Historians have emphasized the political and social challenges faced by clergy there, in some ways completing the narrative of long, slow declension that Perry Miller outlined for Puritan New England.[32] For historians of religion in the early national period, disestablishment and its consequences then set the stage for new stories. Morse's anxieties intertwined with the "upstart" energies of "frontier" Methodist and Baptist preachers to produce a new, post-Revolutionary religious culture. Although few academics would agree with Robert Baird that the United States' Protestant culture was part of a divine covenant, those writing about the early republic nonetheless enjoy the benefits of a religious bull market when staking the claims of their subject's importance.[33]

In the last years of the twentieth century, public audiences and scholars alike followed Isaac's embrace of a malleable role for religion in the

Revolutionary era. It acted as an essential if nonspecific influence on anti-authoritarian (and thus anti-British) sentiment before the war (via the Great Awakening), and, more concretely, as an inspiration for an almost providential disestablishment in the Revolution's aftermath. The dominance of this interpretation, importantly, left plenty of space for Butler's version of a "secular" Revolution, as the key political events of the 1770s and early 1780s were simply sidestepped. Historians of American religion found plenty of topics in other eras, and new contributions to the field of religion and the Revolution came primarily from the recognition that groups beyond white Protestant males had received far too little attention.

In 1994, Ronald Hoffman and Peter Albert published an edited collection on the subject (the last such effort prior to the current one) titled *Religion in a Revolutionary Age*. Its distinguished list of authors revisited the role of colonial religious life (including the Great Awakening) in setting the stage for the Revolution; updated the field with studies of women, Americans, working-class Philadelphians, and Southern evangelicals; and delved into questions of religion and political culture. These latter essays skewed towards questions of constitution writing and the religious politics of the early republic.[34] By the beginning of the twenty-first century, arguments that religion was important to the American Revolution—precisely the argument that public audiences often seek—focused largely on the limited moments of the Great Awakening, the Bishop Controversy, and the path to disestablishment. In short, most of the tumultuous events that created the United States seemed to fade in importance from the study of religion and the Revolution.

This narrative hollowing out of the American Revolution reached beyond the study of religion. Around the turn of the twenty-first century, the place of the American nation in early American historiography shifted as historians grappled with the changing nature of political power in a post-9/11, multipolar world.[35] Deep research into the connections sustained by colonists across the Atlantic and across the American continent in the early modern era convinced historians that colonists became more invested in being British the closer they came to the Revolution, and studies of the prewar period, previously assumed to have been the hearth for a sense of distinctive American nationhood, languished.

In terms of religion, work by Linda Colley, Brendan McConville, Carla Pestana, and Owen Stanwood, for example, demonstrated how deeply colonists were invested in Britain's Protestant empire. Susan Juster's study of transatlantic prophecy culture integrated English and American contexts into a collective whole.[36] Less closely tied to religion, a new wave of loyalist studies, as well as reassessments of how wide or deep commitment to the patriot cause really was, built the argument that resistance to Britain was perhaps a minority cause. Interest in the transatlantic slave trade, the global slave-based economy, and the dynamics of abolitionism highlighted the conservative and sometimes reactionary nature of the American Revolution. Indeed, the revitalization of studies on the transatlantic Age of Revolutions—this time including the Haitian Revolution, which R. R. Palmer's pivotal 1959 work, *The Age of Democratic Revolution*, had largely left out—made the American Revolution seem comparatively *un*revolutionary in its implications.[37]

Scholarly pendulums being what they are, the American Revolution has made a comeback, but not in a way that provides much comfort to those who believe a "religious" founding era was essential for a stable nation. A series of conferences and pathbreaking new works on the Revolution have emerged since 2010. The shape of the new Revolution looks very different from that of the old one, however. This new version reflects the more troubled state of American politics in the post–Cold War world, and it has been seen as less reassuring to those who seek unity in the Revolutionary era (religious or not) on which to build national identity. The wartime years have come roaring back as a topic, but without the prerequisite American unity born of religion that historians of an earlier generation described. Where the likes of Bridenbaugh, Bailyn, and Bloch outlined how religion helped unite Americans in the 1760s and early 1770s, Robert Parkinson's highly influential 2016 work, *The Common Cause: Creating Race and Nation in the American Revolution*, answers the same question about national unity by charting how, *after* 1775, patriot leaders and allied newspaper editors built support for the fight against the British by fueling fears of slave revolt and Indigenous attack. The two arguments are not incompatible, but juxtaposing them raises the question of which mattered more—religious arguments that persuaded a few early leaders, John Adams among them, to join the Revolutionary movement or the exclusionary process by which those early movers brought an often unwilling population along for the ride?[38]

As the United States passes its 250th birthday, most historians seem to argue for the latter option, a fact that has largely sidelined the relevance of those arguments about Revolutionary ideology that gave religion pride of place a few decades ago. Instead, historians now depict a Revolutionary era that was experienced erratically by a diverse population, only some of whom were religious, only some of whom wanted revolution, and only some of whom benefited from it. In the words of the historian Virginia DeJohn Anderson, "For people who lived through it, the Revolution was . . . confusing. Political upheaval and warfare intruded upon their households and communities, causing unprecedented disruptions and forcing them to take actions with unpredictable consequences."[39] Religion as a primary subject is largely peripheral to the causal issues of this more disruptive and disjointed American Revolution. It is a version of the past that both Jedidiah Morse and Robert Baird would have rejected because its participants lacked both shared piety and national unity, though its secular narrative would likely raise no objections from Jon Butler. And yet as the United States endures an era of globalization, internal political turmoil, and sharp partisan division it is arguably a more appropriate and fruitful version of the Revolution for the present moment than those late–Cold War paeons to national unity or serendipitous disestablishment.

As the essays in this volume demonstrate, historians of religion have hardly been idle while the interpretive trends of the Revolutionary era have shifted. Important scholarly innovations have opened new terrain for investigation. Two trends warrant attention. First, many religion specialists have embraced questions and methods described as *lived religion,* a term associated with the Puritanism scholar David D. Hall. A way of bringing together the study of religious practice and religious meaning, this approach entails, according to the religious studies scholar Robert Orsi, "a fundamental rethinking of what religion is and of what it means to be 'religious.' Religion is not only not sui generis, distinct from other dimensions of experience called 'profane.' Religion comes into being in an ongoing, dynamic relationship with the realities of everyday life." Studying lived religion thus allows "religion" to be a more fluid concept, existing more comfortably with those aspects of life from which it has often been excluded or exempted.[40] It is also worth noting that historians of eighteenth-century religion have emphasized time frames and geographies that stretch beyond the bounds of religion and the American Revolution. They therefore often forefront subjects that do not neatly fit into that topic. Relevant studies, such as those by Sylvester Johnson, Susan Juster, and Linda Gregerson, have integrated religion into the dynamics of empire, for example, often working across multiple early modern empires. Key insights in this field include the ways that early modern religious ideas and institutions functioned to enhance state power.[41]

This more flexible understanding of religious subjects lends itself well to a second focus of recent work on eighteenth-century religion, that of religious experiences and influences outside dominant Protestant Christian institutions. Of course, the motivations to diversify understandings of our religious past predate the focus on lived religion, but as such topics often require methods and understandings of religion that reach beyond the denominational archive, the two trends are mutually reinforcing. Important studies have diversified the populations and religious communities under investigation. Betty Wood and Sylvia Frey's pathbreaking work on African American religion, *Come Shouting to Zion*, published in 1998, demonstrated the ways that religion influenced and shaped Black experiences throughout the colonial period and beyond it.[42] Books by Catherine Brekus and Susan Juster on women's experiences have broadened and diversified our understanding of how women engaged both their faith and their politics.[43] Works by Rachel Wheeler, Linford Fisher, and David Silverman trace the diverse experiences of Indigenous Christians across the eighteenth century.[44] Richard Godbeer and Sarah Crabtree have opened new investigations into colonial and Revolutionary Quaker communities, each with a sophisticated understanding of the transatlantic experiences of their subjects. Maura Farrelly has done the same for Catholics.[45] Early American Jews too have received considerable recent attention.[46] Finally, Kathryn Gin Lum has investigated the relationship between religion and race across the long sweep of colonial and American history.[47]

The result of such work is that scholars of eighteenth-century religion consider within their purview a far wider range of peoples, topics, and sources than were generally included in the discussions of religion and the American Revolution in the twentieth century. Unsurprisingly, these shifts in the historiography of American religion mirror those in the scholarship on the American Revolution described above, as the diversity of American experiences and connections between British North American, transatlantic, and transcontinental have taken center stage.

These developments have come at a cost, however. Transatlantic approaches, longer chronologies, and a wider range of potential "religious" peoples and topics have each led to a de-emphasizing of the American Revolution as a distinct and specific event in American religious history, once again leaving the field a bit stranded. In other words, historiographical trends have made it difficult for historians of religion and the American Revolution to easily bring their discussions directly into conversation with ongoing public concerns of the sort raised in the 2022 Pew study.

Were Americans motivated by their faith when they rebelled? Was the United States founded as a Christian nation? Was religious disestablishment a natural outgrowth of the American fight for "liberty"? While many Americans still expect these questions to sit at the center of discussions of religion and the American Revolution, they seem off-kilter to historians who study the era.

These questions demand reframing. Does it matter whether the revolutionaries of the late 1760s were motivated by faith if the Revolutionary movement was a fringe effort in those years? Is it more important that Protestants were numerically significant though internally divided or that they were politically dominant? When we talk about Americans' religion during the Revolutionary era, when is it appropriate to talk just about those who had political voices, and when do we need different categories? Personal experience suggests that such complications often fall on deaf (or at least disinterested) ears at cocktail parties. Yet the topic of religion and the American Revolution can and does still have an important place in the story of American religion and in studies of the American Revolution, a fact demonstrated by both the essays in this volume and much other recent work.[48] To put a finer point on it, Butler's comment that the conflict was secular in nature (and historians' widespread agreement with him) does not make the study of religion in that era pointless. Moreover, in many ways the baggage we bring to the topic as the country passes its 250th anniversary is much the same as it was when it passed its twenty-fifth or its fiftieth, though perhaps now turned on its head. Jedidiah Morse wanted to depict the American Revolution as a providential event because he needed to believe that the United States (and his place in it) could be more stable than its tumultuous youth would suggest.

In our destabilized political moment, Americans may well find solace in just the opposite truth: religious unity was *not* a prerequisite for the creation of the United States (or, by extension, its longevity) or for effective political unification. People from shared religious backgrounds divided over crucial questions of policy in the past as they do today. Playing politics with religion is nothing new. Neither is experiencing the events of the world through the lens of one's faith. The primary course of events in the Revolutionary era, as Butler asserted, found its causes outside religion, but religious tools, communities, experiences, and choices mattered to the people who lived through it. By once again bringing the subject of religion and the American Revolution into shared focus, and by doing so in the context of an American revolution that is more recognizable in our present circumstances than it is mythological, the participants in the present volume demonstrate the many ways that religion and the American Revolution is once again a vibrant field of study that speaks to concerns of the present moment, while also integrating it into scholarly understandings of the past.

The American Revolution that emerges from the essays that follow shaped and transformed American religious history, even in those areas where important continuities persisted, such as for Indigenous Christians or in evangelical discussions of slavery. Collectively, they investigate a wide range of religious movements, regions, and topics, though no such volume could ever claim to touch all the possible avenues for investigation. In general, the disruptions caused by the Revolution play catalytic roles in these discussions, even as these authors draw on longer time frames for context and also trace the Revolution's consequences. The people who appear in these essays dealt with the dislocations of occupation and political violence. They grappled with theological and political questions, and they turned to coreligionists for support. The legal transformations that unfolded during the Revolution remain central. But rather than reopening the story of Thomas Jefferson and James Madison's Virginia, the authors here suggest a complex and diverse reassessment of the relationship between religion and political forms that touched both minority religious groups and those who sought to sustain Protestant religious forms in a new era. And if the connections between religion and the state were complicated, the same is even more true for religion and slavery—a topic that is enduringly important to both popular and academic audiences because of its centrality to the national conscience.

Our investigations start in a traditional place: the religious ritual of the fast day, a mainstay of public life in colonial British America, especially in New England. But rather than emphasizing the events' unifying capacities, Spencer McBride discusses national fast days of the early Revolutionary period as a moment when "Congress was crafting an alliance with colonial clergymen and effectively coopting their pulpits." An essentially political act had political consequences; McBride argues that fast days became moments of "polarization," forcing often uncertain populations (and clergy) to decide where they stood on issues they may well have rather avoided. As he writes, such rituals also "made it more difficult for colonists to keep their opinions on the imperial crisis private." Although the nation's first fast day in 1775 was widely celebrated by revolution-leaning clergy as a triumph of public unity, it also saw anti-Quaker violence in Philadelphia. Public religion was an important tool for Congress, but its usage did not guarantee or in all cases further support for the Revolutionary cause.

Peter Walker examines another public religious ritual, the process of oath taking. Like McBride, Walker situates his story in a longer context, one in which oaths were seen by their swearers as divine promises to God. While a rich historiography has explored the experience of Anglican loyalists through the war years, Walker takes these discussions in a fresh direction. He argues that being asked to take an oath against the king, which was seen by loyalist Anglicans as a violation of their ordination oaths, became an "instrument to create new communities of conscience." In an era when freedom of conscience was an important and ascendent moral value, the oaths required by revolutionaries permitted those who objected to constitute themselves as "independent moral subject[s]." As Walker points out, however, such oaths were administered selectively. Thus while McBride shows fast days to be moments that forced individuals into the political scene en masse, the moral actors Walker finds to have been created by oaths were defined by "religion, race, and gender." In these two essays, public religion functioned as an important tool in the Revolutionary era, yet in each case reader attention is directed to the disruptions and fissures that emerged alongside the increasingly powerful Revolutionary movement.

Jessica Nelson shifts our attention to New England's Indigenous communities, and alongside Revolutionary ruptures she also finds continuities. As Nelson writes, "Although the war itself caused disruption and loss to Native communities, many of these communities relied upon Christianity in similar ways throughout the late eighteenth century—even after the emergence of the United States." Nonetheless, Nelson also argues that Christian Algonquian and Haudenosaunee peoples used "Christian rhetoric and a shared sense of Christian identity" to "build intertribal relationships throughout the shifting geopolitical circumstances of the era." This argument highlights the distinctiveness of the Indigenous experience in the Revolution, and it also brings that story into conversation with that of other American religious groups for whom religious connections served as means to negotiate political change.

The Jews studied by Adam Jortner also fall into this category, as a community that used religious networks to manage political change. Jortner's essay, along with Peter Walker's on Anglicans and Christopher Jones's on

Methodists, is one of only three essays in the volume to focus on a particular denomination. Moreover, it is the only one of the three to focus on the years before, during, and after the Revolution. This fact is worth noting, because it highlights the comparative unimportance of denominational categories to the study of the era. Only a few groups faced distinctive religious challenges.[49] As Jortner argues, Jews faced both dramatic wartime disruptions and then significant reorganization in the war's aftermath. European and colonial Jews had derived their communal existence from membership in government-recognized synagogue communities. After the Revolution, as the new state and federal governments embraced secular citizenship, American synagogues became "institution[s] based on choice" rather than the primary or exclusive arbiters of Jewish cultural membership. Jews fought for, and in many places gained, full rights of citizenships, but they also experienced dramatic changes to the organization of internal Jewish life.

Michael Baysa returns us to the question of how we understand what counts as "dominant" in religious culture, while continuing to emphasize how destabilizing the war was to religious life. His careful narrative of the challenges faced by Universalists, including the prominent patriot clergyman Charles Chauncy, in publishing their works suggests that the story we have learned about the development of American Protestant theology is incomplete. He shows that writers like Chauncy circulated manuscripts and participated in public conversations about religion even when the war shuttered presses, thus challenging the tendency of scholars to assume that the record of print culture matched public opinion. Attending to these alternative textual conversations has a significant payoff, Baysa argues. The energy of anti-Universalist publishing in the early republic—a factor that some have ascribed to the overweening ascendency of evangelicalism—may well have arisen from the vibrancy of Universalist textual circulation during the Revolution.

Alyssa Penick's essay turns to the question of disestablishment in the Chesapeake, using an approach that incorporates the very different colonies of Virginia and Maryland into a single discussion. She challenges a traditional story that has "compressed revolution and disestablishment into a single event" and argues instead that non-Anglicans in both Chesapeake states felt that religious freedom was far from secure in the early 1780s. For those who lived through the Revolution, therefore, disestablishment was not an obvious or inevitable outcome of the struggle for political freedom from Britain in the 1770s. Penick argues that advocates for religious liberty in the 1780s "changed the story of '76" in such a way as to insist that religious liberty had been a goal from the start and that the sacrifices of the war necessitated "full religious equality." Like the essays that come before, Pennick's also argues that the violence and struggle of the Revolution played an important role in the era's religious transformations. Moreover, she argues, advocates for religious liberty *created* the idea that freedom of religion was intrinsic to the Revolution, a "fact" that in many public contexts remains uncontested to this day.

The next pair of essays, by Christopher Jones and Peter Choi, address important questions about the consequences of the Revolution for the evangelical community. Historians of that topic have, in the decades since the publication of Nathan O. Hatch's *Democratization of American Christianity*, generally assumed a synergistic relationship between republican political theology, disestablishment, and expansive evangelical energy. Jones complicates this conversation by demonstrating how diverse groups of Methodists found that seeking "freedom" after the Revolution required migration either within or outside the United States. The Revolution, he argues, did not just lead to Methodist growth but also led to divided Methodists with different understandings of how to seek "liberty." Throughout these essays, the Revolution separates as often as it unites.

Choi tackles the subject of slavery and evangelicals. The contradiction of a political movement for "freedom" undertaken by a state that protected slavery has been noted since before the Revolution broke out, and it has lost none of its saliency. In recent years, Choi and other historians have elucidated the centuries-long intertwining of religious institutions and theologies with the dynamics of the slave trade and plantation slavery, as well as the compromises American evangelicals made with slavery in the antebellum era. Their work has complicated an older narrative that depicted slavery as a primarily economic institution that was ultimately challenged by the religiously inspired Quakers and evangelicals. Choi deepens this discussion by identifying four overlapping and often conflicting strands of white evangelical thought on slavery, explaining how that movement managed to appear simultaneously radical and reactionary. At the same time, by tracing the "rise and fall of evangelical abolition" he provides a clear narrative arc: white evangelicals, even those who maintained the strongest antislavery positions, did not sustain the abolition movement either within evangelicalism or within the broader culture.

The final two essays in this collection address the ways that American Protestants incorporated the impulses of the Revolution into their religious lives in the early republic. Shelby Balik investigates household religion. Although religious cultures can be profoundly conservative, devotional literature aimed at white families across the new United States shows important shifts away from monarchical subjecthood and toward the constitution of a Protestant political citizenship. Describing a world that Jedidiah Morse certainly inhabited, she argues that "many Americans—and especially reformed Protestant ministers—were convinced" that the "republic's salvation . . . depended on the patriotic efforts of pious families." Family prayer, she demonstrates, was "both practical religion and practical politics," as households moved into the gap created by the loss of institutional religious establishments. Revolutionary politics were tamed inside patriarchal homes.

Seth Perry too charts the incorporation of the Revolution into a more conservative post-Revolutionary era, tracing how the Methodist itinerant Lorenzo Dow appropriated and plagiarized writings by the atheistic radical Thomas Paine. When employed by the likes of Dow, Paine's rhetoric was used "to support an imbrication of religion and the state that [Paine] never intended to endorse." In other words, Perry suggests that evangelicals continued to find resonance in Revolutionary rhetoric, even as they embraced the more conservative Protestant culture of the early republic. They tamed the radical into a new acceptable form. As Perry writes, "Dow domesticated Paine's formerly incendiary rhetoric into a discourse of American liberty that suited an audience of slaveholders"—an apt synecdoche for the end of the Revolutionary era.

THE ESSAYS in this collection result from the Sons of the American Revolution's 2021 annual conference in Providence, Rhode Island. That organization, like this volume, seeks to further understanding of the nation's founding, under the premise that the events of the American Revolution are crucial not just to the past but to the present. At its conclusion, the SAR's organizer, Joe Dooley, commented that the discussions had been fascinating but not at all what he had expected. His surprise reflects the challenges of engaging this topic. As part of the effort to create a usable past out of the Revolutionary era, centuries of Americans have looked to religion in the American Revolutionary era in order to assess the health, purpose, or sustainability of their republic. For much of that time academic historians, when they wrote about religion, supported those efforts, sometimes out of ideological agreement, sometimes because it aligned with other academic or political perspectives.

Yet in the present moment, the story of the American Revolution and the place of religion in it appears more fraught than ever. Religion unified some Americans, but it was also a tool of statecraft that divided as it united. Throughout the colonial period, Christianity had been an important force that crossed racial lines, and yet religion did not serve to unite all Americans, or even all Christian Americans, across those racial lines in the Revolution. Some Americans gained religious liberty through the Revolution, but not all interpreted that liberty in the same way, and not all chose to stay within the boundaries of the new United States. Finally, the Revolution changed how Americans worshipped and what they believed, as they brought their religious lives into line with their new political forms. Ultimately, the essays in this volume argue that religion *mattered* to Americans of the Revolutionary era but did not unify in any neat and tidy way. And perhaps this is the final lesson for those who look to the founding period to understand whether the country is on the correct path. Then, as now, there were many American religious histories.

Notes

1. The Pew study and its findings can be found at https://www.pewresearch.org/religion/2022/10/27/45-of-americans-say-u-s-should-be-a-christian-nation/. For detailed information about the order and phrasing of these questions, see "Topline," p. 8.
2. Jon Butler, *Awash in a Sea of Faith: Christianizing the American People* (Cambridge, MA: Harvard University Press, 1990), 195. The term *secular* has undergone considerable theoretical development since 1990. It is used here and throughout this essay in its more popular sense of "not religious." Good entry points into the theory of secularity are Michael Warner, Jonathan VanAntwerpen, and Craig J Calhoun, eds., *Varieties of Secularism in a Secular Age* (Cambridge, MA: Harvard University Press, 2010), esp. the essay by Jon Butler; Tracy Fessenden, *Culture and Redemption: Religion, the Secular, and American Literature* (Princeton, NJ: Princeton University Press, 2007); and Talal Asad, *Formations of the Secular: Christianity, Islam, Modernity* (Stanford: Stanford University Press, 2003).
3. Butler, *Awash in a Sea of Faith*, 195.
4. For a biography of Morse, see Joseph W. Phillips, *Jedidiah Morse and New England Congregationalism* (New Brunswick, NJ: Rutgers University Press, 1983).

5. Jedidiah Morse, *A Sermon Exhibiting the Present Dangers, and Consequent Duties of the Citizens of the United States of America* (New York, 1799), 9. For an exploration of Morse and the role of these statements in the early nineteenth century, see Kate Carté Engel, "Triangulating Religion and the American Revolution Through Jedidiah Morse," Commonplace, accessed April 18, 2025, https://commonplace.online/article/triangulating-religion-and-the-american-revolution-through-jedidiah-morse/.
6. "From John Adams to Massachusetts Militia, 11 October 1798," Founders Online, National Archives, https://founders.archives.gov/documents/Adams/99-02-02-3102.
7. George Washington, Farewell Address Online by Gerhard Peters and John T. Woolley, The American Presidency Project, https://www.presidency.ucsb.edu/node/200675.
8. Morse, *Sermon Exhibiting the Present Dangers, and Consequent Duties*, 9.
9. For the Illuminati scare, see Carté Engel, "Triangulating Religion"; Jonathan J. Den Hartog, *Patriotism and Piety* (Charlottesville: University of Virginia Press, 2015); and Bryan Waterman, "The Bavarian Illuminati, the Early American Novel, and Histories of the Public Sphere," *William and Mary Quarterly*, 3d ser., 62 (2005): 9–30. See also Jonathan D. Sassi, *A Republic of Righteousness: The Public Christianity of the Post-Revolutionary New England Clergy* (New York: Oxford University Press, 2001).
10. For the history of skepticism and responses to it, see Christopher Grasso, *Skepticism and American Faith: From the Revolution to the Civil War* (New York: Oxford University Press, 2018); and Amanda Porterfield, *Conceived in Doubt: Religion and Politics in the New American Nation* (Chicago: University of Chicago Press, 2012).
11. David Sehat, *The Myth of American Religious Freedom* (New York: Oxford University Press, 2011), 36. See also Den Hartog, *Patriotism and Piety*, chap. 2; Neil Brody Miller, "'Proper Subjects for Public Inquiry': The First Unitarian Controversy and the Transformation of Federalist Print Culture," *Early American Literature* 43 (2008): 101–35; and K. Alan Snyder, "Foundations of Liberty: The Christian Republicanism of Timothy Dwight and Jedidiah Morse," *New England Quarterly* 56 (1983): 382–97.
12. Michael D. Hattem, *Past and Prologue: Politics and Memory in the American Revolution* (New Haven, CT: Yale University Press, 2020), 163–64.
13. "From John Adams to Jedidiah Morse, 29 November 1815," Founders Online, National Archives, https://founders.archives.gov/documents/Adams/99-02-02-6547.
14. Jedidiah Morse, *Annals of the American Revolution; or, A record of the causes and events which produced, and terminated in the establishment and independence of the American Republic* (Hartford, CT, 1824), 195–96.

15. See "To John Adams from Jedidiah Morse, 2 December 1815," Founders Online, National Archives, https://founders.archives.gov/documents/Adams/99-02-02-6549. The Adams Papers online place these two letters in reverse order, with the request for a providential history *after* the religiously oriented response. The two have the same date, and the response mentions the lateness of the day. Therefore, I have interpreted the second letter as a response.
16. "From John Adams to Jedidiah Morse, 2 December 1815," Founders Online, National Archives, https://founders.archives.gov/documents/Adams/99-02-02-6548.
17. Patrick Henry, "'And I Don't Care What It Is': The Tradition-History of a Civil Religion Proof-Text," *Journal of the American Academy of Religion* 49 (1981): 35–49.
18. Robert Baird, *Religion in America, or, An Account of the Origin, Progress, Relation to the State, and Present Condition of the Evangelical Churches in the United States: With Notices of the Unevangelical Denominations* (New York, 1844), 101–2. For a discussion of Baird's work in the context of the historiography of American religion, see Catherine A. Brekus, "Contested Words: History, America, Religion," *William and Mary Quarterly*, 3d ser., 75 (2018): 3–36.
19. Baird, *Religion in America*, 102.
20. Baird, *Religion in America*, 103.
21. Joseph Story, *Commentaries on the Constitution*, 3 vols. (Boston: Hilliard, Gray, 1833), vol. 3, doc. 69, § 1869, https://press-pubs.uchicago.edu/founders/documents/amendI_religions69.html, quoted in Baird, *Religion in America*, 117.
22. Edmund S. Morgan, "The Puritan Ethic and the American Revolution," *William and Mary Quarterly*, 3d ser., 24 (1967): 4–43. See also Sarah Rivett, "Early American Religion in a Postsecular Age," *Proceedings of the Modern Language Association* 128 (2013): 989–95.
23. Alan Heimert, *Religion and the American Mind, from the Great Awakening to the Revolution* (Cambridge, MA: Harvard University Press, 1966); Patricia U. Bonomi, *Under the Cope of Heaven: Religion, Society, and Politics in Colonial America* (1986; updated ed., New York: Oxford University Press, 2003); Harry S. Stout, "Religion, Communications, and the Ideological Origins of the American Revolution," *William and Mary Quarterly*, 3d ser., 34 (1977): 519–41; Rhys Isaac, *The Transformation of Virginia, 1740–1790* (Chapel Hill: University of North Carolina Press, 1982). In very different forms, these arguments resonate in Susan Juster, "The Evangelical Ascendency in Revolutionary America," in *The Oxford Handbook of the American Revolution*, ed. Jane Kamensky and Edward G. Gray (New York: Oxford

University Press, 2013), 407–26; and Christopher Beneke, *Beyond Toleration: The Religious Origins of American Pluralism* (New York: Oxford University Press, 2006). After historians grappled with the challenge presented to the idea of the "Great Awakening" presented by Jon Butler in "Enthusiasm Described and Decried: The Great Awakening as Interpretive Fiction," *Journal of American History* 69 (1982): 305–25, investigations into the mid-century revivals have been rejuvenated in both transatlantic and regional contexts. They do not, however, tend to make causal arguments about the Revolution. See, e.g., Frank Lambert, *Inventing the "Great Awakening"* (Princeton, NJ: Princeton University Press, 1999); and Douglas Leo Winiarski, *Darkness Falls on the Land of Light: Experiencing Religious Awakenings in Eighteenth-Century New England* (Chapel Hill: University of North Carolina Press, 2017).

24. John M. Murrin, "No Awakening, No Revolution? More Counterfactual Speculations," *Reviews in American History* 11 (June 1983): 161–71, quote on 167.
25. Thomas S. Kidd, *God of Liberty: A Religious History of the American Revolution* (New York: Basic Books, 2010), 25.
26. Carl Bridenbaugh, *Mitre and Sceptre: Transatlantic Faiths, Ideas, Personalities, and Politics, 1689–1775* (New York: Oxford University Press, 1962).
27. Bernard Bailyn, *The Ideological Origins of the American Revolution*, enlarged ed. (Cambridge, MA: Belknap Press of Harvard University Press, 1992), quote on 251; see also 246–71.
28. Nathan O. Hatch, *The Sacred Cause of Liberty: Republican Thought and the Millennium in Revolutionary New England* (New Haven, CT: Yale University Press, 1977); Ruth Bloch, *Visionary Republic: Millennial Themes in American Thought, 1756–1800* (Cambridge: Cambridge University Press, 1985). J. C. D. Clark, *The Language of Liberty, 1660–1832: Political Discourse and Social Dynamics in the Anglo-American World* (Cambridge: Cambridge University Press, 1993); James B. Bell, *A War of Religion: Dissenters, Anglicans, and the American Revolution* (Basingstoke: Palgrave Macmillan, 2008).
29. Gordon Wood, "Religion and the American Revolution," in *New Directions in American Religious History*, ed. Harry S. Stout and D. G. Hart (New York: Oxford University Press, 1997), 173–205, quote on 175. For more recent discussions along the same lines, see Gary L. Steward, *Justifying Revolution: The American Clergy's Argument for Political Resistance, 1750–1776* (New York: Oxford University Press, 2021); and S. Scott Rohrer, *The Folly of Revolution: Thomas Bradbury Chandler and the Loyalist Mind in a Democratic Age* (University Park: Pennsylvania State University Press, 2022).

30. Isaac, *Transformation of Virginia*, quote on [271].
31. There is an expansive literature on disestablishment, particularly in Virginia. See, e.g., Thomas E. Buckley, *Establishing Religious Freedom: Jefferson's Statute in Virginia* (Charlottesville: University of Virginia Press, 2013); John A. Ragosta, *Wellspring of Liberty: How Virginia's Religious Dissenters Helped Win the American Revolution and Secured Religious Liberty* (New York: Oxford University Press, 2010); and Jewel L. Spangler, *Virginians Reborn: Anglican Monopoly, Evangelical Dissent, and the Rise of the Baptists in the Late Eighteenth Century* (Charlottesville: University of Virginia Press, 2008). For a more recent version of investigations into this topic, see Sarah Barringer Gordon, "The First Wall of Separation Between Church and State: Slavery and Disestablishment in Late-Eighteenth-Century Virginia," *Journal of Southern History* 85 (February 2019): 61–104. The best work on the state-by-state process of disestablishment is Carl H. Esbeck and Jonathan J. Den Hartog, eds., *Disestablishment and Religious Dissent: Church-State Relations in the New American States, 1776–1833* (Columbia: University of Missouri Press, 2019). See also Thomas J. Curry, *The First Freedoms: Church and State in America to the Passage of the First Amendment* (New York: Oxford University Press, 1986).
32. Sassi, *Republic of Righteousness;* Christopher Grasso, *A Speaking Aristocracy: Transforming Public Discourse in Eighteenth-Century Connecticut* (Chapel Hill: University of North Carolina Press, 1999).
33. For an example of religion, particularly evangelicalism, as a dominant cultural force, see Daniel Walker Howe, *What Hath God Wrought: The Transformation of America, 1815–1848* (New York: Oxford University Press, 2007). For an excellent summary of recent interpretive themes of this period, see Grasso, *Skepticism and American Faith*, 514n4, as well as the surrounding discussion in Grasso's part 1.
34. Ronald Hoffman and Peter J. Albert, eds., *Religion in a Revolutionary Age* (Charlottesville: University of Virginia Press, 1994). For a historiographical treatment from the same era, see John F. Wilson, "Religion and Revolution in American History," *Journal of Interdisciplinary History* 23 (1993): 597–613.
35. The historiography of the Atlantic turn in early American history is vast. Eliga H. Gould, "Comparing Atlantic Histories," *Reviews in American History* 38 (2010): 8–16, provides a good starting point.
36. Linda Colley, *Britons: Forging the Nation, 1707–1837* (New Haven, CT: Yale University Press, 1992); Carla Gardina Pestana, *Protestant Empire: Religion and the Making of the British Atlantic World* (Philadelphia: University of Pennsylvania Press, 2009); Brendan McConville, *The King's Three Faces: The Rise and Fall of Royal America, 1688–1776* (Chapel Hill: University of North Carolina Press, 2006); Owen Stanwood, *The Empire Reformed: English America in the Age of the Glorious Revolution* (Philadelphia: University

of Pennsylvania Press, 2011); Susan Juster, *Doomsayers: Anglo-American Prophecy in the Age of Revolution* (Philadelphia: University of Pennsylvania Press, 2003). See also Katherine Carté, *Religion and the American Revolution: An Imperial History* (Chapel Hill: University of North Carolina Press, 2021). The interpretation that the colonies grew closer to the metropole across the eighteenth century has been associated with the terms *convergence* and *Anglicization*. See Ignacio Gallup-Diaz, Andrew Shankman, and David J. Silverman, eds., *Anglicizing America: Empire, Revolution, Republic* (Philadelphia: University of Pennsylvania Press, 2015).

37. For the seminal work in renewed loyalist studies, see Maya Jasanoff, *Liberty's Exiles: American Loyalists in the Revolutionary World* (New York: Knopf, 2011); for efforts to estimate rates of loyalism and support for the Revolutionary movement, see Michael A. McDonnell, "The Struggle Within: Colonial Politics on the Eve of Independence," in Kamensky and Gray, *Oxford Handbook of the American Revolution*. Also essential for reinterpreting the dynamics behind support for the Revolutionary movement has been Woody Holton, *Forced Founders: Indians, Debtors, Slaves, and the Making of the American Revolution in Virginia* (Chapel Hill: University of North Carolina Press, 1999). For the transatlantic abolition movement and the Revolution, see Christopher Leslie Brown, *Moral Capital: Foundations of British Abolitionism* (Chapel Hill: University of North Carolina Press, 2006). For the Age of Revolutions, see R. R. Palmer, *The Age of the Democratic Revolution: A Political History of Europe and America, 1760–1800* (Princeton, NJ: Princeton University Press, 1959). and Sarah Knott, "Narrating the Age of Revolution," *William and Mary Quarterly*, 3d ser., 73 (January 2015): 3–36. Brendan McConville critiques some of these moves in "Going Continental? Romantic Transnationalism and Contemporary Interpretation of the American Revolution," *Journal of the Early Republic* 39 (2019): 539–46.

38. Robert G. Parkinson, *The Common Cause: Creating Race and Nation in the American Revolution* (Chapel Hill: University of North Carolina Press, 2016). As the United States prepared to commemorate the 250th anniversary of the American Revolution, scholars published a series of historiographical surveys of the study of the American Revolution. See, e.g., T. H. Breen, Kathleen Duval, Leslie M. Harris, Michael D. Hattem, and Serena Zabin, "The Revolution at 250: A Conversation," *Journal of the Early Republic* 44 (2024): 513–79; Michael D. Hattem, "Revolution Lost? Vast Early America, National History, and the American Revolution," *William and Mary Quarterly*, 3d ser., 78 (2021): 269–74; Michael A. McDonnell and David Waldstreicher, "Revolution in the Quarterly? A Historiographical Analysis," *William and Mary Quarterly*. 3d ser., 74 (2017): 633–66; and Patrick Spero and Michael Zuckerman, eds, *The American Revolution*

Reborn (Philadelphia: University of Pennsylvania Press, 2016). Although the absence of religion from recent discussions is often noted, it is not a primary focus of any recent historiographical discussions. For works on religion that fit within this framework, see Roberto Oscar Flores de Apodaca, "Praying Soldiers: How Continental Soldiers Experienced Religion During the Revolutionary War, 1775–1783," *Early American* 20 (2022): 440–65; Anna Vincenzi, "'Mutation in Dominion' or Revolution? The American Revolution as Seen from Papal Rome," *Early American Studies* 20 (2022): 466–505; Carté, *Religion and the American Revolution;* William Harrison Taylor, *Unity in Christ and Country: American Presbyterians in the Revolutionary Era, 1758–1801* (Tuscaloosa: University of Alabama Press, 2017); Spencer W. McBride, *Pulpit and Nation: Clergymen and the Politics of Revolutionary America* (Charlottesville: University of Virginia Press, 2016); and James P. Byrd, *Sacred Scripture, Sacred War: The Bible and the American Revolution* (New York: Oxford University Press, 2013). For a version of the American Revolution that integrates Protestant sentiment into social revolt, see Brendan McConville, *The Brethren: A Story of Faith and Conspiracy in Revolutionary America* (Cambridge, MA: Harvard University Press, 2021).

39. Virginia DeJohn Anderson, *The Martyr and the Traitor: Nathan Hale, Moses Dunbar, and the American Revolution* (New York: Oxford University Press, 2017), 3.

40. The concept of lived religion in American religious history is elaborated most fully in two edited collections: David D. Hall, ed., *Lived Religion in America: Toward a History of Practice* (Princeton, NJ: Princeton University Press, 1997), esp. Hall's introduction and Robert Orsi's essay, "Everyday Miracles: The Study of Lived Religion," quote on 7; and Laurie F. Maffly-Kipp, Leigh E. Schmidt, and Mark Valeri, eds., *Practicing Protestants: Histories of Christian Life in America, 1630–1965* (Baltimore: Johns Hopkins University Press, 2006).

41. For influential collections that work across this era, see Linda Gregerson and Susan Juster, *Empires of God: Religious Encounters in the Early Modern Atlantic* (Philadelphia: University of Pennsylvania Press, 2011); Sylvester A. Johnson, *African American Religions, 1500–2000: Colonialism, Democracy, and Freedom* (New York: Cambridge University Press, 2015); Stephanie L. Kirk and Sarah Rivett, eds., *Religious Transformations in the Early Modern Americas* (Philadelphia: University of Pennsylvania Press, 2014); and Pestana, *Protestant Empire.* Important work on the intersection of slavery and religion also falls into this category. See, e.g., Travis F. Glasson, *Mastering Christianity: Missionary Anglicanism and Slavery in the Atlantic World* (New York: Oxford University Press, 2012); Rebecca Anne Goetz, *The Baptism of Early Virginia: How Christianity Created Race* (Baltimore: Johns Hopkins

University Press, 2012); and Katharine Gerbner, *Christian Slavery: Conversion and Race in the Protestant Atlantic World* (Philadelphia: University of Pennsylvania Press, 2018). For a recent historiographical treatment of early American religion, see Brekus, "Contested Words."

42. Sylvia R. Frey and Betty Wood, *Come Shouting to Zion: African American Protestantism in the American South and British Caribbean to 1830* (Chapel Hill: University of North Carolina Press, 1998). Jon Sensbach's work has also been particularly important here, for demonstrating the experiences of early African American Protestants. See Jon F. Sensbach, *A Separate Canaan: The Making of an Afro-Moravian World in North Carolina, 1763–1840* (Chapel Hill: University of North Carolina Press, 1998); and Sensbach, *Rebecca's Revival: Creating Black Christianity in the Atlantic World* (Cambridge, MA: Harvard University Press, 2005). See also John W. Catron, *Embracing Protestantism: Black Identities in the Atlantic World* (Gainesville: University Press of Florida, 2016); and, most recently, Alexis Wells-Oghoghomeh, *The Souls of Womenfolk: The Religious Cultures of Enslaved Women in the Lower South* (Chapel Hill: University of North Carolina Press, 2021). For racial diversity in early American congregations, see Richard Boles, *Dividing the Faith: The Rise of Segregated Churches in the Early American North* (New York: New York University Press, 2020); and Charles F. Irons, *The Origins of Proslavery Christianity: White and Black Evangelicals in Colonial and Antebellum Virginia* (Chapel Hill: University of North Carolina Press, 2008).

43. Catherine A. Brekus, *Strangers and Pilgrims: Female Preaching in America, 1740–1845* (Chapel Hill: University of North Carolina Press, 1998); Brekus, *Sarah Osborn's World: The Rise of Evangelical Christianity in Early America* (New Haven, CT: Yale University Press, 2013); Susan Juster, *Disorderly Women: Sexual Politics and Evangelicalism in Revolutionary New England* (Ithaca, NY: Cornell University Press, 1994).

44. Rachel M. Wheeler, *To Live upon Hope: Mohicans and Missionaries in the Eighteenth-Century Northeast* (Ithaca, NY: Cornell University Press, 2008); David J. Silverman, *Red Brethren: The Brothertown and Stockbridge Indians and the Problem of Race in Early America* (Ithaca, NY: Cornell University Press, 2010); Linford D. Fisher, *The Indian Great Awakening: Religion and the Shaping of Native Cultures in Early America* (New York: Oxford University Press, 2012).

45. Richard Godbeer, *World of Trouble: A Philadelphia Quaker Family's Journey Through the American Revolution* (New Haven, CT: Yale University Press, 2019); Sarah Crabtree, *Holy Nation: The Transatlantic Quaker Ministry in an Age of Revolution* (Chicago: University of Chicago Press, 2015); Maura Jane Farrelly, *Papist Patriots: The Making of an American Catholic Identity* (New York: Oxford University Press, 2012).

46. Adam Jortner, *A Promised Land: Jewish Patriots, the American Revolution, and the Birth of Religious Freedom* (New York: Oxford University Press, 2024); William Pencak, *Jews and Gentiles in Early America, 1654–1800* (Ann Arbor: University of Michigan Press, 2005).
47. Kathryn Gin Lum, *Heathen: Religion and Race in American History* (Cambridge, MA: Harvard University Press, 2022). In this context see also Mark R. Valeri, *The Opening of the Protestant Mind: How Anglo-American Protestants Embraced Religious Liberty* (New York: Oxford University Press, 2023).
48. Scholars continue to write on religion and the Revolution, though often in ways that sidestep the question whether religion was important to the Revolution as a whole. One area of persistent interest is the religion of the "founding fathers." The topic draws popular attention, and because those individuals were self-evidently important to the Revolution, their religious views also carry weight. See Andrew Porwancher, *The Jewish World of Alexander Hamilton* (Princeton, NJ: Princeton University Press, 2021); Sara Georgini, *Household Gods: The Religious Lives of the Adams Family* (New York: Oxford University Press, 2019); Daniel L. Dreisbach, *Reading the Bible with the Founding Fathers* (New York: Oxford University Press, 2017); J. Patrick Mullins, *Father of Liberty: Jonathan Mayhew and the Principles of the American Revolution* (Lawrence: University of Kansas Press, 2017); Gideon Mailer, *John Witherspoon's American Revolution* (Chapel Hill: University of North Carolina Press, 2017); and Gregg L. Frazer, *The Religious Beliefs of America's Founders: Reason, Revelation, and Revolution* (Lawrence: University Press of Kansas, 2012). John Fea, *Was America Founded as a Christian Nation? A Historical Introduction* (Louisville: Westminster John Knox, 2011), provides an overview of the subject for public audiences that brings scholarly discussions and popular discussions together. As noted above, another set of historians has delved deeply into the religious culture of the early republic, examining the long-term consequences of religious disestablishment and the fragmentation initially set off by the evangelical revivals of the mid-eighteenth century, as well as the cultural conflict between skepticism or deism—inheritors of the Enlightenment—and the forces of evangelical Protestantism. These investigations have made important contributions to understanding religion and the exercise of political or cultural power, but because of their focus on the nineteenth century, the history of religion in the American Revolutionary era, as opposed to its aftermath, is peripheral. For post-Revolutionary disestablishment, especially in the context of New England and its revivals, see Shelby M. Balik, *Rally the Scattered Believers: Northern New England's Religious Geography* (Bloomington: University of Indiana Press, 2014); and Winiarski, *Darkness Falls*. An older but still important work in this conversation is

Stephen A. Marini, *Radical Sects of Revolutionary New England* (Cambridge, MA: Harvard University Press, 1982). For the cultural conflicts between faith and its various opposites, see Grasso, *Skepticism and American Faith*; Eric R. Schlereth, *An Age of Infidels: The Politics of Religious Controversy in the Early United States* (Philadelphia: University of Pennsylvania Press, 2013); and Porterfield, *Conceived in Doubt*. In addition to speaking to the Revolutionary era, these works also challenge the connections drawn between the American republic and evangelicalism by Nathan O. Hatch's seminal book *The Democratization of American* Christianity (New Haven, CT: Yale University Press, 1989). Sehat's *Myth of American Religious Freedom* is also important to this discussion of the early republic. For an intellectual survey of the whole period, see Mark Noll's *America's God: From Jonathan Edwards to Abraham Lincoln* (New York: Oxford University Press, 2002), which investigates the theological process by which American Protestants came to terms with republicanism as well as the intellectual trends of the Enlightenment.

49. No volume could cover every such example. For recent works on Quakers and Catholics specifically, see n. 45 above. For the Moravians, a topic that could stand updating, see Kenneth G. Hamilton, *John Ettwein and the Moravian Church During the Revolutionary Period* (Bethlehem, PA: Times Publishing, 1940).

Religious Ritual and Public Polarization in the American Revolution

SPENCER W. MCBRIDE

★

American revolutionaries did not invent the public ritual of communal fasting and prayer. Similarly, the American Revolution was not the first time that the liturgy in the Church of England's Book of Common Prayer became the topic of political debate. Even so, during the Revolution congressionally appointed fast days and the proposed substitution of Congress for the king and Parliament in Anglican prayers polarized communities throughout Great Britain's North American colonies. These colonists' decisions to either fast or feast on days of fasting signaled to neighbors their allegiances in the imperial conflict. Similarly, an Anglican clergymen's decision on whether to omit the king from prayers indicated a stance on a crisis that for them was simultaneously political and ecclesiastical. Some were eager to fast for the Revolution or to pray for Congress instead of the king. Others were staunch opponents of such acts, and many colonists were conflicted.

Considering the ways that fast days polarized American communities during the Revolution alongside the experiences of Anglican clergymen, who were forced to weigh their ecclesiastical oaths with political and ministerial considerations, illuminates the fraught nature of choosing sides in the American Revolution. In times of peace as well as in times of war, religious ritual blurs the boundaries of private and public life. But during the Revolutionary War, rituals such as fast days did so with particularly high stakes, forcing American colonists to navigate entangled webs of identity and allegiance that could have devastating effects on their futures. The public nature of these religious rituals and their political ramifications often destroyed the middle ground between rebellion and loyalty and forced moderate, conflicted, and neutral colonists to openly join one side or the other.

In 1775, when the First Continental Congress considered a motion for a continental day of fasting and prayer, they drew from a rich English tradition. At times of public crisis and often in response to royal declarations, English men and women would collectively abstain from food and drink on an appointed day and congregate in chapels throughout the country to hear sermons crafted by clergymen to address the crisis at hand. When English settlers invaded the Atlantic Seaboard of North America to establish colonies, they brought the practice with them. This ritual was common in New England. In fact, at times a colony or town could declare too many fast days, inspiring critics to argue that fast days held too regularly stripped the ritual of much of its significance. Colonies to the south, such as Virginia, similarly observed fast days, but the rituals were far less common and typically associated with particularly disruptive events, such as the English Civil War.[1] If employed strategically, fast days could be effective public rituals, mobilizing a population to rise up in support of a cause, be it war with a foreign country or the suppression of internal rebellion.

Those in Congress who supported a fast day declaration were optimistic about its power to mobilize colonists to resist the controversial imperial policies of Parliament and to boost support for the newly formed Continental Army. For instance, John Adams envisioned "millions on their knees at once before their Great Creator, imploring . . . his Smiles on American Councils and Arms." He believed that fast days would prompt the clergy to "engage with a fervor that will produce wonderful effects."[2]

In fact, the clergy was an essential part of this plan. Although continental in scope, the fast day that Congress was contemplating was reliant on local compliance. If local congregations refused to participate in the event, the declaration would prove an empty gesture and could even signal congressional weakness. But if clergymen sympathetic to the patriot cause could entice their congregations to fast and then to gather to pray, the public ritual could realize its potential.

By declaring a day of fasting and prayer, Congress was crafting an alliance with colonial clergymen and effectively coopting their pulpits. Such an alliance with the clergy throughout the colonies offered a partial solution to problems Congress faced at the time of its inception. In 1775 the Continental Congress had not firmly established its legitimacy and effectiveness as a governing body. The "national" perch of Congress contributed to this problem of public perception. At this time there were relatively few "national" figures, men whose reputations were known and respected throughout the thirteen colonies. Average colonists in British North America tended to be familiar with the political leadership of their own colonies and perhaps those of neighboring colonies. However, colonists living outside New England were unlikely to know of delegates such as John Adams at this time, just as New Englanders were unlikely to know who the delegates from Virginia were, except for George Washington. Accordingly, congressional communications sent through local committees of correspondence would lack the established authority inherent in known local politicians. Through fast days Congress was attempting to bridge this gap by reaching out to the people's clerical leaders. By urging the clergy to lead fast day observations and preach to their congregations on the spiritual justification and necessity of resisting Great Britain's imperial policies, Congress was delivering its message through individuals known and trusted by local audiences. Fast days turned participating clergymen and churches into political forums, adjuncts of and advocates for Congress.[3]

Looking back, it is not surprising that America's Revolutionary leadership reached out to the clergy to forge a political alliance. The clergy were among the most educated men in colonial society, typically well read and trained to speak persuasively. Many clergymen educated at American colleges witnessed firsthand the politicization of college faculties in the 1750s and 1760s, as the curricula of those institutions became increasingly concerned with preparing students to better serve the state. Furthermore, several clergymen had displayed a willingness to speak out on political matters affecting the entire continent during the Stamp Act crisis of 1765. These moments of political activism did not result in an enduring clerical participation in the political sphere, but they allowed secular leaders to see the potential effectiveness of the clergy therein. Hence, it was both reasonable and realistic for Congress to expect the clergymen who accepted their invitation to preach politics on fast days to become potent extensions of Congress and its protests.[4]

It was also reasonable for Congress to predict that the day of fasting would unite the colonists as a people. Modern nations have frequently used public rites to nurture a common identity, and the public observance of a fast day was no different. Although fast days were not particularly festive, they still served the purpose of a public holiday. By collectively taking a break from life's ordinary events to focus for an entire day on the extraordinary, people in each colony would share the same experience: abstaining from food and drink, engaging in a concert of prayer, and listening to their respective ministers preach on the providential mission of America. While not every colonist would participate in the fast, the appearance of consensus was crucial to the ritual's efficacy in establishing a common identity.[5]

After some debate Congress resolved that July 20, 1775, would "be observed, by the inhabitants of all the English colonies on this continent, as a day of public humiliation, fasting and prayer." The official proclamation urged colonists to abstain from food and drink on the appointed day and "to abstain from servile labour and recreation on said day."[6] The news spread quickly throughout the colonies, and clergymen began to prepare sermons for the occasion.

Reports of that first congressionally declared fast day suggest that it met, and in some cases exceeded, the expectations of delegates. In a letter to his wife, Abigail, John Adams wrote from Philadelphia that "the Fast was observed here with a Decorum and solemnity, never before seen ever on a Sabbath. The Clergy of all Denominations, here preach Politicks and War in a manner that I never heard in N. England. They are a flame of Fire."[7] Clergymen in other colonies similarly reported packed chapels and fiery political sermons on the first fast day.[8]

Of course, clergymen adamantly opposed to the resistance led by Congress refused to participate. Samuel Seabury locked the doors of his Connecticut church to prevent parishioners from gathering there despite his refusal to lead worship services on the occasion. Seabury was an ardent loyalist from the beginning of the conflict, and locking the church was a clear public statement of his political opposition to Congress. When arrested by a militant party of the Sons of Liberty in 1776, Seabury was accused of subverting the American cause and forced to stand trial. Among the accusations the impromptu court brought against him was his refusal to open his church to Americans desiring to observe the fast. In his own defense, Seabury pled ignorance, insisting that he had not been informed of the fast day. The credibility of his defense is questionable, however, as the fast day proclamation appeared in newspapers throughout the colony and was distributed as a broadside in the area as well. Surely Seabury was well aware of the fast. In the spirit of Revolutionary rituals, his refusal to participate amounted to a public statement of his loyalty to Great Britain and his dismissal of congressional legitimacy.[9] Other avowed loyalist clergymen recognized that their refusal to observe the fast day could result in backlash from patriots in their congregations. Such was the case for Jacob Bailey of Pownalborough, Massachusetts (now Dresden, Maine), who after refusing to observe the fast day and openly railing against Congress was "severely threatened" by local patriots and eventually had to flee to Canada.[10]

A closer look at fast day observance and its consequences reveals that while the ritual rallied avowed patriots and loyalists to their respective sides, it pushed many colonists who were more moderate or entirely neutral to one side or the other. This was especially the case in American cities. As the historian Benjamin Carp has demonstrated, the largest and most concentrated populations of patriots lived in cities and interacted daily with the largest and most concentrated populations of loyalists. This juxtaposition of demographic extremes often gave the already difficult decision between revolution and loyalty an even greater sense of urgency.[11] Accordingly, fast day participation throughout the War of Independence was more consistent in American cities than it was in rural settlements, perhaps because there was a greater need for city dwellers to publicly demonstrate where their allegiances lay. Public rituals such as the observation of fast days made it more difficult for colonists to keep their opinions on the imperial crisis private. If they attended a fast day sermon, they were thought to be sympathetic to the Revolution. If they did not attend, they were suspected of loyalism and, by extension, opposition to the patriot cause.

Such reasoning appears to be what led patriots into the streets of Philadelphia on the first fast day to commit acts of destruction. This was the same fast day observance that Adams had celebrated as exceeding the solemnity of typical Sabbath observance. Perhaps he had missed the violent outburst altogether or, more likely, he had chosen to omit it in his report home. According to reports, patriots smashed the windows of the city's Quaker shopkeepers, who had kept their places of business open on the fast day. While fast days seemingly united Philadelphians in the city's churches, it divided them in the streets.[12]

The abstention of the Quaker community from the fast day was based on their belief in pacifism, but this fast day mob chose to interpret Quaker pacifism as opposition to the patriot cause. Such an attack on Philadelphia's Quaker businesses associated with the 1775 fast day illustrates the way in which American revolutionaries could hypocritically persecute political and religious dissenters under the banner of liberty and providentialism. In this instance, many of Philadelphia's elite used the fast day to further scapegoat the city's Quaker population, constituting yet another episode in a long-running local power struggle between Philadelphians allied with the Penn family and the city's small but influential Quaker population and its allies. Although city leaders urged citizens on subsequent fast days to "forebear from any kind of insult to [Quakers], or any others who may . . . refuse to keep the said fast," the city's anti-Quaker temperament demonstrated in the 1775 fast day riot did not dissipate.[13]

Recent immigrants to Philadelphia such as Thomas Paine tapped into this local power struggle, recognizing that its polarizing effect could be used to promote a continental revolution. Paine became an especially harsh critic of the Society of Friends despite the strong Quaker influence on his early education. As the historian Jane E. Calvert persuasively argues, Paine used the Quakers as "a convenient foil and the means of rallying the non-Quaker Pennsylvanians against Great Britain."[14] He consistently equated the society's pacifism with passivity and at other times conflated it with loyalism; both were gross mischaracterizations of the Quakers' political stance. Paine's anti-Quaker diatribes in popular pamphlets such as *Common Sense* and *The Crisis* fit into the "common cause" rhetoric in which Revolutionary spokesmen vilified dissenters. American patriots were standing up for their liberties while denying the same to their neighbors who had different opinions.[15] Thus, fast days did not occur in a political or cultural vacuum. Instead, they presented patriot opportunists an additional avenue for pursuing their political ambitions, local or national. Furthermore, the poor treatment of Philadelphia Quakers appears to have pushed some away from a position of true neutrality and toward loyalism.

Some clergymen who were opposed to Congress and the Continental Army it had formed still observed the fast day but did so in a strategic manner to block their parishioners from hearing rousing patriotic sermons at other churches on the occasion. "It has been a serious & solemn & I hope sincere Fast!," Ezra Stiles wrote in his journal, describing the 1775 fast day observance in the city. "I suppose all congregations in town kept it. With Reluctance indeed the Church of England just read prayers at XI o'clock, but without preaching or afternoon service." Stiles was accusing his religious rivals of hypocrisy, claiming that the city's Anglican clergymen were uninterested in the fast day's cause. Instead, their pro forma fast day observance "was rather policy to prevent the church from going to the Meetings [of other denominations]—for they abominate this fast."[16]

Stiles and others like him recognized that fast day observance was a vital battlefield for public opinion. One could protest Congress and the Revolution by abstaining from the event or even by holding it as an empty ritual intended only to keep men and women from participating elsewhere. At stake were the hearts and minds of the American people.

While fast days galvanized clergy and laity of all Christian denominations in the colonies, Anglican clergymen wrestled with a liturgical question of their own: whether to pray, or not to pray, for King George III and Parliament. The impetus for this question was the arrival in their cities and towns in 1776 of news of the Declaration of Independence. With this news many Americans clamored for a change to the liturgy of the Church of England in the colonies, one that reflected their new political status.

Anglican priests in the colonies, like their counterparts in England, had each taken an oath of loyalty to the church and to the king as its ecclesiastical head. In theory, this meant that no matter what they thought about the fairness of imperial policies regulating affairs in British North America, no matter what side they identified with amid political protests that eventually transformed into violent revolution, these clergymen were to remain true to their oaths. And replacing king and Parliament with Congress in the liturgy would certainly run counter to that oath.

For clergymen such as Samuel Seabury of Connecticut, as well as Thomas Chandler and Myles Cooper, both of whom led congregations in the loyalist hotbed of New York City, the decision was an easy one. All three decided early in the imperial conflict that they would remain absolutely loyal to the king as their political and ecclesiastical leader. And for years after Chandler and Cooper fled to England, they remained convinced that their decision had been the correct one. Nor did Seabury ever publicly express regret for his principled stand, not even after leveraging his fortuitously timed ordination as a bishop in Scotland into a prominent place in the newly formed American Episcopal Church.[17]

But what of the Anglican clergymen for whom this decision was more ambiguous, the men who sorted through an assortment of conflicted personal feelings and external political pressures to make their decision about the alteration of the liturgy? What do their experiences teach us about the galvanizing effect this liturgical question had on the clerical community and, by extension, their congregations? Could altering the liturgy have been more about individual survival and the survival of the Church of England in the erstwhile colonies turned states than it was about political and religious principles? Indeed, surviving documents suggest that for certain Anglican clergymen at least, the decision to pray or not to pray for the king was more about an ordering of ecclesiastical priorities than it was about a principled stand on the question of revolution or loyalty.

Removing prayers for the king from the Church of England's Book of Common Prayer and replacing them with prayers for the Continental Congress seems to have started in Virginia. In 1776, after Virginia's leaders at home sent instructions to their delegates in Philadelphia to move for independence, the former appointed a committee of Virginia churchmen to alter the church's prayers in expectation of the Declaration of Independence.[18] Adapting the worship of the established church to the altered character of Virginia's government was not simply a pragmatic act. It also served as a clear signal to Virginia's Anglican population that where their relationship with Great Britain was concerned they had reached a point of no return.

In Philadelphia, the decision to alter the liturgy was made by the vestries of the city's congregations in the days immediately following the adoption of the Declaration of Independence in Congress. The choice made by Jacob Duché, rector of Christ Church, to support the liturgical change is particularly illuminating. The first chaplain to serve in the Continental Congress, Duché quickly won praise from nearly all the delegates as a gifted orator and an ally in Congress's goal to coordinate resistance to the imperial policies of Great Britain. In his first prayer in Congress, he warned that Britain was in danger of losing the favor of Providence and its central role in God's plan for the moral redemption of mankind. Then when Congress declared independence and the vestry at Christ Church moved to "omit those petitions in the Liturgy wherein the King of Great Britain is prayed for," Duché supported it.[19] However, in October 1776 he resigned his chaplaincy, citing as reasons his poor health and a need to focus on his congregation. Nevertheless, in carrying out his regular ecclesiastical duties, he continued to recite the altered versions of the prayers during worship services.[20]

Then Duché's circumstances changed. In September 1777 the British army descended on Philadelphia. Congress and a large number of patriots fled, and the army occupied the city. Duché, however, remained. On the first Sunday following the start of the British occupation, Duché prepared to lead his congregation in its worship services, but on this day his pews were filled to the brim with British soldiers. Duché had an important decision to make. He could read the day's prayer as prescribed by the Church of England, or he could read the altered version. Duché chose the former. Perhaps he hoped that one penitent act of loyalty would be enough to compensate for the patriotic preaching of the previous three years. But he had no such luck. When he exited the church after the service, he was arrested and imprisoned by British officers.[21]

The British only held Duché captive for one night, but he left any of his remaining patriotism in his cell. Perhaps as a condition for his release, Duché wrote a letter to George Washington imploring him to surrender to the British. In explaining his change of heart, Duché insisted that he had never supported independence. Indeed, he said that the Declaration had contributed to his decision to resign the chaplaincy. He thought that independence was a step too far in opposing British imperial policy, as unjust as Duché may have thought that policy was. But there was more to this priest's delayed confession than apprehension over the issue of independence. He cited his low opinion of the men then in Congress and questioned their ability to successfully prosecute the war. As he saw it, the deficiencies in Congress were compounded further by the deficiencies of the army it created. The lack of martial discipline and the frequent desertions all made the war a hopeless endeavor for Washington, and Duché believed that his inevitable defeat would have stinging consequence for American life for years to come. "Humanity itself," Duché implored the general, "calls upon you to desist."[22]

Of course, Washington did not desist. But he did send Duché's letter to Congress, which in turn had it published. As a result, Duché was forced to flee to England to preserve his livelihood and maybe even his life. Yet, this assessment of Duché as a patriot experiencing a conflict of conscience over independence raises a significant question: how could a man conflicted over the prospect of American independence so readily alter the liturgy following the adoption of the Declaration of Independence? Did he merely lose his nerve once the British occupied his city? Was he simply a man of weak resolve who went in whatever direction the wind blew? Or was it self-preservation? Perhaps he feared that if he opposed the motion of the vestry to alter the prayers, he would be deemed a loyalist and persecuted as such. He had, after all, witnessed one of his clerical assistants, Thomas Coombé, brought to the brink of execution for his abandonment of the patriot cause earlier that year. Only the mediation of Duché and Reverend William White, who persuaded the incensed Philadelphians to deport him rather than kill him, had spared Coombé's life. Ultimately, it is hard to know what Duché's motives were.

Yet, Duché's alteration of the liturgy may alternatively be seen as an effort to preserve the Church of England in America, as an insistence on praying for the king might have driven any and all patriots from Anglican congregations. So, where Duché appears to have been motivated, at least in part, by self-preservation, several Anglican clergymen altered the liturgy with the aforementioned goal of preserving their congregations—and the larger church in North America—amid the storm of revolution. Indeed, several Anglican clergymen in Boston who did not initially agree to stop praying for the king and Parliament eventually acquiesced to patriot demands and commenced praying for Congress in their stead. One of these clergymen, Reverend Edward Bass, explained that because he believed the Revolution was certain to fail, omitting the king from prayers was a short-term concession he made for a long-term benefit, namely, the preservation of his church and his ministry. He feared that even in the aftermath of a failed revolution, if the Church of England appeared unresponsive to the wishes and political inclination of many of its parishioners, such obstinacy would do irreparable damage to the church's prospects in a region of the American colonies so dominated by the Congregationalists that it was already struggling to maintain its presence.[23] In essence, Bass compromised, negotiating the ecclesiastical and political elements of his ministerial oath, but to use a biblical metaphor, he believed he had chosen the better part.

Thomas Paine's insistence that the American Revolution was a time "that tried men's souls" was as true, if not more so, for the American clergy as it was for the American laity. Perhaps the same can be said for the Anglican clergymen in America when compared with their ecclesiastical counterparts in other denominations. Choosing a side in the Revolution could be a difficult task for many of these priests. The process entailed far more than simply forming an opinion on the extent to which Parliament was violating the colonists' rights as Englishmen. Among numerous other considerations, clergymen, like their lay counterparts, had to take into account their prospects for protecting themselves, their families, and their livelihoods on the basis of the choices they made. While it is tempting to privilege historical accounts of zealous patriots and adamant loyalists throwing caution to the wind by allowing ideological principles alone to guide their decision making, in reality most took a far more measured approach to American protests and, eventually, independence. In the case of Anglican clergymen, this often measured approach included weighing the alteration of the church's liturgy and their respective oaths against other considerations.

Personal connections and circumstances also seemed to play a role in the political steps taken by certain Anglican clergymen during the war and their fate in its aftermath, even if they had remained staunch loyalists. Consider the cases of four different priests in Virginia. Late in the war Reverends John Brice, William Andrews, Thomas Price, and William Harrison fled to British lines. After the surrender at Yorktown, American forces took these men prisoner. All four were charged with treason, but none was convicted. Two of the four experienced a loss of prestige and access to the pulpit in America as a result. Bruce returned to Princess Anne County, where he was never again considered for clerical or political stations and quietly lived out the rest of his life. Andrews fled to England in recognition of the bleakness of his prospects in America. The two other clergymen, Price and Harrison, immediately resumed their parochial duties, almost as if nothing had happened.[24]

How do we explain the double standard? Price and Harrison were members of the gentry, and Bruce and Andrews were not. In fact, the Prices and the Harrisons were among the so-called first families of Virginia, whose wealth and extensive landholdings afforded them significant power and influence in the state. Price's and Harrison's familial ties trumped their loyalist positions during the war, demonstrating that even in the most patriotic regions of the country a loyalist could return to a prominent social and cultural place if he was connected to the right people,[25] or in the aforementioned case of Samuel Seabury in Connecticut, if he held some form of leverage over his patriot counterparts in the church. Personal and family situations, along with other social and ecclesiastical circumstances, often combined in the way that they factored into the political decisions made by Anglican clergymen during the Revolution.

Yet, the navigation of the social and political disruptions caused by the Revolution started with a choice between revolution and loyalism, and for many Anglican clergymen this liturgical conflict forced that choice. Perhaps some were loath to publicize their stance, whether they were conflicted or neutral on the matter, or were committed to one side or the other and feared the backlash of making their sentiments public. For the Anglican clergy in the colonies, the question of praying for the king and Parliament effectively eroded the political middle ground or unraveled any privacy covering their personal political views.

HISTORIANS HAVE written extensively on loyalists and patriots in the American Revolution. As a result, we have a fairly good idea of colonists' myriad motives and justifications for choosing one side or the other in the conflict. However, those who were caught somewhere between the two sides remain understudied by comparison. Moderate or conflicting views of the war led many colonists to abstain from choosing a side. Still others were truly neutral in the affair. The extent to which religious views informed the opinions of this group is unclear, but public religious rituals clearly contributed to the erosion of a tenable political middle ground.

Fast days and liturgical debates had a similar, if more subtle, effect on political mobilization as the loyalty oaths mandated by local councils on safety. Forcing citizens to take an oath of loyalty to the United States of America helped transform the Revolution into a civil war, forcing conflicted or willfully neutral individuals to choose a side. A person's refusal to take such an oath, such as in the case of Rev. John Zubly of Georgia, was often read as an indication of support for the British. Even when Zubly offered to take a "halfway" oath instead, pledging his allegiance to Georgia but not to the United States, the local council on safety confiscated his property and banished him from the state.[26]

Fast days and debates over liturgical politics were less dramatic than loyalty oaths but had a similar effect. They simultaneously galvanized and polarized Americans. While these events are often associated with the infusion of religious language and symbolism into the rhetoric of the Revolution, they represent important components of political mobilization in a conflict that was at once international and domestic.

For historians of the American Revolution there is a particular reason to lament polarizing effects of religious rituals on the public. Polarization contracts the range of expressed public opinions. In the case of the American colonists such polarization obscured—and in some cases obliterated—the nuance of public opinion about the conflict. Accordingly, historians in the present know a lot about the motives of loyalists and revolutionaries but far less about those positioned in between—the moderates, the conflicted, and the neutral. Religious ritual helped to galvanize the American public during the Revolution and to erode the political middle ground to the extent that an unknown number of Americans kept their true, often complicated feelings about the conflict private. Now many of these views are lost to history, in part because of the effectiveness of public religious rituals in mobilizing the public during the American Revolution.

Notes

1. Spencer W. McBride, *Pulpit and Nation: Clergymen and the Politics of Revolutionary America* (Charlottesville: University of Virginia Press, 2017), 12–16. On the history of fast day observance in colonial America, see David D. Hall, *Worlds of Wonder, Days of Judgement: Popular Religious Belief in Early New England* (New York: Knopf, 1989), 170–71; and W. DeLoss Love Jr., *Fast and Thanksgiving Days of New England* (Boston: Houghton Mifflin, 1895). On the less frequent observance of fast days in colonies south of New England, see John F. Berens, *Providence and Patriotism in Early America, 1640–1815* (Charlottesville: University of Virginia Press, 1978), 32–35; and Rhys Isaac, *The Transformation of Virginia, 1740–1790* (Chapel Hill: University of North Carolina Press, 1982), 243–45. For more on the role of fast days in the colonists' conceptions of providentialism, see Nicholas Guyatt, *Providence and the Invention of the United States, 1607–1876* (New York: Cambridge University Press, 2007). For more on fast days and how their observance fit in the development of religious rhetoric surrounding the Revolutionary War, see James H. Hutson, *Religion and the Founding of the American Republic* (Washington, DC: Library of Congress, 1998), 55; and Thomas S. Kidd, *God of Liberty: A Religious History of the American Revolution* (New York: Basic Books, 2010), 125. On the role that rituals such as fast days played in unifying disparate groups during and after the American Revolution, see Derek H. Davis, *Religion and the Continental Congress, 1774–1789: Contributions to Original Intent* (New York: Oxford University Press, 2000), 88; Benjamin H. Irvin, *Clothed in the Robes of Sovereignty: The Continental Congress and the People Out of Doors* (New York: Oxford University Press, 2011), 7–8; and David Waldstreicher, *In the Midst of Perpetual Fetes: The Making of American Nationalism* (Chapel Hill: University of North Carolina Press, 1997), 34–35.
2. John Adams to Abigail Adams, June 11 and 17, 1775, Adams Family Papers: An Electronic Archive, Massachusetts Historical Society, https://www.masshist.org/digitaladams/archive/doc?id=L17750611ja.
3. As an example of Americans' unfamiliarity with new national political figures in Congress, when Thomas Jefferson visited Rhode Island in 1784, a Providence newspaper included a description of Jefferson's recent accomplishments in order to explain to its readers precisely who their

distinguished visitor was. Coincidently, this is also the first instance on record of Jefferson being publicly credited with authorship of the Declaration of Independence. The original dateline read "Providence, June 19, 1784." The description was reprinted in several New England newspapers, such as Boston's *American Herald*, June 28, 1784. See also Andrew Burstein and Nancy Isenberg, *Madison and Jefferson* (New York: Random House, 2010), 110.

4. On the education of clergymen and the politicization of college faculties in the 1750s and 1760s, which precipitated and encouraged the politicization of students during the Revolution, see David W. Robson, *Educating Republicans: The College in the Era of the American Revolution, 1750–1800* (Westport, CT: Greenwood, 1985), 22, 29–50; and J. David Hoeveler, *Creating the American Mind: Intellect and Politics in the Colonial Colleges* (Lanham, MD: Rowman & Littlefield, 2002), 347–49. For examples of the political activism of clergymen during the Stamp Act crisis, see Benjamin Throop, *A Thanksgiving Sermon, Upon the Occasion, of the Glorious News of the Repeal of the Stamp Act* (New-London, CT, 1766); and Charles Chauncey, *A Discourse on "The Good News from a Far Country"* (Boston, 176, reprinted in *The Pulpit of the American Revolution; or, the Political Sermons of the Period of 1776*, ed. John Wingate Thornton [New York: B. Franklin, 1970], 105–45). On the role of clergymen in the diffusion of information in colonial New England, see Richard D. Brown, *Knowledge Is Power: The Diffusion of Information in Early America, 1775–1800* (New York: Oxford University Press, 1989), 65–81. See also McBride, *Pulpit and Nation*, 18.
5. Matthew Dennis, *Red, White, and Blue Letter Days: An American Calendar* (Ithaca, NY: Cornell University Press, 2002), 40–41. On the role of ritual in the Revolution, see Peter Shaw, *American Patriots and the Rituals of Revolution* (Cambridge, MA: Harvard University Press, 1981). On the appearance of consensus for festive rites, see Waldstreicher, *In the Midst of Perpetual Fetes*, 8–9, 14.
6. "Resolution for a Fast," June 12, 1775, in *Journals of the Continental Congress, 1774–1789*, vol. 2, ed. Worthington C. Ford (Washington, DC: Library of Congress 1905), 87.
7. John Adams to Abigail Adams, July 23, 1775, Adams Family Papers: An Electronic Archive, Massachusetts Historical Society, https://www.masshist.org/digitaladams/archive/doc?id=L17750723jasecond.
8. McBride, *Pulpit and Nation*, 30–37.
9. Bruce E. Steiner, *Samuel Seabury, 1729–1796: A Study in the High Church Tradition* (Athens: Ohio University Press, 1971), 156–64.
10. Jacob Bailey to anonymous, n.d., quoted in James S. Leamon, *The Reverend Jacob Bailey, Maine Loyalist: For God, King, Country, and for Self* (Amherst: University of Massachusetts Press, 2012), 110.

11. Benjamin L. Carp, *Rebels Rising: Cities and the American Revolution* (New York: Oxford University Press, 2007), 5–9, 13–17, 225.
12. On the destruction of Quaker property on the 1775 fast day in Philadelphia, see Christopher Marshall, diary, July 20, 1775, Christopher Marshall Papers, 1774–1781, Historical Society of Pennsylvania. See also Irvin, *Clothed in the Robes of Sovereignty*, 115.
13. Committee of Inspection and Observance, "In Committee Chamber," May 16, 1776, Historical Society of Pennsylvania; Tara Strauch, "Open for Business: Philadelphia Quakers, Thanksgiving, and the Limits of Revolutionary Religious Freedom," *Church History* 85, no. 1 (March 2016): 133–39.
14. Jane E. Calvert, "Thomas Paine, Quakerism, and the Limits of Religious Liberty During the American Revolution," in *Selected Writings of Thomas Paine*, ed. Ian Shapiro and Jane E. Calvert (New Haven, CT: Yale University Press, 2014), 547–66.
15. Calvert, "Thomas Paine, Quakerism, and the Limits of Religious Liberty."
16. Ezra Stiles, diary, July 20, 1775, in *The Literary Diary of Ezra Stiles*, ed. Franklin Bowditch Dexter, 3 vols. (New York: Charles Scribner's Sons, 1901), 1:591.
17. McBride, *Pulpit and Nation*,70–80.
18. G. MacLaren Brydon, "Revision of the Prayer Book by an American Civil Legislature," *Historical Magazine of the Protestant Episcopal Church* 19, no. 2 (June 1950): 133–38.
19. Edward Duffield Neill, "Rev. Jacob Duché: The First Chaplain of Congress," *Pennsylvania Magazine of History and Biography* 2, no. 1 (1878): 66–67.
20. McBride, *Pulpit and Nation*, 53–60.
21. McBride, *Pulpit and Nation*, 59–60.
22. Jacob Duché to George Washington, October 8, 1777, in *The Washington-Duché Letters*, ed. Worthington Chauncey Ford (New York, 1890).
23. On Bass and other Anglican clergymen in Boston who agreed to patriot demands that they stop praying for the king, see Leamon, *Reverend Jacob Bailey*, 115–16.
24. Otto Lohrenz, "The Advantage of Rank and Status: Thomas Price, a Loyalist Parson of Revolutionary Virginia," *Historian* 60, no. 3 (Spring 1998): 561–77.
25. Lohrenz, "Advantage of Rank and Status." See also McBride, *Pulpit and Nation*, 79.
26. John J. Zubly, "To the Grand Jury of the County of Chatham," in "*A Warm and Zealous Spirit": John J. Zubly and the American Revolution, a Selection of His Writings*, ed. Randall M. Miller (Mercer, GA: Mercer University Press, 1982), 165–70.

Thomas Barton's Crisis of Conscience

Community, Salvation, and Oaths of Allegiance on the Pennsylvania Frontier

PETER W. WALKER

★

At the end of 1778, Rev. Thomas Barton and his wife, Esther (Rittenhouse) Barton, arrived in British-held New York City as loyalist refugees.[1] They were fleeing from the frontier town of Lancaster, Pennsylvania, where Thomas had been an Anglican clergyman and missionary of the Society for the Propagation of the Gospel (SPG). He had made his opposition to American independence known, first by refusing to perform the Anglican church service without the customary prayers for King George III and then by refusing to take the oath of allegiance required by the new state. After the legal penalties for the latter crime were significantly ramped up, Barton petitioned the Pennsylvania Assembly asking to be excused on conscientious grounds from taking the oath. The assembly denied his petition, prompting his flight to New York. Esther accompanied him even though the oath had not been demanded of her.[2]

From New York, Barton wrote to the secretary of the SPG detailing the misery caused by his forced removal from his home, his children, and his congregation. He reported that every single one of the SPG missionaries in Pennsylvania had undergone a similar ordeal, insisting that their treatment constituted nothing less than religious persecution. They had "suffer'd a Persecution as cruel as the Bed of Procrustes," he wrote, invoking a common metaphor drawn from Greek mythology: just as Procrustes had stretched his victims or cut off their legs to make their bodies fit an iron bed, so persecutors had mutilated consciences by forcing devout Anglicans to conform to an external standard.[3] Barton undoubtedly received some measure of satisfaction when his correspondent replied acknowledging the tremendous sufferings the missionaries had borne for their loyalty. They "have made Sacrifices to Britain that will astonish Posterity," the secretary wrote. "Let them not be called *Friends* [of Britain];—let them be called *Martyrs*."[4]

Questions around oaths were central to Barton's identity as a martyr and a victim of persecution. Loyalists and neutralists alike complained of the hypocrisy of revolutionaries who spoke about liberty while mercilessly oppressing dissent. The American Revolution was a "minority project," in Rebecca Brannon's words, imposed, often by force, on the disaffected.[5] Barton, though, was accusing the Pennsylvania Assembly not just of tyranny but of something far worse: religious persecution. This accusation referred to his refusal to swear allegiance to the new state, as well as his fealty to the unaltered Anglican church service. For Americans in this era, oath taking was a religious act. Barton's petition to be excused from the oath of allegiance and his insistence that the assembly was persecuting him by rejecting his petition do not make sense unless we recognize that the oath held a spiritual and theological significance, which distinguished it categorically from a mere legal contract or secular promise. Barton's ordeal thus offers a starting point for considering the use of this longstanding but contentious religious instrument to create new communities of conscience during the American Revolution. Fundamental to this project was the construction of an independent moral subject, defined by religion, race, and gender and endowed with the capacity to choose to swear allegiance or refuse to do so.

Historians have long recognized the important role of oaths of allegiance in the story of American independence. Oaths were imposed by the newly independent American states, the British military authorities, patriot committees of safety, and Revolutionary crowds (or, in loyalist eyes, "mobs"). Lists of subscribers to these oaths survive, providing invaluable evidence of popular allegiances and politicization, as well as of patriot suppression of dissent.[6] By carefully reading these lists, historians have shown that individuals often swore oaths to both sides and honored neither, exploiting and frustrating expectations of absolute loyalty.[7] However, they have only recently begun to consider the religious dimensions of oaths of allegiance.[8] Few have recognized the accompanying theological apparatus, which was thought to make an oath an effective guarantor of allegiance in the first place. This theological apparatus shaped the Revolutionary contest over allegiance in important ways, above all by ensuring that loyalism often took the form of conscientious objection and martyrdom.

As the rich body of scholarship on the early modern oath attests, oaths once held a religious significance that today has been largely lost.[9] Oaths by definition invoked God as an underwriter to the truth of a statement. An oath was thus a contract "with God involved as a party, rather than merely a witness."[10] For the seventeenth-century archbishop of Canterbury John Tillotson, an oath was "a sacred thing . . . an act of religion and an invocation of the name of God." It gave the swearer access to God, constituting a form of worship. Conversely, breaking an oath had dreadful consequences. It was a "provisional self-curse."[11] Perjury was not just a crime but a sin, one that clerical authorities considered worse than homicide. For this reason, they agreed that oaths should be taken only with the utmost solemnity and only when absolutely necessary, to avoid setting snares for the soul. This was why Quakers refused to take them. Puritans were also wary of them.

The early modern state sought to harness the profound power of oaths for its own political ends. It did so precisely because the oath was understood as a soteriological contract, not a merely legal one. Oaths concerned salvation. There could be no more consequential guarantee of political allegiance, no more effective way to bind subjects to sovereign or political nation together. England therefore saw a proliferating series of state oaths from the Tudor period on. These involved the nation, not just the individual, in a relationship with God. The nation's earthly and spiritual well-being, even its eschatological destiny, became tied to the keeping of national oaths.

Eventually, the proliferation of oaths of allegiance caused problems for the state. Oaths depended for their efficacy on the inviolability of conscience and thus invited conscientious resistance to them.[12] Over the course of the early modern period, conscience was gradually transformed from "a moral and legal guarantor of political conformity" to "a resource for resistance to the claims of the state."[13] Especially contentious was the imposition of new state oaths that contradicted those imposed by preceding regimes. This was a common occurrence, given early modern England's religio-political turmoil: from the whiplash back and forth of the Tudor Reformation to the seventeenth-century civil wars to the "Glorious Revolution" of 1688. To what extent was an individual bound by an old oath? Did swearing a new oath constitute perjury? Some authorities maintained that the swearer was bound by an oath even if it had been imposed by violence; others suggested that such an oath was unlawful, or simply redundant if subsequent circumstances made its fulfillment impossible. Potential justifications for renouncing obsolete oaths thus existed, but there was by no means a consensus on this question.[14] For this reason, fealty to preexisting oaths offered a powerful tool of resistance to those seeking to undermine the demands of the state.[15]

This longer history illuminates the struggles over community, conscience, and oaths of allegiance that took place during the American Revolution. When independence was declared, many Americans—various officeholders, including the clergy, as well as naturalized foreign Protestants—had previously sworn oaths of allegiance to the Crown.[16] These oaths were a coercive religious instrument designed to hold the empire together.[17] When they failed to contain the political disputes, Kevin Murphy has shown, the revolutionaries returned to this same coercive instrument in their efforts to forge a new political community.[18] The element of coercion is exposed by loyalist objections to the Revolutionary oaths. Loyalists argued that patriots' refusal to accommodate those who had already sworn oaths of allegiance constituted religious persecution: they were coercing individuals into jeopardizing their salvation. This was a powerful, unsettling critique, and it resonated with audiences beyond the loyalists themselves.[19] Focusing on the religious dimensions of oaths of allegiance, and opposition to them, thus invites us to see the American Revolution as a crisis of conscience, not only a crisis of individual consciences[20] but also a crisis of conscience as a political category, calling into question the very capacity of the oath to hold a community together.

Oaths of Office and Prayers for the King: The Loyalist Church of England Clergy

This essay considers these issues raised by oaths through a case study of Thomas Barton and his refusal to swear allegiance to the state of Pennsylvania. During the Revolution, many categories of Americans were caught between the conflicting demands of different oaths, but none more so than the Church of England clergy. All had taken certain oaths of office when they were ordained. Taking these oaths was a religious act and a key part of the ordination ritual whereby they received clerical status. They included an oath of allegiance to George III and an oath to conduct church service according to the Book of Common Prayer. After independence was declared, the Revolutionary authorities imposed new oaths of allegiance and outlawed the prayers for the king contained in the prayer book. Individual clergy responded in different ways, but many concluded that the patriots' demands were incompatible with their ordination oaths.

Partly for this reason, the colonial Anglican clergy were disproportionately loyalists, especially in New England and the Mid-Atlantic. This is, of course, a generalization. Many factors besides the institutional influence of the Church of England shaped the decisions of individual clergy: their theological priorities, political sympathies, social networks, local political contexts, and individual personalities.[21] The SPG exercised a particularly strong pull toward loyalism, not least because it supported its missionaries financially and actively enforced their political allegiance. Thus, every single SPG missionary in Pennsylvania refused to swear allegiance to the state, whereas all but one of the Anglican clergy of Philadelphia did so; the latter were independent of the SPG and were funded entirely by their congregations.[22] We should not assume that the loyalist clergy were somehow more "religious" than the patriots: both sides had theological justifications for their positions; individuals were always driven by multiple, overlapping motivations; and attempting to identify anyone's innermost beliefs is a fool's errand. My focus here is less on Barton's reasons for choosing loyalism and more on his moral critique of the Revolution in general and its use of oaths of allegiance in particular.

The Anglican church service was a key point of conflict between Anglicanism and the imperatives of American independence. Anglican worship followed a set form laid out in the Book of Common Prayer. The Church of England was a state church, and one of its functions was to sacralize the political community. To this end, the officiating minister was supposed to pray for the monarch and their well-being, that God grant the monarch "victory over all his enemies" and protect the people from "sedition, privy conspiracy, and rebellion."[23] Unsurprisingly, the revolutionaries objected to these prayers, and after declaring independence they passed treason laws against them. The choice to read or not to read these prayers immediately became a litmus test for the Anglican clergy's political allegiance. The clergy were under immense pressure to make a clear statement one way or the other, given the power of public religion to authorize independence or delegitimize it.[24] Some clergy believed that omitting the prayers was an expedient justified by the political emergency. Others replaced them with prayers for Congress, on the grounds that they should be for the nation's political leaders whoever they happened to be. Loyalists among the Anglican clergy refused to modify the prayers and closed their churches rather than officiate without them.[25]

For the loyalist clergy, an important argument against omitting or modifying the prayers for the king was that doing so contradicted their ordination oaths. Whether or not a minor departure from the Book of Common Prayer was acceptable in the abstract, they argued, they could not make this modification themselves. Rev. William Clark, for example, explained to his congregation that "by Vows, Oaths & Subscriptions, which have been made on Earth & recorded in Heaven, I am obliged to act as a Dutiful Subject of His Most Gracious Majesty King George the Third; and to the Constant use of the Liturgy of that Church of which, under GOD, he is the head."[26] To modify the content of the church service, Clark reasoned, would be to break his ordination oaths and thus damn himself by committing the sin of perjury.

The precise wording of the Anglican clergy's ordination oaths is therefore crucially important. Canon law required ordinands to swear the oath of allegiance ("I, A. B. do sincerely promise and swear, that I will be faithful, and bear true allegiance [to the present monarch]") and the oath of supremacy (denying the ecclesiastical and spiritual authority of the pope). They also had to sign a declaration that the Church of England's Thirty-Nine Articles of Religion were "agreeable to the Word of God" and that the Book of Common Prayer contained "nothing contrary to the Word of God"; and they had to promise to "use the Form in the said Book prescribed in public Prayer . . . and none other."[27] In addition, the 1662 Act of Uniformity, passed after the Restoration, required clergy to take the following oath when installed in office: "I A. B. do declare my unfeigned assent and consent to all and everything contained and prescribed in and by [the Book of Common Prayer]."[28] Finally, the same act required those clergy involved in the education of youth to take an additional oath when installed: "I A. B. do declare that it is not lawful upon any pretense whatsoever to take arms against the King and that I do abhor that traitorous position . . . and that I will conform to the liturgy of the Church of England as it is now by law established."[29]

To what extent did these oaths prohibit the Anglican clergy from supporting the Revolution? This question was debatable. The oath taken by educators provided the strongest justification for loyalism, but only some of the clergy had taken it.[30] The other oaths were more ambiguous. The oath of allegiance to George III could be construed as having become obsolete or impossible to fulfil, but if it was understood as binding, this would absolutely prohibit the swearing of a new oath of allegiance. In addition, the promise to use the "form" of the Book of Common Prayer "and none other" raised further questions, given the revolutionaries' efforts to stop Anglicans from praying for the king. What exactly was meant by the "form" of the prayer book? Who could authorize a departure from it, and under what circumstances?[31] Like many colonial Americans, the Anglican clergy were deeply invested in British history, and they turned to it for answers to these questions.[32]

From an Anglican point of view, the most relevant precedent was the oaths imposed by William and Mary after the "Glorious Revolution." These were refused by four hundred Anglican clergymen known as nonjurors, whose refusal to take the new oath led to the nonjuring schism in the Church of England. Their opposition to foreswearing helped constitute Jacobitism's deeply religious character.[33] Both jurors and nonjurors were themselves divided over whether to offer active allegiance or passive submission. Thus, there were four distinct positions. Some jurors were active supporters of the Williamite monarchy who gladly swore the new oaths of allegiance and held that the old oaths had been made redundant when James vacated the throne. Other jurors believed that James remained ruler de jure but acknowledged that William and Mary were now rulers de facto; they were therefore content to offer passive submission, if not active allegiance. They argued that the new Williamite oaths only recognized William and Mary as rulers de facto, and they were therefore willing to take them. Indeed, it is possible that the wording of the Williamite oaths was deliberately chosen to provide this accommodation. Likewise, some nonjurors were outright Jacobites who held that James was ruler de jure and therefore demanded their full and undivided allegiance; they actively worked for the restoration of the deposed Stuart dynasty. Others recognized James as ruler de jure and passively submitted to William and Mary as rulers de facto, but they rejected the idea that it was somehow possible to take the Williamite oaths while doing so. This latter group were dangerous because there was only a thin line between conscientious objection to foreswearing and actively plotting against the new monarchy. Nevertheless, their coreligionists recognized that their arguments against foreswearing were sound, and there were meaningful efforts to accommodate the nonjuring conscience.[34]

Understanding the different lines of argument over the earlier Williamite oaths helps us better understand the later conflict over oaths of allegiance in the American Revolution. Like active Jacobites, active loyalists held that George III was still the de jure ruler of the American colonies, that oaths of allegiance taken to him were still valid, and that new oaths of allegiance to the Revolutionary authorities were inherently unlawful. According to this logic, no one who had sworn allegiance to George III could lawfully submit to the Revolutionary authorities in any way until the king himself released them from their allegiance to him (as eventually happened in 1783 with the Peace of Paris). Meanwhile, passive loyalists, like passive nonjurors, accepted the revolutionaries as rulers de facto, though not de jure, and recognized the duty of passive submission on this basis. Here, however, an important difference between the American Revolution and the "Glorious" Revolution becomes apparent: the American revolutionaries were far less willing to accept passive submission. The oaths they imposed simply did not accommodate the consciences of those who recognized George III as ruler de jure. They were also far more skeptical of the idea that Americans who refused to swear new oaths of allegiance could be anything other than active loyalists.

Thomas Barton and the Pennsylvania Test Act

The complex theological issues involved in these debates explain why Rev. Thomas Barton, the Lancaster loyalist and SPG missionary, accused the revolutionaries of religious persecution.[35] From the beginning of the imperial crisis, Barton expressed his desire to stay out of the political disputes. He sympathized with the patriots' grievances but refused to countenance rebellion. Yet in the frontier town of Lancaster, loyalists were isolated and vulnerable. In these circumstances, neutrality offered the safest means of self-preservation, not to mention continuation of Anglican religious service. This was a consistent theme in Barton's letters to the SPG. In 1775 he noted that he had "drop'd no Politics" in his correspondence with them since he was "no Politician." "I always thought it ill became a Minister of the Gospel to set up for a Minister of State," he explained, simply praying for a "happy Reconciliation."[36]

Neutrality became harder after independence was declared, and Barton soon fell afoul of Pennsylvania's stringent treason laws. First, Pennsylvania imposed an oath of allegiance on voters, thereby disenfranchising, according to contemporary estimates, about half of the potential electorate.[37] Then in June 1777 it passed the Test Act, requiring all white adult males to take an oath of allegiance to the state. The Test Act excluded white adult men who refused to take the oath from the new political community. They were subject to imprisonment if they traveled outside their county and suffered a range of civil penalties. The Test Act required the following oath: "I, A. B., do swear . . . that I renounce and refuse all allegiance to George the Third, King of Great Britain, his heirs and successors, and that I will be faithful and bear true allegiance to the commonwealth of Pennsylvania as a free and independent state." The swearer also promised not to interfere with this freedom and independence and to report others' efforts to do so.[38]

For Barton and many others, what made the oath unconscionable was its requirement that he abjure the allegiance to George III that he had previously made by his ordination oaths. In this sense, the Pennsylvania test oath was considerably stricter than the earlier oath of allegiance to William and Mary, which could be interpreted as requiring only passive submission to the de facto rulers. The Pennsylvania test oath, by contrast, unambiguously demanded that the new authorities be recognized as the de jure rulers. The oath was controversial even among patriots, because so many citizens considered themselves unable to take it.[39] It was precisely because the inhabitants of the state were so divided in their attitudes to the Revolution that its Test Act was exceptionally strict. The "conception of a corporate, homogenous 'people' was not merely assumed; it was also enforced," Aaron Sullivan explains.[40]

The authors of the Pennsylvania Test Act were fully aware of these niceties. Pennsylvania had a long history of political contention over the theology of oath taking, given Quakers' conscientious refusal to take any oaths whatsoever. The right of affirmation was protected by the colony's first Frame of Government, and it was repeatedly contested by the Quakers' political enemies. In 1772 the colony made allowances for religious groups who objected to the conventional rituals of oath taking (such as kneeling and kissing the Bible). The Pennsylvania Constitution of 1776 required all legislative representatives to swear allegiance to the state and "profess, but distinctly not swear, to a belief in God" (in Tara Strauch's words). The 1777 Test Act also recognized the right of affirmation for specific religious communities (such as the Quakers). In other areas, then, Pennsylvania revolutionaries were keenly aware of conscientious objections to oaths and made extensive efforts to accommodate them.[41] They would have fully understood the theological concerns about foreswearing expressed by Barton and others. Elsewhere, the revolutionaries argued that oaths of allegiance to the Crown were void because George III was held to have broken *his* coronation oaths by, among other actions, "establishing" Roman Catholicism in Quebec.[42] However, this was as far as the authors of the Pennsylvania Test Act were willing to go toward accommodating dissenting consciences, given the demands of republican ideology and the exigencies of wartime.

Not only did the Test Act explicitly exclude loyalists from the political community but, because it only applied to white adult men, it also implicitly excluded Black people, Indigenous Americans, women, and children, grouping them together and denying them the moral *capacity* to take an oath. Contemporaneous British law likewise considered the testimony of non-white and non-Christian witnesses to be inadmissible or unreliable on the grounds that they could not be credible oath takers. For example, an East India Company legal brief of 1778 argued that Muslim witnesses were less credible than Christians, explaining that "the credit due to an oath depends on our believing that the person who swears is impressed with a sense of religion . . . and a dread of the punishment . . . against perjury."[43] In the Pennsylvania Test Act, likewise, religion, race, and gender worked together to construct an independent moral subject granted the capacity to take an oath or refuse to do so. Unintentionally, then, it invited white male loyalists to leverage their privileged moral status into an attack on the Revolution. Barton did exactly this.

By refusing to take the oath, Barton became exposed not just to the legal penalties prescribed by the Test Act but also to popular violence. He took "every prudent Step to give no Offence," he told the SPG, yet had his life threatened. Some of his fellow missionaries, meanwhile, were "drag'd from their Homes, assaulted with Stones & Dirt, duck'd in water, obliged to flee for their Lives, driven from their Habitations & Families, laid under Arrests, & imprison'd!"[44] While lamenting this violence, Barton also believed that the persecution was generating a religious revival. With his church closed, his congregation were forced to meet "in Secret . . . having somewhat the Appearance of the Persuasion of the primitive [i.e., early] Christians." The experience "kindled & encreas'd their Zeal, & united them the closer together." Barton suggested that this revival took place predominately among women. Since the Test Act prevented men from leaving their counties, women traveled into Lancaster County to have their children catechized and christened. Barton met them at the county border.[45]

Barton pleaded with the state of Pennsylvania to grant him exemption from the Test Act on grounds of conscience. After Pennsylvania began mandating imprisonment for those who refused to swear the test oath, Barton petitioned the General Assembly for exemption from the part of the oath requiring him to abjure the king.[46] He explained that he and the other missionaries could not "in Conscience" abjure George III but were willing to submit passively to the new Revolutionary authorities. Indeed, they were necessarily apolitical by virtue of their status as clergymen. He cited the SPG's instructions to "inculcate Submission to Government" while taking "special care to give no Offence" to it. Thus, he insisted that the missionaries were "exempted by their Office, from taking any active Part on either Side." Indeed, they had "not intermeddled, directly or indirectly, in the present melancholy Contest." Even more than regular clergy, he continued, missionaries were necessarily unconcerned with civil affairs. He claimed that exemption from the test oath was "the same Indulgence, which Missionaries, both Protestant and Papist, of almost all Christian Nations, have experienced." He concluded by hoping that the Assembly members, as "Christians & Protestants . . . will pay due Regard to religious Scruples, however different they may be from their own." In short, Barton argued that exemption from the test oath was a question of religious toleration.[47] These arguments did not persuade the Assembly, which rejected Barton's petition and instead gave him permission to emigrate. He and Esther immediately fled to New York City, leaving their children behind.[48]

In New York, Thomas Barton began retelling his story with a new emphasis: his refusal to take the test oath made him a loyalist martyr. There, he wrote the letter discussed at the beginning of this essay, detailing the suffering and "persecution" borne by the Pennsylvania missionaries and prompting the SPG secretary to refer to them as "martyrs." The language of martyrdom was intended to advance the loyalists' moral case against the American Revolution, but this was not a conventional species of political argument. Even in exile in New York, safely under the protection of the British military, Barton refrained from arguing that the new Revolutionary authorities were *wholly* illegitimate. He complained to the SPG: "We have not intermeddled with any Matters inconsistent with our own Callings & Functions. We have studied to be quiet, & to give no Offence to the present Rulers. We have obey'd the Laws & Government, now in Being, as far as our Conscience, and prior Obligations would permit."[49] Barton here recognized the Revolutionary authorities—the "present Rulers . . . now in Being"—as rulers de facto and acknowledged his duty of submission to them. Thus, the Test Act was not entirely illegitimate: it was possible for others to take the test oath in good conscience. As Barton explained, "My heart assures me, that many conscientious and good men have conformed to the test-act, yet my own conscience always revolted at the abjuration part of it."[50] Barton, then, criticized the revolutionaries not for usurping royal rule in America but for failing to accommodate the consciences of those who scrupled against coerced ideological conformity.

There was tension in this line of argument. Barton held that Pennsylvania was committing religious persecution because the missionaries were *not* politically opposed to the Revolution. Had they been so, the revolutionaries would have been guilty of nothing worse than treating their political enemies uncharitably. At this point, Barton found himself in a bind. The revolutionaries, he believed, had discredited themselves, but he himself could not push this line of attack without justifying their treatment of him. Thus, in his letter to the SPG, after accusing the revolutionaries of religious persecution, Barton apologized "for having already gone so far beyond my Line, & ventured on the Field of POLITICS."[51] All this talk of religious persecution made only for an indirect attack on the Revolution, as Barton himself recognized.

What, then, was Barton hoping to achieve by comparing the loyalist clergy to persecuted martyrs? In Lancaster, Barton used this performance to resist the Revolutionary state; in New York, he used it to cultivate favor with the British authorities. Ultimately, though, he was more concerned with the religious implications of martyrdom. Martyrdom, following the template of Christ's crucifixion and resurrection, is not about death but about rebirth. Barton, likewise, hoped that the missionaries' martyrdom would sow the seeds of spiritual and political revival.[52] "Notwithstanding the present depressed & persecuted state of the Church of England here," he wrote to the SPG, "she will, one Day, rise triumphant & be the Glory of the New World." By gladly suffering persecution, her clergy had demonstrated "her Moderation & Peaceableness," thus "recommend[ing] her & them to the Esteem & attention of the People." Above all, Barton hoped their suffering would secure government support for the colonial Church of England: "Should the Church of England, at the Conclusion of these Troubles, be a *little* cherished by the Government . . . she will certainly flourish & grow more than ever."[53] Even as the Pennsylvania revolutionaries used the oath of allegiance to forge and enforce a new political community, Barton used his conscientious opposition to that oath to form alternative, competing communities around martyrdom and voluntary suffering.[54]

By representing himself as a martyr, Barton repurposed the Pennsylvania test oath. Its authors hoped that it would prove a bond strong enough to forge a new political community out of a reluctant and divided people. They fully understood the element of coercion this involved; indeed, they believed that coercion was necessary to allow the Revolution to survive the emergency of wartime. For Barton, the oath of allegiance was illegitimate and thus made the state that imposed it guilty of persecution. Rather than binding his conscience to the state, the test oath instead became an occasion for him to play conscientious objector and thus forge alternative communities of conscience through the voluntary embrace of martyrdom.

What made Barton such an effective martyr was his privileged status as an independent moral subject deemed capable of taking an oath. The irony is that this status was awarded to him by the Pennsylvania Test Act itself. While Thomas Barton made considerable moral capital out of his refusal of the oath, Esther's sufferings are all but invisible in the archival record and were never deemed by contemporaries to be as consequential as her husband's. The Pennsylvania test oath offers just one example of the way that religion worked alongside race, gender, and property to make and remake power relationships in the Revolutionary era.

Barton's political decisions cannot be understood as a simple, mechanistic consequence of his religious commitments: his Anglicanism was one of many factors shaping his loyalism. What his maneuverings instead demonstrate is that for many Americans in this era, questions of allegiance were connected to questions of salvation and cannot be understood apart from them. There is a simple but important historiographical point to be made here. This essay has sought to recover the religious dimensions of taking (or not taking) an oath by bringing scholarship on the Revolutionary oaths of allegiance into conversation with the rich historiography on the oath in early modern Europe.[55] Our understanding of the American Revolution would benefit from attention to the ever more sophisticated models that early modernists have offered for understanding the religio-political conflicts that followed in the wake of the "long Reformation."[56] This is not just a generic plea for historians to "take religion seriously"; more concretely, it is a plea for historians of the American Revolution to relinquish its historiographical exceptionalism and instead interpret it in a geographically and chronologically wider framework.[57]

Focusing on the religious dimensions of the Revolutionary oaths of allegiance shows how the patriots initially struggled to achieve a clean break with old-world modes of religious coercion and their attendant political problems. It is true that Pennsylvania's new constitution secured loyalty by protecting the rights of conscience with extensive concessions to religious minorities, including protecting the right of specific communities to substitute an affirmation for an oath. Yet for everyone else it continued to use the oath of allegiance to coerce the consciences of potential dissidents. Indeed, the 1777 test oath was actually less tolerant in this regard than the Williamite oaths imposed nearly a century earlier, perhaps because Pennsylvania made such extensive concessions to conscience elsewhere. Ultimately, the test oath defined as illegitimate any religion that precluded political allegiance. This is why loyalism so often took the form of martyrdom. This kind of conscientious resistance was deeply unsettling, and it actively shaped the debate about religious liberty in the new republic. The federal constitution was written with the knowledge that Pennsylvania's Test Act had transformed political dissent into martyrdom. As Tara Strauch has shown, the constitution's prohibition of religious tests was intended to make good on this lesson, and yet the framers were unwilling to abandon entirely the oath's unique coercive power, which survives to this day in the presidential oath of office.[58]

Notes

1. I would like to thank Kate Carté, the participants in the Sons of the American Revolution conference "Religion and the American Revolution," the two anonymous reviewers for the University of Virginia Press, and Kevin Murphy, who provided me with an invaluable reading list of secondary sources when this essay was at an early stage.
2. James P. Myers, *The Ordeal of Thomas Barton: Anglican Missionary in the Pennsylvania Backcountry, 1755–1780* (Bethlehem, PA: Lehigh University Press, 2010), 140–45.
3. For another example, in 1771 Lord Mansfield described the case of the Chamberlain of London versus Allen Evans as creating "a most exquisite dilemma . . . as bad a persecution as that of Procrustes. If they are too short, stretch them, if they are too long, lop them." *Political Register, and Impartial Review of New Books* 8 (1771): 156.
4. University of Oxford, Bodleian Libraries, USPG Archive (henceforth USPG), B21/36: Thomas Barton to the SPG, New York, January 8, 1779.
5. Rebecca Brannon, "Loyalists and the American Revolution," in *Oxford Research Encyclopedia of American History*, ed. Jon Butler (Oxford: Oxford University Press, 2014), 4. See also Holger Hoock, *Scars of Independence:*

America's Violent Birth (New York: Crown, 2017); and Janice Potter, *The Liberty We Seek: Loyalist Ideology in Colonial New York and Massachusetts* (Cambridge, MA: Harvard University Press, 1983), 15–38. For Pennsylvania, see Jane E. Calvert, "Thomas Paine, Quakerism, and the Limits of Religious Liberty During the American Revolution," in *Selected Writings of Thomas Paine*, ed. Ian Shapiro and Jane E. Calvert (New Haven, CT: Yale University Press, 2014), 602–29; Richard Godbeer, *World of Trouble: A Philadelphia Quaker Family's Journey Through the American Revolution* (New Haven, CT: Yale University Press, 2020); and Aaron Sullivan, "Uncommon Cause: The Challenges of Disaffection in Revolutionary Pennsylvania," in *The American Revolution Reborn*, ed. Patrick Spero and Michael Zuckerman (Philadelphia: University of Pennsylvania Press, 2016), 48–67.

6. T. H. Breen, *The Will of the People: The Revolutionary Birth of America* (Cambridge, MA: Harvard University Press, 2019), 138–40, 144–46; Joshua Canale, "'When a State Abounds in Rascals': New York's Revolutionary Era Committees for Public Safety, 1775–1783," *Journal of the Early Republic* 39, no. 2 (2019): 203–38.
7. Christopher F. Minty, "'Of One Hart and One Mind': Local Institutions and Allegiance during the American Revolution," *Early American Studies* 15, no. 1 (2017): 99–132; Donald F. Johnson, *Occupied America: British Military Rule and the Experience of Revolution* (Philadelphia: University of Pennsylvania Press, 2020), 147–48.
8. Kevin Murphy, "Coercion and Sworn Bond in the Eighteenth-Century British Atlantic" (PhD diss., Stony Brook University, 2023); Tara E. Strauch, "Taking Oaths and Giving Thanks: Ritual and Religion in Revolutionary America" (PhD diss., University of South Carolina, 2013); Tara Thompson Strauch, "Oaths and Christian Belief in the New Nation, 1776–1789," in *Religion and the State: Europe and North America in the Seventeenth and Eighteenth Centuries*, ed. Josh B. Stein and Sargon G. Donabed (Lanham, MD: Lexington Books, 2012), 127–42.
9. Murphy, "Coercion and Sworn Bond," 12–65; Thea Cervone, *Sworn Bond in Tudor England: Oaths, Vows and Covenants in Civil Life and Literature* (Jefferson, NC: McFarland, 2011); Conal Condren, *Argument and Authority in Early Modern England: The Presupposition of Oaths and Offices* (Cambridge: Cambridge University Press, 2006); Jonathan Gray, *Oaths and the English Reformation* (Cambridge: Cambridge University Press, 2013); David Martin Jones, *Conscience and Allegiance in Seventeenth Century England: The Political Significance of Oaths and Engagements* (Rochester, NY: University of Rochester Press, 1999); Caroline Robbins, "Selden's Pills: State Oaths in England, 1558–1714," *Huntington Library Quarterly* 35, no. 4 (1972): 303–21; John Spurr, "A Profane History of Early Modern Oaths," *Transactions of the*

Royal Historical Society, 6th ser., 11 (2001): 37–63; Stefania Tutino, *Law and Conscience: Catholicism in Early Modern England, 1570–1625* (Aldershot: Ashgate, 2007); Edward Vallance, *Revolutionary England and the National Covenant: State Oaths, Protestantism, and the Political Nation, 1553–1682* (Woodbridge, UK: Boydell, 2005); John Walter, *Covenanting Citizens: The Protestation Oath and Popular Culture in the English Revolution* (Oxford: Oxford University Press, 2017); Perez Zagorin, *Ways of Lying: Dissimulation, Persecution and Conformity in Early Modern Europe* (Cambridge, MA: Harvard University Press, 1990); Edmund Leites, ed., *Conscience and Casuistry in Early Modern Europe* (Cambridge: Cambridge University Press, 1988); Edward Vallance and Harald Braun, eds., *Contexts of Conscience in Early Modern Europe, 1500–1700* (Basingstoke: Palgrave Macmillan, 2004).

10. Vallance, *Revolutionary England*, 2.
11. Spurr, "Profane History," 38.
12. John Spurr, "'The Strongest Bond of Conscience': Oaths and the Limits of Tolerance in Early Modern England," in Vallance and Braun, *Contexts of Conscience*, 151–65.
13. Jones, *Conscience and Allegiance*, 2–3.
14. Murphy, "Coercion and Sworn Bond," 3, 8; Gray, *Oaths and the English Reformation*, 35, 41; Robbins, "Selden's Pills," 304.
15. L. M. Hawkins, *Allegiance in Church and State: The Problem of the Nonjurors in the English Revolution* (London: George Routledge, 1928), 34–55.
16. Strauch, "Taking Oaths and Giving Thanks," 45.
17. A. J. B. Johnston, "Borderland Worries: Loyalty Oaths in Acadie / Nova Scotia," *French Colonial History* 4 (2003): 31–48; Patrick Fagan, *Divided Loyalties: The Question of the Oath for Irish Catholics in the Eighteenth Century* (Dublin: Four Courts, 1997); Alasdair Raffe, "Scottish State Oaths and the Revolution of 1688–1690," in *Scotland in the Age of Two Revolutions*, ed. Sharon Adams and Julia Goodare (Woodbridge, UK: Boydell, 2014), 173–91.
18. Murphy, "Coercion and Sworn Bond," 192–306.
19. Strauch, "Taking Oaths and Giving Thanks," 84–87.
20. Michael Kammen, "The American Revolution as a *Crise de Conscience*: The Case of New York," in *Society, Freedom, and Conscience: The American Revolution in Virginia, Massachusetts, and New York*, ed. Richard M. Jellison (New York: Norton, 1976), 125–89.
21. Nancy L. Rhoden, *Revolutionary Anglicanism: The Colonial Church of England Clergy During the American Revolution* (Basingstoke: Macmillan, 1999); Spencer McBride, *Pulpit and Nation: Clergymen and the Politics of Revolutionary America* (Charlottesville: University of Virginia Press, 2016), 68–101; James B. Bell, *A War of Religion: Dissenters, Anglicans, and the American Revolution* (Basingstoke: Palgrave Macmillan, 2008), 123–221.

22. William Pencak, "Out of Many, One: Pennsylvania's Loyalist Clergy in the American Revolution," in *Pennsylvania's Revolution*, ed. Pencak (University Park: Pennsylvania State University Press, 2010), 97–120.
23. Book of Common Prayer, 1762 ed., Morning Prayer, Evening Prayer, and The Litany.
24. Katherine Carté, *Religion and the American Revolution: An Imperial History* (Chapel Hill: University of North Carolina Press, 2021), 169–206.
25. See Spencer McBride's essay in this volume.
26. USPG B22/339: [William Clark], Address to People of Dedham and Stoughton, March 1777.
27. For the oaths of allegiance and supremacy, see Rupert Bursell, "The Clerical Oath of Allegiance," *Ecclesiastical Law Journal* 17, no. 3 (2015): 299. For subscription to the Book of Common Prayer and the Thirty-Nine Articles, see Robert Phillimore, *The Ecclesiastical Law of the Church of England*, vol. 1 (London: H. Sweet, 1873), 125–26.
28. Rupert Bursell, "The Clerical Declaration of Assent," *Ecclesiastical Law Journal* 18, no. 2 (2016): 166; XIV Carol. II., sections 2 and 4 (spelling modernized).
29. XIV Carol. II., section 6 (spelling modernized).
30. This point has been misunderstood by some historians, such as Pencak in "Out of Many, One," 97, 118fn.
31. Even aside from the question of allegiance, this was a legally murky area, marked by conflicting interpretations of the ability of the royal supremacy to authorize what was called "special worship." Bursell, "Clerical Declaration," 168–71.
32. Michael D. Hattem, *Past and Prologue: Politics and Memory in the American Revolution* (New Haven: Yale University Press, 2021), 21–125.
33. Paul Kléber Monod, *Jacobitism and the English People, 1688–1788* (Cambridge: Cambridge University Press, 1989), 138–45; David Parrish, *Jacobitism and Anti-Jacobitism in the British Atlantic World, 1688–1727* (Woodbridge, UK: Boydell, 2017), 43–61.
34. Jones, *Conscience and Allegiance*, 201–22, 462–74; Charles F. Mullet, "Religion, Politics, and Oaths in the Glorious Revolution," *Review of Politics* 10, no. 4 (1948): 465–66; Robbins, "Selden's Pills," 319; Hawkins, *Allegiance in Church and State*, 105–30.
35. I have relied particularly on Myers, *Ordeal of Thomas Barton*. See also Marvin F. Russell, "Thomas Barton and Pennsylvania's Colonial Frontier," *Pennsylvania History* 46, no. 4 (1979): 312–34; John B. Frantz and William Pencak, "Introduction: Pennsylvania and Its Three Revolutions," in *The American Revolution in the Pennsylvania Hinterland*, ed. Frantz and Pencak (University Park: Pennsylvania State University Press, 1998), xix–xx; Karen Guenther, "Berks County," in Frantz and Pencak, *Beyond*

Philadelphia, 75; Pencak, "Out of Many, One"; Mark Häberlein, *The Practice of Pluralism: Congregational Life and Religious Diversity in Lancaster, Pennsylvania, 1730–1820* (University Park: Pennsylvania State University Press, 2009), 107–29.

36. USPG B21/27: Thomas Barton to the SPG, Lancaster, October 20, 1775.
37. Brett Palfreyman, "The Nonjuror Problem in Pennsylvania," in *The Consequences of Loyalism*, ed. Rebecca Brannon and Joseph S. Moore (Columbia: University of South Carolina Press, 2019), 164.
38. Kenneth Owen, *Political Community in Revolutionary Pennsylvania, 1774–1800* (Oxford: Oxford University Press, 2018), 48; *The Statutes at Large of Pennsylvania from 1682 to 1801* (Clarence M. Busch, 1903), 110–14.
39. Owen, *Political Community*, 48.
40. Aaron Sullivan, *The Disaffected: Britain's Occupation of Philadelphia During the American Revolution* (Philadelphia: University of Pennsylvania Press, 2019), 15–17, 19–44, quotation p. 42; Murphy, "Coercion and Sworn Bond," 291–94.
41. J. William Frost, "Adjusting to New Conditions in Britain and America, 1690–1700," in *The Quakers, 1656–1723: The Evolution of an Alternative Community*, ed. Richard C. Allen and Rosemary Anne Moore (University Park: Pennsylvania State University Press, 2018), 194–97; Strauch, "Taking Oaths and Giving Thanks," 60–68; Strauch, "Oaths and Christian Belief," 130; Jane E. Calvert, *Quaker Constitutionalism and the Political Thought of John Dickinson* (Cambridge: Cambridge University Press, 2009), 258–59.
42. Strauch, "Taking Oaths and Giving Thanks," 56–57, 59.
43. Lauren A. Benton, *Law and Colonial Cultures: Legal Regimes in World History, 1400–1900* (Cambridge: Cambridge University Press, 2002), 18, 167–209, esp. 173, 179, 185, 191, quotation p. 147; Karen A. Macfarlane, "'Does He Know the Danger of an Oath'?: Oaths, Religion, Ethnicity and the Advent of the Adversarial Criminal Trial in the Eighteenth Century," *Immigrants & Minorities* 31, no. 3 (2013): 317–45. See also Murphy, "Coercion and Sworn Bond," 66–123.
44. USPG B21/30: Thomas Barton to the SPG, Lancaster, November 25, 1776. Daniel Batwell was indeed dragged through a river. James P. Myers Jr., "Homeland Security in the Pennsylvania Backcountry, 1777–1778: The Example of the Reverend Mr. Daniel Batwelle, SPG," *Pennsylvania History* 78, no. 3 (2011): 247–71.
45. USPG B21/36: Thomas Barton to the SPG, New York, January 8, 1779.
46. *Statutes at Large of Pennsylvania from 1682 to 1801*, 147–49, 238–45; USPG B21/35: Thomas Barton to the SPG, New York, December 15, 1778.
47. USPG B32/32: [Thomas Barton], "Case of the Missionaries of Pennsylvania," Lancaster, May 20, 1778.

48. Theodore W. Jeffries, "Thomas Barton (1730–1780): Victim of the Revolution," *Journal of the Lancaster County Historical Society* 81, no. 1 (1977): 60; USPG B21/31: "Warrant from Executive Council of PA for Rev. Thomas Barton to Remove to NY," September 17, 1778; USPG B21/35: Thomas Barton to the SPG, New York, December 15, 1778.
49. USPG B21/36.
50. Thomas Barton to John De Hart, New York, January 30, 1779, quoted in William Barton, *Memoirs of the Life of David Rittenhouse* (Philadelphia: Edward Parker, 1813), 279–80.
51. USPG B21/36.
52. Peter W. Walker, "Religion, Politics, and Martyrdom in the American Revolution: The Loyalist Church of England Clergy," in *A Companion to American Religious History*, ed. Benjamin E. Park (Hoboken, NJ: Wiley-Blackwell, 2021), 59–70.
53. USPG B21/37: Thomas Barton to the SPG, New York, October 25, 1779.
54. For a similar example, see Frost, "Adjusting to New Conditions," 195.
55. See Strauch, "Taking Oaths and Giving Thanks," 20, 24, 28–51.
56. For another example of scholarship that uses long-term religious contexts to frame the American Revolution, see Evan Haefeli, ed., *Against Popery: Britain, Empire, and Anti-Catholicism* (Charlottesville: University of Virginia Press, 2020). My argument that historians should pay attention to long-term religious *contexts* should not be taken to imply that the Revolution had long-term religious *causes*.
57. For the Revolution's historiographical exceptionalism, see Hattem, *Past and Prologue*, 141–245. For the relationship between early American and early modern history, see Merry E. Wiesner-Hanks, *What Is Early Modern History?* (Cambridge: Polity Press, 2021); and Liz Covart, "Popular and Public History," *Journal of Early Modern History* 25, no. 6 (2021): 547–59.
58. Strauch, "Taking Oaths and Giving Thanks," 84–127; Murphy, "Coercion and Sworn Bond," 316–22.

"Singing Psalms, We Went in Amongst Them"

Native Christianity, Relationships, and Continuity Across the Revolutionary War Period

JESSICA LAUREN NELSON

★

> The former Kings of England Use to let the People in this Country have their Freedom and Liberty; but the present King of England wants to make them Slaves to himself. . . . And now I think you must See who is the oppressor, and who are the oppressed. . . . It is Wright for Peaceable [people] to Defend themselves when Wicked People fall upon them without Reason or Cause, then they can look up to Heaven to their God, and he will help them.
>
> —Samson Occom to the Oneida Tribe, 1775

This description of the conflict between King George III and the American colonies would certainly have pleased any advocate for independence. It portrays God as on the side of the oppressed, making this war not only a battle for political control over a territory but a duel of morality as well. The author of this letter and the intended recipients, however, were not American colonists. It was written by Rev. Samson Occom (Mohegan/Brothertown) to the Oneida tribes living just south of Lake Ontario. He was advising the Oneida to remain as neutral as possible during the war. If, however, they needed to join in the conflict, he suggested, they should fight for the Americans.

For Occom, as for most peoples of the North American continent in the late eighteenth century, religion was not something that could be separated from the minutiae of daily life—nor from the massive geopolitical changes taking place around the world. Indigenous people, especially those living on the Atlantic coast or in the trans-Appalachian West, were perhaps among the most impacted by the American Revolution. One of the causes of the war was colonial frustration at the Proclamation Line of 1763, by which the British monarchy had nominally prohibited colonial settlement west of a line roughly located along the Appalachian Mountain range to prevent conflict with Native tribes in the region. The emergent United States quickly disregarded the idea of limiting westward expansion of the new nation, erasing the Proclamation Line and sending troops as far west as the Illinois River during the Revolutionary War to try to establish American influence far across the continent.

Nevertheless, a case study of Christian Algonquian and Haudenosaunee people in New England shows surprising continuity in religious practice before, during, and after the Revolutionary War. Although the war itself caused disruption and loss to Native communities, many of these communities relied upon Christianity in similar ways throughout the late eighteenth century—even after the emergence of the United States. The Native people studied in this essay found Christian education, theology, denominational affiliation, and other forms of engagement with Christianity to be helpful in navigating the harsh realities of settler colonialism, although never sufficient to fully ameliorate white racial prejudice. More importantly, Christian rhetoric and a shared sense of Christian identity helped build intertribal relationships throughout the shifting geopolitical circumstances of the late colonial and early national periods. As a strategy for *survivance*—a term coined by the Anishinaabe scholar Gerald Vizenor to describe the creative process of enduring—many Native people in New England formed connections between themselves and others via Christianity.[1] The title of this essay, "Singing Psalms, We Went in Amongst Them," is a line from Samson Occom's diary describing the day he arrived at the Brothertown settlement, a Native Christian community. The entry recounts that at the moment Occom arrived in Brothertown, its members were engaged in a Christian prayer service; but at a metaphorical level, the quote also illustrates how Native people could strengthen relationships amongst themselves via Christianity.[2]

This essay focuses particularly on the Oneida, the Brothertown (now the Brothertown Indian Nation), and the Stockbridge (now the

Stockbridge-Munsee Band of Mohicans), as well as a few other coastal New England Algonquian tribes. The Oneida, one of the six tribes of the Haudenosaunee, with homelands located south of Lake Ontario, largely converted to Christianity in the early eighteenth century. The ethnogenesis of Brothertown lies with seven small New England tribes. Under the leadership of Occom, Joseph Johnson (Mohegan/Brothertown), and David Fowler (Montauk/Brothertown), portions of those tribes united to voluntarily relocate to upstate New York in the eighteenth century, founding a new tribe known as Eeyamquittoowauconnuck, or Brothertown, in 1785, with Christianity as a central pillar of identity.[3] Stockbridge, located in western Massachusetts among the Mahican people, was founded as a Christian Indian town under the Puritan minister John Sergeant in 1737 (followed by the Congregationalist Jonathan Edwards for several years in the 1750s). By the late eighteenth century, encroachment from Anglo-American settlements had made Native life in the Stockbridge village untenable, and the majority of the Native residents moved further west into Oneida lands in the 1780s.

My analysis centers primarily on the ways that these groups deployed Christian identity as a tool of diplomacy and relationship building. In emphasizing the material and political uses of Christian rhetoric, I do not mean to suggest that the people studied in this essay intentionally identified as Christian solely due to material factors, in a way that somehow made their commitment to Christianity less internalized or authentic. As Joel W. Martin and Mark A. Nicholas argued in 2010, the question whether a conversion is "authentic" is often only applied to non-white converts to Christianity.[4] In the history of these tribes, the question of authentic conversion preoccupied white missionaries. Seventeenth-century Puritans frequently complained about Native converts "backsliding," and the eighteenth-century Congregationalist Eleazar Wheelock, for example, worried that Native schoolteachers might "turn savage when they were out of the reach of the English."[5] The anthropologist Webb Keane has argued that the search for sincerity in conversion is a particularly Protestant preoccupation; Keane's framework brings a religious focus to the sociologist James C. Scott's observation that dominant groups often believe that the deference expressed by oppressed groups is "'only' a performance" and "discount its authenticity."[6]

Yet the same power structures that encouraged white missionaries to doubt the authenticity of Native Christianity have historically also sidelined Native critiques of white missionaries' authenticity. Occom accused the Wheelock family (father Eleazar and son John) of simply using Occom for fundraising purposes, arguing that although the Wheelocks "may speak or write with seeming concern for the Indians," their language was simply a "cloak, to get something for [themselves]."[7] Rev. William Apess (Pequot), an ordained Methodist minister, asked in a scathing 1827 essay on white discrimination against Indians, "My white brother . . . why do you who profess his gospel and to have his spirit, act so contrary to it?"[8] If Natives' Christianity was to be questioned, so too should the Christianity of Anglo-American colonists.

In both cases, however, trying to categorize expressions of Christian identity as true or false is less useful than what Martin and Nicholas advocate for, a "recognition for complexity."[9] Recent scholarship has, in fact, broken out of the tired authentic/inauthentic binary when analyzing Native Christianity. Examples include Ryan Carr's recent study on Samson Occom's Christian theology as a part of, not an exception to, his traditionalist Mohegan heritage; Edward E. Andrews's work on Native and Black missionaries in the seventeenth, eighteenth, and early nineteenth centuries; and Lisa Brooks's analysis of Native cultural persistence in Native New England.[10] Moreover, this type of analysis moves beyond the concept of religion as an internal belief system, which relies on an assumed distinction between the material and spiritual planes. Instead, as mentioned in the introductory paragraphs of this essay, not only were Occom and other Native Christians unable to separate their religious practice from the minutiae of daily life but *they showed no interest in doing so*. Rosalyn LaPier (Blackfeet/Metis), a contemporary scholar of Blackfeet culture, notes that Blackfeet belief systems teach that knowledge of the invisible or supernatural world brings about greater knowledge of the visible world and that together they lead to "a deeper understanding of how the universe work[s]."[11] As the introductory quote demonstrated, Occom interpreted the outbreak of the Revolutionary War through a lens of Christian morality; it was a worldview that helped him understand how the universe worked. This essay examines how Native Christianity functioned as a factor in relationship building and diplomacy, served practical goals for Native people in Anglo-American contexts, and had communicative power across multiple groups. If we consider Christianity as a system of knowledge about the world rather than a set of beliefs, these Native Christians' understanding of the practical efficaciousness of Christianity was itself constituent of their worldview.

Native Christianity in Anglo-American Contexts

In the mid-eighteenth century, Native people became more deeply involved with Christian missionaries and institutions. Of course, Christianity had been a part of the English colonization process since the beginning. The ability of Native intermediaries such as John Sassamon (Massachusett, c. 1620–1675), Daniel Takawambait (Natick, c. 1652–1716), or the Hannit family (Wampanoag, documented in Experience Mayhew's *Indian Converts* from the 1620s through 1727) to operate within colonial society often, although not always, depended on their acceptance of Christianity.[12] As colonization continued to dispossess Algonquian people of their lands in the eighteenth century, however, many showed increased interest in education in English literacy as a strategy for defending their lands, an education that typically came unavoidably entangled with Christian ideology. In colonial New England, Moor's Indian Charity School, operated by the Congregationalist minister Eleazer Wheelock, looms large. Established in 1754 and originating in a request made by a Pequot woman, Sarah Occum, for Wheelock to educate her son Samson, the school taught sixty Native students from Algonquian, Haudenosaunee, and Delaware communities to serve as Christian missionaries.[13] Several graduates of the school would go on to teach in schools for Indigenous children themselves, both in coastal New England and in Haudenosaunee territory. Involvement with Christian institutions was not limited exclusively to education. Native membership in Christian churches increased in the 1740s, especially in New Light congregations.[14]

One of the benefits that accrued to some Native Christians in the decades surrounding the American Revolution was the opportunity to be paid schoolteachers in Native communities. In 1765, for example, the newly formed Connecticut Board of the Society in Scotland for Propagating Christian Knowledge (SSPCK) declared that the Moor's students Joseph Wooley (Delaware), David Fowler (Montauk/Brothertown), and Hezekiah Calvin (Delaware) had demonstrated their capacity to serve as schoolteachers, for which they would be compensated by the SSPCK.[15] The year prior, the Boston Board of the Company for the Propagation of the Gospel in New England agreed to sponsor Occom as a missionary to the Haudenosaunee in exchange for an annual salary of £30 and the repayment of debts he had accumulated.[16]

Although the funders changed, the practice of training and paying Native schoolteachers continued after the Revolutionary War. The state of

New York paid Elijah Wampy (Brothertown) to teach school in Brothertown in the spring of 1797.[17] Later that year, the state-appointed overseers for the Brothertown reported that a "sober young Indian woman" (identified elsewhere as Hannah Fowler, Brothertown) had taught school over the summer, marking the first time that an Indigenous woman was officially recognized by the state government as a schoolteacher.[18] In Stockbridge, a missionary report published by the Scottish Society for the Propagation of Faith in 1833 commented that three Stockbridge women had taught school at some point in the past decades.[19] Archival evidence only identifies two of these women, Mary Doxtator Peters and Electa Quinney, but the records indicate that both were paid by either missionary societies or the state between 1815 and 1833.[20] Peters's funding for her schools rested explicitly on her reputation among white communities as a good Christian woman. In 1821, a committee from a Presbyterian church in Onondaga Hollow, New York, wrote a fundraising letter on Peters's behalf, stating: "We the subscribers, inhabitants of the town of Onondaga certify to the benevolent that we are well acquainted with the Indian Woman who is the bearer, Mary Doxtator [Peters]. We know her to be a woman of good moral character & have reason to believe she is a sincere Christian. . . . Hoping she will find favor in the eyes of those who feel for the woes of suffering humanity & appreciate the debt which the American people owe to Aboriginal inhabitants of this country we give her this paper."[21] Peters's reputation helped her gather the material goods necessary to promote Stockbridge's economic independence by teaching Stockbridge women to weave cloth and freeing the tribe from reliance on white merchants for their clothing.[22] Back in Connecticut, white missionary organizations also continued to carry out Eleazar Wheelock's paternalistic desire to train a cadre of Indigenous schoolteachers: in 1817 the American Board of Commissioners for Foreign Missions founded the Foreign Mission School in Cornwall, Connecticut, with an initial student body made up primarily of Indigenous students from mainland North America.[23]

The practice of paying Indigenous schoolteachers, however, dwindled in the early republic. In 1826 the Foreign Mission School closed because of opposition from Connecticut locals, who were up in arms after a male Cherokee student at the school married a white woman from the town. After Quinney's time as a schoolteacher in Stockbridge ended after her marriage in 1835, no other payments to male or female Native schoolteachers were recorded among the Stockbridge, the Brothertown, or the Oneida. The experiences of Indigenous Christian schoolteachers therefore challenge the idea that the American Revolution changed religious practice. Rather, their experiences show continuity across the late colonial and early Republic periods; it was the growing strength of the United States and the Jacksonian-era tendency to push for removal rather than assimilation that changed the paradigm.

The role of schoolteacher was not the only role sought by Christian Native men; some also became ordained ministers. In 1759 Samson Occom was ordained by the Presbyterian Church, making him the first documented ordained Native minister in British North America.[24] The church council that examined Occom before his ordination, comprising several Anglo-American ministers ordained by the Presbyterian Church, concluded that he was "in good measure qualified for the work of gospel ministry" and approved his ordination.[25] Ordination, even informally carried out, functioned as a social credential that could be used when interacting with Anglo-American society both before and after the American Revolution. In 1763, for example, a group of seven New England ministers (including Wheelock) agreed that Samuel Ashpo (Mohegan) should be sent to preach to the Oneida village of Jeningo, given that there was "not the least probability of introducing an English Missionary, at present, by Reason of the deep rooted Prejudices So many of them have imbibed against the English."[26] Ashpo had been ordained as a minister by a council of Native separatists in Mohegan; although Wheelock and others disparaged this form of ordination, they could not deny Ashpo's leadership skills and religious authority among the Mohegans and decided that his missionary endeavors were still worth sponsoring.[27] After the American Revolution, Occom was mentioned in a 1788 treaty signed between the state of New York and the Oneida. In setting new boundaries after land acquisition by New York, the treaty described the Brothertown as "under the pastoral care of the Rev. Samson Occom."[28] The use of the title "Reverend" to describe Occom indicates that status as an ordained minister transcended geopolitical boundaries, functioning in much the same way in the pre-Revolutionary American colonies as it did in an independent United States. In the early nineteenth century, other Native men would seek and acquire ordination: among the best known are Eleazar Williams (Mohawk), an Episcopalian sent by Canadian bishops as a missionary to the Oneida in 1817; William Apess (Pequot), who was ordained a

Methodist minister in 1829; and Joseph Amos (Mashpee), who became head pastor of the Mashpee Baptist church in 1834 and served Indian Christian communities in coastal New England until his death in 1869.[29]

Native Christian schoolteachers and ministers were sometimes selected to carry out diplomatic or evangelistic missions on behalf of white missionaries, societies, or nations. In 1764 Wheelock sent Occom to Haudenosaunee lands near Lake Ontario to promote Moor's school among the Tuscarora, Mohawk, and Oneida tribes, noting that he believed Occom would be particularly influential among them.[30] In 1775 the Connecticut Assembly paid Joseph Johnson £12 to travel to Haudenosaunee territory and take a wampum belt to the Oneida as a sign of peace. As the allegiance of the Haudenosaunee became more critical as the Revolutionary War continued, the Continental Congress funded diplomatic missions to the various Six Nations tribes. In 1776 they paid Jacob Fowler (Montauk/Brothertown) £66 for his time spent among the Oneida advocating for the patriot cause. Fowler was a well-known Christian: he had been a student at Moor's and had been employed by the Society in Scotland for Propagating Christian Knowledge as a schoolteacher in Onowadagegh, a Mohawk village, in the 1760s. Both before and during the American Revolution, Anglo-American missionaries, soldiers, and politicians relied upon Native men to serve as intermediaries.

Despite the occasional advantages of identifying as Christian in Anglo-American society, these benefits never completely ameliorated white racial prejudice. Occom, Joseph Johnson, and David Fowler (Montauk/Brothertown) all bitterly complained about their salaries when they graduated from Moor's and began teaching in grammar schools themselves; they knew they were being paid less than the white teachers. In a 1773 letter to the Connecticut governor Jonathan Trumbull, Joseph Johnson concluded that this discrepancy was based simply on colonists' belief that "an Indian don't deserve to have as much as an English man."[31] Occom complained that the fundraising campaigns he carried out benefited Eleazar Wheelock more than they benefited Occom or Native people. "[Wheelock] has done little or no good to the Indians with all the money we collected in England . . . all that money has done, it has made the Doctor's family very grand in the world," Occom wrote.[32] As Samuel Niles (Narragansett) asked the white missionary Joseph Fish, "To what purpose do we build Schoolhouse, set up preaching, and lay ourselves out for Public Benefit here, When all our lands are like to be sold under us, and we turned off, we don't know where?"[33] Perhaps the clearest image of Christianity's failure to protect Indigenous people comes from a complaint written in 1787 by Charlestown Narragansetts. There, a group of Narragansetts had built a church where they could conduct their Sunday services. However, it had become commonplace that "whilst the people are peaceably gathered together, performing their devotion, many of the loose, disorderly, vain, and thoughtless sally upon the Meeting, replete with language horrid to the ear, and behavior disagreeable to behold, to the great grief and disturbance of [church attendees]."[34] Even Christian services, when conducted by Native people, failed to gain respect from their white neighbors.

Christianity and Intertribal Diplomacy

Although Christian theology and identity proved insufficient to achieve Native equality within Anglo-American society, it was an important and successful means of creating connections between Native people. In the mid-eighteenth century, new styles of worship and preaching embraced by Great Awakening preachers opened up opportunities for Native men to establish new congregations based on doctrinal differences while also breaking away from the oversight of white missionaries. For example, in the 1740s the white minister Joseph Park brought revivalist-style Christianity to his Congregationalist mission church among the Narragansetts in Charlestown. Shortly thereafter, Narragansetts began holding their own prayer services during the week, under the leadership of the recent convert Samuel Niles (Narragansett). Eventually, he formed an Indian Separatist church, which soon attracted Pequot attendees as well, forming a multitribal congregation.[35]

A striking example of how Christianity could solidify connections among different tribes is the ethnogenesis of Brothertown between 1770 and 1785. The idea for Brothertown had been conceptualized by Samson Occom, Joseph Johnson, and several others in the early 1770s as a new path forward for coastal New England Native people. The idea was to move together to a new location, farther away from white settlement, and create a new community centered on a Christian Indian identity. In March 1773, representatives from several Christianized New England tribes—namely, Mohegan, Farmington Tunxis, Niantic, Stonington Pequots, Narragansett, Montauk, and Mashantucket Pequots—gathered to discuss the possibility of moving elsewhere. Eventually, they decided upon Oneida territory, where many of the men involved had already spent time as schoolteachers or missionary translators.[36] In the fall of 1773, the

Oneida agreed to grant the New England Indians a tract of land ten miles square within Oneida territory, but they asked for representatives of the tribes to visit them and settle the details over the winter, when their hunting season had ended.[37]

Accordingly, in early 1774 Joseph Johnson and an unnamed Narragansett, Montauk, or Tunxis companion met with the Oneida in their homelands.[38] The meetings between the Oneida and Johnson stretched over four days, which was common for Haudenosaunee deliberations.[39] Johnson's initial speech relied primarily on traditional Haudenosaunee protocols, not Christianity. He addressed the Oneida as "older brothers" and asked them to "consider of us, and harken to us, as to a younger Brother." He also took a silver pipe and tobacco to give to the Oneida as a symbol of the relationship being formed between the Oneida and the New England Indians. Although Johnson made occasional references to God in his speech—stating that he and his people "rejoice that God gave us favor in the eyes of his Honor Sir William Johnson, and we rejoice that God gave us favor in your eyes"—he did not explicitly refer to Christianity as a point of connection between the two communities.[40] He did, however, give a sermon to the assembled Oneida two days later, on a Sunday morning. It was a classic Great Awakening–style call to conversion, detailing the biblical examples of individuals who had repented contrasted with those who had not.

After Johnson's sermon, the Oneida described the shared Christian identity between the groups as a central reason for their offer of land. "Brethren, perhaps it was the Lord that steered your minds this way," they stated in a speech on the second day of the negotiations. "Maybe it is his will and pleasure that ye should come up here, and live alongside of us, your Brethren." In fact, the Oneida only laid out two expectations for the new tribe: "The first and chief is Religion, or to follow the directions given to us in God's Word. The second is to concur with the unchristianized Nations, so far as will promote peace and tranquility in our Land." Recognizing that not all the Haudenosaunee professed Christianity, the Oneida urged some caution in evangelization efforts but still warmly welcomed the Christian tribes. Their unity would rest on their shared recognition of the Christian God: "Let us have one Rule, even God our Maker, Who dwells in Heaven above, who is the father of us all." With this foundation, the two communities would have "one head, one heart, and one Blood."[41] Johnson's reply echoed the Oneida's religious language. "If it is not the will of God all our Councils and purposes will come to nought or all will be in vain," he acknowledged. "But if it please God, and it opens your hearts to pity us and to receive us as a young Brother and help us in every deed, then will we come up, and settle together in peace."[42] Once the Oneida had invoked Christian rhetoric as a language of diplomacy within the negotiations, Johnson was quick to reciprocate.

This pattern was repeated as Johnson promoted and fundraised for the impending move. When describing the Brothertown movement to white Christians, Johnson portrayed it as a missionizing endeavor: he stated that one of the goals of the removal was to preach to the "Indians that border on your extensive frontiers" and "instruct them in the great things of your holy religion."[43] When communicating with potential members of Brothertown from the seven tribes, however, Johnson never mentioned the idea of a Christian utopia or suggested that the purpose of the emigration was to evangelize far-off tribes. Instead, he focused on the physical needs of the tribes and the prospects of a better future with greater material comfort. Indeed, as Ryan Carr has argued, Brothertown was a "political community" that "possessed sources of cohesion that went beyond 'Christian fellowship.'"[44] Although most Brothertown members identified as Christian, church attendance and denominational affiliation varied within the tribe; for example, Baptist and Methodist congregations formed in the late 1790s, each with their own Brothertown minister, in addition to the Congregationalist church led by Occom.[45] Johnson's diaries and letters make it clear that he saw the world through a Christian lens, but his negotiation strategies with others also show that he understood when and how to deploy Christianity rhetoric to influence others.

Although I have argued that Native Christian religious expression shows continuity throughout the late eighteenth and early nineteenth centuries, the Revolutionary War did disrupt the timeline of Brothertown's formation. The move was originally planned for the spring of 1775, but with the outbreak of violence between colonists and the British in Boston in April of that year, only sixteen out of the anticipated sixty made the move, Samsom Occom being among those who stayed home.[46] The migrating party seems to have been made up entirely of men, and within a few months most of this delegation had returned to New England to be with their families.[47] The potential income from renting or selling their homelands in New England became more uncertain with the outbreak of war, and colonists' opinion of the removal plan also changed. Native relationships transversing regions, like that of the Oneida and the future Brothertown, appeared more suspicious to patriots during the Revolutionary War, and according to Joseph Johnson, they caused the governor of Connecticut to wonder whether the tribes might be plotting to "unite to join his Majesty's troops."[48] Moreover, Indigenous men were often compelled to join the Continental Army or perform other service for the patriot cause.[49] Coastal New England tribes, already reduced in size by the long-term effects of colonization, lost upwards of 20 percent of their male population to the war. One of the primary originators of the Brothertown movement, Joseph Johnson, worked as a messenger for the patriot cause in the early years of the war and died under unknown circumstances at some point between June 1776 and May 1777.[50]

The idea of Brothertown persisted, however, despite the warfare and losses. Several Brothertown families took shelter in Stockbridge, Massachusetts, during the war.[51] While there is little documentation of this period, the Stockbridge must have welcomed the Brothertown, given that the two tribes would share similar trajectories after the war. Moreover, the Brothertown choice of Stockbridge as a place of refuge was likely grounded in the Christian identity of Stockbridge. Stockbridge was located about 150 miles from the Brothertown tract in Oneida, so the move would not have been a simple matter.

In 1782, with the Revolutionary War dying down, the Brothertown recommenced their move to Oneida territory; first were those who had stayed in Stockbridge, and then in subsequent years groups of fifty to one hundred from New England moved.[52] When the Brothertown founders left Stockbridge to go to their new settlement, many Stockbridge Indians followed suit.[53] Stockbridge had also faced a heavy influx of white settlers, who overtook the town and superseded the settlement's original identity as a mission site for Native people.[54] Perhaps influenced by the Brothertown, the majority of the Stockbridge, under the leadership of the sachem Hendrick Aupaumut, also decided to relocate westward. Documents from as early as 1785 indicate that the Oneida had bequeathed a tract of land to the Stockbridge before the move began, similar to their conveyance to the Brothertown.[55] The 1788 treaty of Fort Schuyler, which finalized the agreements of the 1784 treaty between the state of New York and the Oneida, included tracts for both the Brothertown and the Stockbridge.[56]

After the Revolutionary War, the Stockbridge tribe connected with other tribes via Christianity as they sought to strengthen their numbers in New York.[57] In the mid-1790s, Hendrick Aupaumut initiated conversations with the Delaware tribe of New Jersey, long considered the "grandfathers" of the Mohicans, inviting them to move to Stockbridge. In 1796 three Delaware chiefs visited Stockbridge to help them decide whether to accept this invitation. Aupaumut's speech on the occasion used a mix of Christian and traditional Indigenous imagery to persuade the Delaware. He noted that in Stockbridge the Delaware would "have the privilege of hearing the glad tidings of the Gospel preached, and your children will be instructed to read and write."[58] But he also peppered his speech with references to Indigenous traditions, specifically to emphasize how the Stockbridge had already and would continue to welcome the Delaware. "I take wees-quos in which our ancestors used to put healing oil, and oil your legs and feet," he told the Delaware chiefs, and "I spread this unnuhkon, or mat, wide on which I put you."[59] These Delaware had also developed an identity that included Christianity; since 1760 many of them had been living at a mission site run by John Brainerd at a location called Brotherton, New Jersey.[60] Eventually they accepted Aupaumut's offer.

The move by the Delaware in some ways further highlighted the connections between Stockbridge and Brothertown. Bartholomew Calvin, one of the Delaware chiefs who agreed on the move to Stockbridge, would have been known to some of the Brothertown founders: his older brother, Hezekiah Calvin, had attended Moor's Indian Charity School along with students like David Fowler and Joseph Johnson.[61] Samuel Kirkland, who had preached to the Oneidas sometimes accompanied by David Fowler, Joseph Johnson, or Hezekiah Calvin, also spent time living in Stockbridge.[62] Daniel Simon, a Narragansett from Charlestown, Rhode Island, who had been educated at Moor's, taught school in Stockbridge for a short period around 1780 and also taught at a school in Brotherton, New Jersey, in 1783.[63] While he never relocated to Brothertown, New York, other members of the Simon family did.[64] Samson Occom frequently preached at both Brothertown and Stockbridge, an arrangement that was formalized in the late summer of 1787, when several Stockbridge leaders requested that Occom serve as a minister to them "in conjunction with Brotherton [*sic;* they were referring to the New York community], if it be agreeable to them."[65] Occom would spend most of the remainder of his life—he died in 1792 at age sixty-nine—traveling between the two communities and holding church services in both. While the two tribes maintained separate governances and identities, their close geographical proximity to each other, their frequent intermarriages and other sharing of resources, and their shared emphasis on both Christianity and

Indigenous identity meant that the two tribes often followed a similar trajectory from the 1780s through the 1830s.

Christian Algonquians like Samson Occom, Hendrick Aupaumut, and Mary Peters espoused a worldview with Christianity as a central element. For them, the Revolutionary War did not in itself drastically reshape their engagement with religion. The Great Awakening, the market revolution, and the encroachment of Anglo-American settlers on their lands certainly impacted their lives, but those forces appeared prior to the Revolution. For Christian Algonquian communities, the Jacksonian removal policies of the 1820s and 1830s had much more impact than the geopolitical changes of half a century prior. Under this threat the Brothertown adopted US citizenship en masse in 1839, a decision that allowed them to own their lands in Wisconsin but disenfranchised the women of the tribe and erased, according to the US federal government, any future claims to tribal sovereignty. The Stockbridge and the Oneida did not apply for US citizenship, but white Protestant missionaries returned to take leadership of Christian communities in their lands until the renaissance of Indigenous activism in the early twentieth century. William Apess, after publishing and preaching against US claims to Mashpee land throughout the early 1830s, stopped preaching in 1836 and died in poverty in New York City five years later. The strategies of survivance that worked in both the late colonial and early republic periods had to change in the face of the growing power of the United States.

Including Native people in the story of religion and the American Revolution, therefore, suggests the usefulness of a different type of periodization, one that decenters the Revolution itself. Yet reshaping the periodization of US history according to Indigenous experiences requires a much deeper integration of Native history and standard American history than has typically been taught. The historian Sarah Pearsall, in her excellent essay "Recentering Indian Women in the American Revolution," analyzed six popular college-level US history textbooks and found that Indigenous experiences were rarely mentioned.[66] As her analysis demonstrates, encountering general references to Indigenous people in history textbooks is difficult enough; specialized analysis through the lens of religion is even more exceptional. Anecdotally, when I reoriented my early US history survey course to center on Indigenous people, students began calling the course the "Native American history class," although I still included all the standard elements of a US history survey course. Students were simply accustomed to a historical narrative that placed Indigenous people on the margins, and changing that focus made the course seem to deal with an entirely new topic. When I workshopped this essay with members of the Calumet & Cross Society, a book club of mostly Brothertown Indian Nation members, this anecdote resonated deeply with them. They had also experienced ways in which their history seemed to be always considered marginal or supplemental to the central themes of broader national histories.

The exclusion of Indigenous people from many mainstream historical narratives is not something that can be corrected simply by incorporating more Native history, however. As Kim Lawson (Heiltsuk Nation) stated in a conference on Indigenous epistemologies: "We're not looking at an issue of paper by paper or record group by record group. It's a whole system of a way of life. Our knowledge systems don't make sense without spirituality. We are asking for respect for a system of knowledge."[67] Engaging with Indigenous histories requires a willingness to acknowledge oral traditions and tribal cultural sovereignty, elements that have sometimes been lacking in traditional historical approaches.

Lawson's reference to spirituality offers another important lesson to scholars. Incorporating the experiences of Native people more deeply into American historiography can also bring to light new ways of understanding the impact of religion and spirituality on historical developments. This does not mean reifying old, stereotypical claims about Native people being "more spiritual" than Europeans: Indigenous people always have and will continue to express a range of religious beliefs and affiliations. It does imply, however, the need for a greater acceptance of different ways of knowing about the world. Rather than attempting to fit the experiences of Native people into existing historical frameworks, the lives and writings of the people studied in this essay invite us to broaden those frameworks altogether.

Notes

This essay's title comes from the Journal of Samson Occom, October 24, 1785, in *The Collected Writings of Samson Occom, Mohegan: Literature and Leadership in Eighteenth-Century Native America*, ed. Joanna Brooks (Oxford: Oxford University Press, 2006), 306. I want to thank the anonymous reviewers, the

Calumet & Cross Society, Bradley Dubos, Megan Fulopp, and the North American Religions Workshop group at Northwestern University for their comments on the manuscript.

1. Gerald Vizenor, "Aesthetics of Survivance: Literary Theory and Practice," in *Survivance: Narratives of Native Presence* (Lincoln: University of Nebraska Press, 2008), 1–25.
2. Journal of Samson Occom, October 24, 1785.
3. The Brothertown Indian Nation prefers the spelling Eeyamquittoowauconnuck, but in transcriptions from handwritten documents the word has sometimes been spelled Eeyawquittoowauconnuck.
4. Joel W. Martin and Mark A. Nicholas, *Native Americans, Christianity, and the Reshaping of the American Religious Landscape* (Chapel Hill: University of North Carolina Press, 2010), 15.
5. Bernd C. Peyer, *The Tutor'd Mind: Indian Missionary-Writers in Antebellum America* (Amherst: University of Massachusetts Press, 1997), 40; Eleazar Wheelock to Andrew Oliver, October 15, 1760, quoted in Margaret Connell Szasz, *Indian Education in the American Colonies, 1607–1783* (Albuquerque: University of New Mexico Press, 1988), 223.
6. Webb Keane, "Sincerity, 'Modernity,' and the Protestants," *Cultural Anthropology* 17, no. 1 (2002): 65–92; James C. Scott, *Domination and the Arts of Resistance: Hidden Transcripts* (New Haven, CT: Yale University Press, 1990), 3.
7. Samson Occom to John Bailey, summer 1783, in *Collected Writings of Samson Occom, Mohegan*, 119–20.
8. William Apess, *The Experiences of Five Christian Indians, of the Pequod Tribe* (Boston: Printed by James B. Dow, 1837), 58, http://archive.org/details/experiencesoffivooapes.
9. Martin and Nicholas, *Native Americans, Christianity*, 15.
10. Ryan Carr, *Samson Occom: Radical Hospitality in the Native Northeast* (New York: Columbia University Press, 2023); Edward E. Andrews, *Native Apostles* (Cambridge, MA: Harvard University Press, 2013); Lisa Tanya Brooks, *The Common Pot: The Recovery of Native Space in the Northeast* (Minneapolis: University of Minnesota Press, 2008), esp. the introduction, where Brooks traces the historiography of Native opposition to the "pure"/"inauthentic" binary.
11. Rosalyn R. LaPier, *Invisible Reality: Storytellers, Storytakers, and the Supernatural World of the Blackfeet* (Lincoln: University of Nebraska Press, 2017), xl.
12. See Kristina Bross, *Dry Bones and Indian Sermons: Praying Indians in Colonial America* (Ithaca, NY: Cornell University Press, 2004); Kristina Bross and Hilary E. Wyss, eds., *Early Native Literacies in New England: A Documentary and Critical Anthology* (Amherst: University of Massachusetts

Press, 2008); Julius H. Rubin, *Tears of Repentance: Christian Indian Identity and Community in Colonial Southern New England* (Lincoln: University of Nebraska Press, 2013); Jacqueline M. Henkel, "Represented Authenticity: Native Voices in Seventeenth-Century Conversion Narratives," *New England Quarterly* 87, no. 1 (2014): 5–45.

13. See Eleazar Wheelock, *A Plain and Faithful Narrative of the Original Design, Rise, Progress and Present State of the Indian Charity-School, at Lebanon in Connecticut* (Boston: Richard and Samuel Draper, 1763); and Samson Occom, "Autobiographical Narrative, Second Draft [September 17, 1768]," in *Collected Writings of Samson Occom, Mohegan*, 54.
14. See Andrews, *Native Apostles;* and Linford D. Fisher, *The Indian Great Awakening: Religion and the Shaping of Native Cultures in Early America* (Oxford: Oxford University Press, 2014).
15. "Several things to be considered & acted upon by the Board . . . ," March 12, 1765, Wheelock Papers, MS 765212.1, Rauner Library, Dartmouth College.
16. Meeting minutes, Commissioners for Propagating the Gospel in New England & parts adjacent, July 25, 1764, Wheelock Papers, MS 764425.2.
17. Thomas Eddy to Joseph Kirkland, May 15, 1797, Brothertown Papers, 1788–1810, New York State Archives, Albany.
18. 1797 Report of the Brothertown Superintendents, Rare Book Room, Brotherton [*sic*] Indian Records, 1774–1804, 15, Rare Book Room, Hamilton College Library, Clinton, NY.
19. Rev. Cutting Marsh, First Scottish Report for 1833, in "Documents Relating to the Stockbridge Mission," *Collections—State Historical Society of Wisconsin*, ed. Reuben Gold Thwaites, vol. 15 (Madison: Democrat Printing Company, 1900), 80.
20. For Peters, see Certificate of Mary Peters by John Sergeant, September 19, 1815, Dean Family Papers, Box 1, Folder 9, and Circular Letter of Rev. James H. Mills et al., January 18, 1821, Dean Family Papers, Box 1, Folder 10, both in Indiana State Archives, Indianapolis. For Quinney, see Karyn Saemann, *Electa Quinney, Stockbridge Teacher* (Madison: Wisconsin Historical Society Press, 2014); Barnes M. Hall, *The Life of Rev. John Clark* (New York: Carlton & Porter, 1856), 109, http://archive.org/details/liferevjohnclaroohallgoog; and Augustus Ambler to the American Board of Commissioners for Foreign Missions, March 23, 1829, in *Collections—State Historical Society of Wisconsin*, 15:47.
21. Circular letter of Rev. James H. Mills and five church elders, January 18, 1821, Dean Family Papers, Box 1, Folder 10, Indiana State Archives.
22. In 1795, the Stockbridge sachem Hendrick Aupaumut mentioned in a letter to Quakers that the tribe's inability to produce their own clothing meant that they were "forced to seek some articles of clothing among the traders; and the traders generally set up great price on their goods." Hendrick

Aupaumut et al. to the Indian Meeting of the Friends' Missionary Society, November 19, 1795, in Samuel Lorenzo Knapp, *The Life of Thomas Eddy* (London: Fry, 1836), 79. See also Dawn Peterson, *Indians in the Family: Adoption and the Politics of Antebellum Expansion* (Cambridge, MA: Harvard University Press, 2017), 69.

23. John Demos, *The Heathen School: A Story of Hope and Betrayal in the Age of the Early Republic* (New York: Vintage, 2014).
24. In the seventeenth and early eighteenth centuries some Native inhabitants of praying towns were designated as deacons or pastors but not formally ordained, which limited the recognition of their status outside their own communities. In Mexico, Indigenous men were permitted to be ordained as priests up until 1555 and after 1585, although the cases of ordination were exceptional and the overall number remained between 1 percent and 5 percent of the clergy, while the church in Peru experimented with ordaining mestizo men between 1576 and 1588. Matthew D. O'Hara, *A Flock Divided: Race, Religion, and Politics in Mexico, 1749–1857* (Durham, NC: Duke University Press, 2009); Ileana Schmidt Diaz de Leon, *Colegio Seminario de Indios de San Gregorio y el Desarrollo de la Indianidad en el Centro de Mexico, 1586–1856* (Guanajuato, Mexico: University of Guanajuato, 2012); Christine Lee, "The Long Road to an Andean Catholic Clergy: From Solórzano to Pèlach I Feliú," *Religions* 10, no. 4 (April 2019): 284, https://doi.org/10.3390/rel10040284. To the best of my knowledge, no Native person was ordained in French Canada during the colonial period.
25. Quoted in William DeLoss Love, *Samson Occom and the Christian Indians of New England* (Chicago: Pilgrim Press, 1899), 52.
26. License for Samuel Ashpo to Preach Among the Indians, May 12, 1761, in *The Letters of Eleazar Wheelock's Indians*, ed. James Dow McCallum (Hanover, NH: Dartmouth College Publications, 1932), 40.
27. Eleazar Wheelock to Gideon Hawley, June 10, 1761, in McCallum, *Letters of Eleazar Wheelock's Indians*, 35. According to McCallum's transcription, Wheelock crossed out the phrase "by the hands of Such Creatures."
28. State of New York, Treaty with the Oneida, September 22, 1788, A0448–79, Recorded Indian Deeds/Treaties, New York State Archives.
29. See Michael Leroy Oberg, *Professional Indian: The American Odyssey of Eleazer Williams* (Philadelphia: University of Pennsylvania Press, 2015); William Apess, *A Son of the Forest: The Experience of William Apes, a Native of the Forest. Comprising a Notice of the Pequod Tribe of Indians* (printed by the author, 1829); and "Amos, Joseph, Rev., 1805–1869," Native Northeast Portal, accessed February 10, 2025, https://nativenortheastportal.com/bio/bibliography/amos-joseph-rev-1805-1869.
30. Eleazar Wheelock to George Whitfield, August 7, 1764, Wheelock Papers, MS 764475.

31. Joseph Johnson to Jonathan Trumbull, early summer 1773, in *To Do Good to My Indian Brethren: The Writings of Joseph Johnson, 1751–1776*, ed. Laura J. Murray (Amherst: University of Massachusetts Press, 1998), 189.
32. Samson Occom to John Bailey, summer 1783, in *Collected Writings of Samson Occom, Mohegan*, 119.
33. Quoted in Joseph Fish, *Old Light on Separate Ways: The Narragansett Diary of Joseph Fish, 1765–1776*, ed. Cheryl L. Simmons and William Scranton Simmons (Hanover, NH: University Press of New England, 1982), 34.
34. David Harry representative of Charleston Narragansetts, to the Honorable General Assembly of Rhode Island, March 1787, Paul Campbell Research Notes, Box 2, Folder 12, Rhode Island Historical Society, Providence.
35. Joseph Fish to Andrew Oliver, November 11, 1762, Miscellaneous Bound Manuscripts, Massachusetts Historical Society, Boston.
36. Joseph Johnson's Address at Kanohaware, January 20, 1774, Wheelock Papers, MS 774120.
37. "Extract from Indian Records," October 15, 1773, in *The Papers of Sir William Johnson*, vol. 12, ed. Milton W. Hamilton (Albany: University of the State of New York, 1957), 1037, http://archive.org/details/papersofsirwilli12johnuoft.
38. See Samson Occom to Eleazar Wheelock, January 6, 1774, in *Collected Writings of Samson Occom, Mohegan*, 109, for the list of men who set out for Oneida. For an explanation of why only two men made it to Oneida, see Joseph Johnson's Address at Kanohaware, January 20, 1774.
39. David J. Silverman, *Red Brethren: The Brothertown and Stockbridge Indians and the Problem of Race in Early America* (Ithaca, NY: Cornell University Press, 2010), 99.
40. Joseph Johnson's Address at Kanohaware, January 20, 1774, Wheelock Papers, MS 774120. Johnson identified this speech as taking place on January 20 but later stated that it had occurred on a Friday, and that Friday was the twenty-first day of January. The speech was filed in the Wheelock Papers (which uses an organization system based on the dates of documents) with the date of January 20, but it seems likely that Johnson simply erred and meant to identify his speech as taking place on Friday, January 21.
41. Oneidas' Second Answer to Joseph Johnson, January 24, 1774, Wheelock Papers, MS 774121.
42. Joseph Johnson's Second Address at Kanohaware, January 24, 1774, Wheelock Papers, MS 774120.
43. Joseph Johnson, editorial, *New York Journal or Advertiser*, December 29, 1774, quoted in Johnson, *To Do Good to My Indian Brethren*, 249.
44. Carr, *Samson Occom*, 165.
45. See Love, *Samson Occom and the Christian Indians of New England*, 283–316.

46. See Johnson, *To Do Good to My Indian Brethren,* 259n; David Fowler to Colonel Guy Johnson, April 8, 1775, in ibid., 259; and Samson Occom to Joseph Johnson, April 14, 1775, in *Collected Writings of Samson Occom, Mohegan,* 111.
47. Oneida tribe to the New England Provinces, June 19, 1775, in Johnson, *To Do Good to My Indian Brethren,* 264.
48. Joseph Johnson to Colonel Guy Johnson, March 25, 1775, in Johnson, *To Do Good to My Indian Brethren,* 258.
49. Joseph Johnson, "Address at Guy Park," March 25, 1775, in Johnson, *To Do Good to My Indian Brethren,* 255.
50. Silverman, *Red Brethren,* 117. See also Committee Report on Mohegan Petition, May 22, 1783, Connecticut State Archives, Hartford, Indian Papers, Series 1, 2:326, transcription available through the Yale Indian Papers Project, http://yipp.yale.edu/annotated-transcription/digcoll2084.
51. Colin G. Calloway, *The American Revolution in Indian Country: Crisis and Diversity in Native American Communities* (New York: Cambridge University Press, 1995), 91–92; Petition of Gideon Commue et al. to the Connecticut Assembly, October 11, 1780, Connecticut State Archives, Indian Papers, Series 1, 2:226.
52. Love, *Samson Occom and the Christian Indians of New England,* 247; Silverman, *Red Brethren,* 122. See also Samuel Kirkland to James Bowdoin, March 10, 1784, Samuel Kirkland Papers, reference yhm-arc-kir-085c, Digital Collections, Hamilton College Library.
53. Silverman, *Red Brethren,* 122. See also Kirkland to Bowdoin, March 10, 1784, Samuel Kirkland Papers.
54. Rachel Wheeler, *To Live upon Hope: Mohicans and Missionaries in the Eighteenth-Century Northeast* (Ithaca, NY: Cornell University Press, 2008), 186. The tribe's modern name is Stockbridge-Munsee Band of Mohicans.
55. Hendrick Aupaumut to Governor George Clinton, April 11, 1795, quoted in William A. Starna, *From Homeland to New Land: A History of the Mahican Indians, 1600–1830* (Lincoln: University of Nebraska Press, 2013), 203.
56. Silverman, *Red Brethren,* 129; Starna, *From Homeland to New Land,* 203–9.
57. Wheeler, *To Live upon Hope,* 39.
58. Speech of Hendrick Aupaumut to the Delawares, October 7, 1796, Henry Simmons Letterbooks, 1:35, Haverford College, Haverford, PA.
59. Speech of Hendrick Aupaumut to the Delawares, October 7, 1796, Henry Simmons Letterbooks, 1:33–35.
60. While spellings of both locations vary, the New Jersey site is typically spelled Brotherton, while the New York / Wisconsin tribe is spelled Brothertown. Given the connections between the New Jersey Delawares at Brotherton and some of the future founders of Brothertown, it is tempting to assume that the name Brothertown was at least partly inspired by the

name of the mission site, but there is no mention of such a connection in the extant sources.

61. Brothertown Peacemaker Caroline K. Andler, "Shawuskukhkung—Bartholomew Scott Calvin," *Brothertown Citizen* (blog), accessed May 13, 2019, https://brothertowncitizen.files.wordpress.com/2016/09/bartholomew-scott-calvin-article-by-caroline-k-andler.pdf; Camilla Townsend et al., "'I Am Old and Weak . . . and You Are Young and Strong . . .': The Intersecting Histories of Rutgers University and the Lenni Lenape," in *Scarlet and Black*, vol. 1, *Slavery and Dispossession in Rutgers History*, ed. Marisa J. Fuentes and Deborah Gray White (New Brunswick, NJ: Rutgers University Press, 2016), 30; McCallum, *Letters of Eleazar Wheelock's Indians*, 293–98.
62. For example, see Kirkland's signature on the petition of Stockbridge Indians to New York Assembly, October 13, 1780, Connecticut State Archives, Indian Papers, Series 1, 2:226.
63. George Flemming, *Brotherton: New Jersey's First and Only Indian Reservation and the Communities of Shamong and Tabernacle That Followed* (Medford, NJ: Plexus, 2005), 71.
64. Petition of Stockbridge Indians to New York Assembly, October 13, 1780, Connecticut State Archives, Indian Papers, Series 1, 2:226; Love, *Samson Occom and the Christian Indians of New England*, 360–61.
65. Mahican-Stockbridge Tribe to Samson Occom, August 17, 1787, in *Collected Writings of Samson Occom, Mohegan*, 154.
66. Sarah M. S. Pearsall, "Recentering Indian Women in the American Revolution," in *Why You Can't Teach United States History Without American Indians*, ed. Susan Sleeper-Smith, Juliana Barr, Jean M. O'Brien, Nancy Shoemaker, and Scott Manning Stevens (Chapel Hill: University of North Carolina Press, 2015), 67n1.
67. Quoted in Ivy Schweitzer, introduction to *Afterlives of Indigenous Archives*, ed. Ivy Schweitzer and Gordon Henry (Hanover, NH: Dartmouth College Press, 2019), 1.

"No Rabbi in All of America"

How the Revolution Remade the Synagogue

ADAM JORTNER

★

In the wake of the American Revolution the new nation's Jewish community continued an old tradition: fighting with one another. Jonas Phillips of Philadelphia blasted his fellow Jews for planning to build a new synagogue seventy-five feet from the street. It needed to be closer, or else Sabbath breakers might "lumber up the yard of the Synagogue with filth and nastiness."[1] Phillips demonstrated his disgust by hiding the synagogue's deeds for several years.[2] The Newport synagogue of 1790 had shofar troubles; their ram's horn was cracked and defective, and "the Blower" was "such a profligate" that the community actually suspended the service "rather than have a Stigma cast on us." In New York, the shokhet was caught faking kosher meat.[3] In Philadelphia, the hazzan "gives precepts they don't mean to follow."[4] Everyone seemed to be making different decisions. It was simply impossible for any synagogue or any Jew to compel any other Jew to follow any particular guidelines. "Anyone can do what he wants," sighed Rebecca Samuel of Virginia. "There is no rabbi in all of America to excommunicate anyone."[5]

Historians of early American Judaism have viewed this lackadaisical approach to religious institutional life with a kind of wan regret; internal feuds, loose interpretation of Jewish law, and intermarriage are read as struggles "to balance assimilation with Jewish distinctiveness."[6] Manuel Josephson described his America of 1790 as a world where demographics swallowed up tradition; American Jews had "no regular system," Josephson wrote, "chiefly owing (in my opinion) to the smallness of their numbers," and therefore "have continually remained in a state of fluctuation. And every new comer introduced something new, either from his own conceit and fancy, or . . . from the Custom of the Congregation where he was bred."[7] Josephson assumed that Jews must have wanted a firm and unyielding synagogue that defined tradition and defended it consistently. If they didn't have such an institution, it was a mistake they were too weak to avoid. Historians have followed suit, largely defining the study of the small Jewish community in antebellum America as the problem of "little Jewishness" (*vinig yidishkayt*), as Haym Solomon famously described his life in republican Philadelphia.[8]

Historians of American Judaism have generally been content to let *vinig yidishkayt* describe the era in American Judaism. Solomon's quip occurs in several overviews of American Jewish history in the shorter introductory chapters, where it functions as the early example of an American Jewish historiography that argues that the American Jewish story is one of struggles *against* Americanization. Having Haym Solomon cry against *vinig yidishkayt* so early in the history of the republic allows an easy connection to the historiography of later generations of European immigrants and their descendants, but it may not be accurate. Solomon's words are not an argument. Moreover, it places the emphasis of Jewish history on what is *not* rather than on what *is*.[9]

For although Rebecca Samuel bemoaned Jewish behaviors in America, she also identified what Jews had in America, not just what they lacked: she described the post-Revolutionary Jewish situation as "a blessing" because "Jew and Gentile are as one." Samuel wished for stricter obedience to Jewish traditions, but at the same time, she appreciated the political rights for Jews.[10] Josephson similarly tempered his complaints about American Judaism with the recognition that American Jews "enjoy every desireable privilege and great preeminence far beyond many of our brethren dispersed in different countries and governments."[11] Unlike in many parts of Europe, Jews did not have to contend with powerful rabbis and synagogues to whom the state had delegated control and authority over the Jews as a class.[12] Synagogues wielded great control over Jewish life, keeping tradition intact, but the state powers that vested synagogues with such authority also restricted or abolished Jewish political rights.

In the United States, the Revolution broke the institutional framework of American Judaism. In its wake came weaker institutions and vastly improved political rights. Neither situation was an accident or a consequence of demographics. The institutions and the rights were deliberately developed by American Jewish patriots in response to the Revolution. Jewish refashioning during and after the Revolution did not come from the process of assimilation. It came from the same issues that have been foundational to the history of Revolutionary and republican Protestantism: religious choice, civil authority in religion and its dissolution, democratization. The Jewish experience in the Revolution demonstrates that these issues were not merely Protestant or Christian questions: American Jews in the wake of the Revolution did not find America and change to fit the country; they joined in the creation of America and changed with the same forces that molded their Christian countrymen. Religious pluralism was not merely the presence of different groups but their active participation and citizenship in a new civic space.[13]

Indeed, the salient fact about Jewish life during the Revolution and the early republic is not that Jews argued with one another but that these political and religious arguments reworked the synagogue as an institution. The American Revolution did not make the Jews any more prone to argument. (In Genesis, the patriarch Abraham argues with God, so Jewish tensions with religious authority are of long standing.) It did provide the conditions for the transformation of the American synagogue into a vehicle of religious choice.

The Revolution also created the conditions for this transformation by extending religious protections to Judaism. The patriot Jews were critical in this respect. In 1780, patriot Jews from across the nation gathered in Philadelphia, the largest American city with a synagogue that was *not* under British rule. The patriot Jews refounded Philadelphia's Mikveh Israel synagogue, writing a new constitution in 1782 that made the congregation more democratic and defined Jewishness as a religious choice. At the same time, the new Mikveh Israel, under the leadership of Gershom Seixas, began pressing for full Jewish rights in the new republic. If Judaism was a choice, and not an inherited class, then Jews too should be counted as citizens of the republic. "Jews are as fond of liberty as other religious societies can be" and possessed "the rights of a free citizen," wrote Seixas and his Mikveh Israel contemporaries.[14]

American Judaism might have gone in this direction even had the Revolution never happened. But the Revolution did happen. The war itself reshaped American Judaism. It split synagogues and eventually increased Jewish rights. The voluntarist model crafted in Philadelphia in 1782 threw off the European model of a synagogue that ruled the Jews and became a place for Jews to debate rules. The complaints of Samuel and Josephson were signs of how American Jews used their religious freedom. *Vinig yidishkayt* was by design.

American Judaism traditionally dates its origins to 1654, with the arrival of twenty-three Brazilian Jewish refugees in Manhattan. The Dutch governor, Peter Stuyvesant, called them "hateful enemies and blasphemers of the name of Christ."[15] The refugees had been Portuguese Jews living under Dutch auspices in Recife; Stuyvesant wanted them shipped back to Portugal, where they would surely be arrested and possibly killed. Stuyvesant's bosses, the Dutch West India Company, denied the governor's request to expel the Jews. Back in Holland, Jews had a protected status, and indeed, the directors wrote, "the Jewish nation in Brazil have at all times been faithful and have striven to guard and maintain that place, risking for that purpose their possessions and their blood."[16]

Myths have embellished the story of the "original twenty-three," but the improved status of Jews in the colonies as compared with their status in continental Europe is true enough.[17] In most European states, Jews were a class, a bureaucratic category, frequently restricted, persecuted, or exiled. At the time of the American Revolution, Jews were not admitted to France, had been expelled from Portugal and Spain, and were only informally admitted into England. Laws throughout the Continent legislated where Jews could live. In Bavaria as late as 1813, laws demanded that no Jews could move to a new area until an existing Jew there died or departed.[18] In these European conditions, synagogues controlled Jewish life, literally: European rulers dealt not with individuals but with local Jewish communities. The synagogue leaders regulated and ruled Jewish communities, becoming a "state within a state" and wielding real power over their coreligionists. All Jews within an area fell under the control of the local synagogue.[19]

But in a handful of Atlantic port cities fewer legal barriers existed, although the Jewish position remained precarious. These "Port Jews" often relied on extensive Atlantic trade networks, primarily centered in the Mediterranean.[20] Still, with few exceptions Jews remained a distinct class of citizens. Jews of Jamaica paid higher taxes and could not vote or hold office; other colonists "petitioned to have these descendants of 'the crucifiers of the blessed Jesus' removed from the islands."[21] A 1705 Virginia law forbade non-Christians, Catholics, and Africans from testifying in court.[22]

Like synagogues in Europe, Atlantic port synagogues functioned as the central cultural and administrative center of Jewish life. Curacao's Mickvé

Israel ruled the Jewish community with punitive measures. In 1756 it declared that Jews could not separate themselves from the synagogue. It forbade Jews from reading prayer in a minyan outside the synagogue or a house of mourning.[23] New York's Shearith Israel did not go quite that far, but it did place a premium on unity and uniformity. Both Ashkenazi and Sephardim "worshipped and accepted the supervision of this one synagogue." Shearith Israel had less prestige and fewer Jews than European synagogues, but it still "exerted control over its members . . . through moral suasion and, if necessary, social ostracism."[24]

Katherine Carté has argued that eighteenth-century British Protestantism was marked by *scaffolding*, connected webs of missionary societies, churches, publication ventures, and clerical networks. This scaffolding enjoyed state support and connected distant Anglicans, Presbyterians, and Congregationalists in a firm Protestant union.[25] Jews had no such scaffolding, and yet on occasion the British colonial state backed synagogues as institutions that spoke for the Jews. In 1755, Solomon Hays defied the elders of Shearith Israel during a raucous Kol Nidre. "Show your authority that you are an elder," Hays demanded of a member of the governing board, who promptly hit Hays in the face. Hays sued the synagogue and the elders, but the court sided with Shearith Israel. After five years of public vitriol, Hays gave "proper submission" to the authority of the synagogue, paid a fine, and was brought back in. His son Barack kept up the tradition, getting into a synagogue fistfight in 1772. In 1770, Manuel Josephson and Joseph Simson got into an argument over prayer shawls that also went to court. One of Josephson's witnesses tried to whip the court into anti-Semitic fervor by assuring them that Jewish elders "would kill many" if not restrained by "Christian law." The court ignored the provocation and again backed the synagogue's power to discipline members. Civil authority supported the synagogue's right to administer religion to Jews.[26]

There were not many such Jews to be concerned with in the British colonies at the time. North America's mainland colonies had few synagogues; in the rebelling thirteen colonies there were only four synagogues in four cities (one each in New York, Philadelphia, Charleston, and Newport). Perhaps one-tenth of 1 percent of the white population of the new United States was Jewish. The larger New World Jewish communities could be found farther south, in the Caribbean. Jamaica, Barbados, Nevis, Martinque, and Curacao all had synagogues that were older and larger than New York's. Indeed, the British colonial zone of Madras in India built a synagogue before New York did.[27]

Gershom Seixas took the pulpit at Shearith Israel under these conditions in 1768. Fistfights quickly became the least of his problems. The imperial crisis consumed New York, and Seixas planted himself firmly on the side of the patriots. Yet the divisions produced by the Revolution did not map onto the congregational squabbles of the previous decade; Josephson and Simson both lined up behind Seixas when he led them out of occupied New York and into patriot Connecticut.

The son of an Ashkenazic mother and a Sephardic father, Seixas described himself as "home-born," which he also chose to render as "Native."[28] He understood both major traditions at Shearith Israel. He conducted services in the Spanish style but peppered his letters with Yiddish terms not used by Sephardic communities—*talis, hatiss, kugel.*[29] He was not a rabbi; there were no yeshivas in North America. The hazzan merely read from the Torah and recited prayers, perhaps training boys for bar mitzvahs or acting as a shokhet.[30] The minutes of Shearith Israel refer to Seixas as "Rev. Mr." rather than "rabbi." The Gentile Isaac Bangs called him a priest.[31]

Seixas took a deist approach to religion. In 1814 he wrote that "50 years ago" he had read Tindal, Toland, and Bolingbroke, which meant that he had read these deist texts as he assumed leadership at Shearith Israel and as the imperial crisis deepened.[32] Throughout his life, Seixas referred to God using vague deist terms like *Almight Providence* or *our divine legislator.*[33] He later read Voltaire, Rousseau, and Priestly, though he refused to deny the divine nature of the Jewish Scriptures.[34] Like Enlightenment Christian thinkers, Seixas held a special place for revealed religion—created by specific divine revelation—while asserting the simultaneous existence of a natural religion that could be understood by all. All humans had to obey "the moral and social law," but only the Jews had "the religious law," from which, he added, "many others have been founded."[35] Indeed, the principles of Judaism were "the sentiments that arise in the human mind when considered in a moral and social sense, and are strictly conformable to reason, abstracted from the principles of true religion."[36] While he was clearly positioning Jewish tradition as closely as possible to deist Protestantism, he did not equate the two. For Seixas, the Jewish tradition had no rivals: "Among the various compositions of Man I never met with any other Sett that can be equaled either for sublimity of Stile or Subject. The ideas are universally true throughout our Prayers & the Language generally elegant & expressive."[37] This deist approach likely inclined him to the Revolution. He got the chance to align with the patriots on May 17, 1776.

The Continental Congress recommended that day as "a day of humiliation, fasting, and prayer" for "all denominations of Christians." Religion and politics were both at work here. As Spencer McBride has argued, the fast day was an explicit effort by the Revolutionary leadership "to forge a political alliance" with the clergy. By encouraging religious leaders to fast and pray at their request, Congress co-opted local leaders, who were often better known and more respected than the Revolutionary leadership, to speak on their behalf, thereby gaining local and religious legitimacy. As John Adams wrote regarding congressional fast days, "The clergy, this way, are but beginning to engage in Politicks, and they engage with a fervour that will produce wonderfull Effects."[38] At the same time, such fast days helped forge a national consciousness, as "people in each colony would share the same experience, abstaining from food and drink, engaging in a concert of prayer, and listening to their respective ministers preach on the providential mission of America."[39]

Seixas joined the May fast, leading Shearith Israel on a day of humiliation and prayer along with their Christian neighbors.[40] The text of the congressional proclamation requested the clergy to pray for American arms, for forgiveness from God, and "for establishing the rights of America on the most honourable and permanent basis."[41] Seixas ignored the specifically Christian language in the proclamation; perhaps he understood the goals of the prayer to be purely social and moral rather than theological. Israelites had their own religious tenets, but when it came to social contracts, a kind of sameness characterized both Jew and Gentile.

Seixas was not alone in separating the confessional from the moral. The Presbyterian preacher and signer of the Declaration of Independence John Witherspoon made much the same point that fast day in New Jersey. When virtue and manners prevail, Witherspoon said from the pulpit, "the attempts of the most powerful enemies to oppress them, are commonly baffled."[42] Yet Witherspoon noted that Christian salvation was not at stake in the crisis; the Revolution was "a commotion, from which religious differences have been so entirely excluded." Witherspoon declared that he had "already endeavored to exhort sinners to repentance," and now he intended to "point out to you the concern which every good man ought to take in the national character and manners." Witherspoon got even more direct: "I do not wish you to oppose any body's religion, but every body's wickedness." Witherspoon and Seixas were both willing to ignore confessional differences to focus on the patriotic and national concerns of "every good man." Indeed, both Seixas and Witherspoon quoted Micah 4:3: "And they shall beat their swords into ploughshares, and their spears into pruning-hooks."[43]

Seixas and the Jewish patriots followed this exact line throughout the Revolution and the early years of the new nation: moral virtue was universal and required for a republic and could be found in all religions. Therefore, Jews and Christians had equal access to the state *as citizens*. What counted was character, not confession; in Carté's formulation, the needs of the new nation outweighed Protestantism.[44] "Obey the law of God handed down to us by our divine Legislator," Seixas declared in 1805, "We shall then be better men & better Citizens."[45] This approach dovetailed with prevailing ideas about civic virtue and Enlightenment notions of a state as contract; the nation was made up of people who joined voluntarily rather than an expression of religious authority or king's demesnes.

As Howe prepared to invade New York, the congregation split. Seixas determined to move the congregation out of the city rather than live under British rule. This "act was fiercely contested" by the Jewish Tories, and Seixas apparently labored to persuade as many as he could to join him.[46] As the British bore down, Seixas locked the synagogue, took the Torah scrolls and other religious objects, and headed out with the patriot Jews to Connecticut. In later years, Seixas would praise God for allowing him to establish this synagogue in exile: he remembered that though "dispersed in various parts of the Country," enough of them were able "to assemble together in union to observe the appointed times & festivals instituted by Divine Authority, agreeably to the rites & ceremonies of our forefathers."[47]

Shearith Israel did not split into equal parts; it appears that most of the Jews went east with Seixas.[48] The division, however, was significant: where there had been one religious community, there were now two. American Protestants developed this knack in the Great Awakening. American Jews did it in the Revolution.

The escape to Connecticut has literally been compared to Moses crossing the Sea of Reeds. Nineteenth-century Jews, wrote the historian Jacob Rader Marcus, "made the hazzan the patriotic hero of New York."[49] Marcus knew that there was no need to embellish Jewish patriotic credentials. Plenty of Jewish Americans joined the patriot cause, supported Congress, and fought in the armies of independence. Jews served at Bunker Hill and at Yorktown.[50] Benjamin Rush thought "the Jews in all the States" were Whigs (patriots).[51] The historian Marcus Rezneck demonstrated that Jews served in the patriot army in direct proportion to their numbers in the general population. That alone revolutionized Jewish life; no Jew could serve as an officer in Europe, and military careers had traditionally been closed to Jews.[52] In the United States, a number of Jews rose to officer rank. Solomon Bush became a colonel, and when a bullet shattered his leg at Brandywine, he became a prisoner of the British—during which time he nevertheless managed to uncover at least one spy. "My wishes," he wrote, "are to be able to get Satisfaction and revenge the Rongs of my injured Country."[53] A full accounting of patriot Jewish service is impractical here, but a word about Jewish service is critical, if only to quash the persistent anti-Semitic rumor that Jews played no role in fighting for rights they later enjoyed. (Or as Mark Twain spat, "In the United States he [the Jew] was created free in the beginning—he did not need to help, of course.")[54]

So, yes, the patriot Jews did bring their Torah with them as they fled across the river. A list of expenses incurred by Seixas "in removing the Scrolls and other Synagogue property to Stratford, Conn" remains in the Shearith Israel archives.[55] Yet at least one scroll remained in New York, where the Tory Jews continued to worship under the leadership of the Hessian Jew Alexander Zuntz, who had arrived with the German mercenaries. British forces continued to provide sideways support for the Tory synagogue; when two British soldiers broke in and vandalized the building, they received multiple lashings from their superior officers.[56]

Thus, Seixas did not just move the synagogue; he *split* the synagogue. There were now a patriot Torah and a Tory Torah. The model of a synagogue commanding and governing all the Jews had foundered. Moreover, it had shipwrecked over political rather than religious divisions. The patriot-Tory split did not map onto any of the manifold divisions already present in the synagogue. Josephson and Simson both fled to Connecticut with Seixas; Barak Hays stayed on.[57] Loyalists from other regions, such as Rachel Pinto of Connecticut and the Hart family of Newport, made their way to Shearith Israel.[58] Jews from occupied Newport—including Seixas's father, Isaac—found their way to patriot Jewish abodes in Connecticut. Ideology rather than religion now split the American synagogue.

The Shearith Israel refugees scattered over various towns, including Danbury and Norwalk, and apparently traveled to Stratford for Jewish holidays in what was likely Connecticut's first minyan.[59] But by 1779 Long Island Sound had become a theater of war. British naval raids became frequent; several towns burned. Samson Mears, a Shearith Israel exile in Norwalk, noted that the destruction of his town coincided with Tish B'Av, the Jewish commemoration of the destruction of the ancient temple in Israel. "We truly celebrated the Anniversary season with all its gloom that our predecessors experienced," he wrote.[60] Isaac Seixas's sister Rebecca could not find her relatives in the wartime confusion. "I made all the inquiry possible to find a way to forward you a few lines, but all in vain," she wrote. "I could not learn where the troubles of America had carried you."[61] Isaac simply wrote, "God send us better times."[62]

By 1780 the Shearith Israel patriots had relocated to Philadelphia. The British had shifted their gaze south. As Savannah and Charleston faced occupying royal authorities, the patriot Jews there faced the same dilemma as the Jews of New York had. Savannah's Jewish patriots went to Charleston. When Charleston fell, they fled again. Of fifty-six Jewish men in Charleston in 1780, only fourteen remained under British rule.[63] Unlike Shearith Israel, Charleston did not have an extra Torah for an even split, so rather than make their own synagogue in exile, they headed north. By 1780 a national collection of patriot Jews had arrived in Philadelphia from New York, Charleston, Savannah, and elsewhere. A "collection of Brethren," the leaders of the synagogue later wrote, "fled here from different parts for refuge . . . that we might meet to offer up our Prayers to the Holy God of Israel."[64]

The institutional experience of Shearith Israel and Seixas was therefore not unique; the Revolution split multiple synagogues along political lines. Some Jews continued to practice in occupied towns, particularly Newport. The decision by patriot Jews to relocate was therefore a political as well as a religious decision. The patriot refuseniks institutionalized this change in 1782, when they refounded their synagogue, Mikveh Israel.

The new Mikveh Israel was formed by patriot Jews from across the nation—an expansion of a political ideology into a religious structure. The existing Philadelphia *adjunta* (governing board) resigned. They were replaced with a national group: Benjamin Seixas of South Carolina, Hayman Levy of New York, Jonas Phillips of Philadelphia and New York, Simon Nathan of French North America. All of them, in one way or another, were refugees from the war.[65]

These refugees' dedication to ideals of individual liberty became clear at the first meeting of the synagogue, which declared that the previous iteration of Mikveh Israel retained "no right or legal power" to establish rules for the community. It had been formed only "according to the custom of other congregations," not as a voluntary choice by free men. Now, however, the subscribers swore to "bind ourselves one to the other that we will assist . . . to form a constitution and rules for the good government of the congregation" in order to "promote our holy religion and establish a proper congregation in this city."[66] The synagogue existed by choice, not by tradition. It had no rights over any Jew except those voluntarily given.

Mikveh Israel arranged for its new constitution to be "laid before the Congregation for their Approbation and that each one of the Congregation shall have a right to give into the said Parnass [i.e., president] & Adjunta in writing, such rules or regulations as he thinks proper to present." For good measure, the constitution was to be read aloud at Passover so that everyone would have a chance to hear it. This would be a community of choice—a contract.[67] By contrast, the original 1770 constitution had stipulated that all members "submit to any orders of the president of the synagogue." In 1770 the president could also withhold all religious courtesies from a member if the president decided the member had insulted the synagogue. This decision could be appealed, but only to the *next* president.[68] But the revised Mikveh Israel offered multiple avenues of redress.[69] In September, someone suggested that any Jew should have the right to speak in a meeting even if he was not a member and had no right to vote. The motion was voted down. The synagogue and the Jewish community were different things.[70]

Seixas got the job as hazzan. He preached the Revolution to his congregants, asking God to "save and prosper the Men of these United States, who are gone forth to War."[71] Beyond this boilerplate, Seixas also promoted providentialism as a kind of creedless national religion, combining it with his Enlightenment ideas of moral virtue and the state. "The many visitations of an almighty providence," he declared in 1789, were signs "that we are suffering under his displeasure." Therefore, Jews ought to acknowledge the duties owed both to themselves and to "the community to which we belong. . . . Behave in such a manner as to give strength and stability to the laws entered into by our representatives." It was "incumbent on us, as Jews, in a more especial manner . . . to be more circumspect in our conduct."[72] The religious life of his congregation, Seixas declared, matched the objectives of the new American government, and both existed by ineffable wisdom of the Almighty.

The "wonderfull effects" from the patriot restructuring of Mikveh Israel included a political corollary. If, as Seixas taught, Jews followed the same moral requirements as everyone else, and if moral virtue rather than creedal statements determined membership in the body politic, and if Jews gave "strength and stability to the laws entered into by our representatives," then Jews were members of the body politic and needed no particular legislative act to achieve citizenship. Synagogues began to pursue the logical conclusion of living in a state without Protestant scaffolding.[73] If the United States was "the only place where the Jews have not suffered persecution," as Seixas wrote in 1810, then he would take action to confirm that Jews would have "every right of citizenship."[74]

Seixas and Mikveh Israel acted as soon as the war ended. Pennsylvania and twelve other states denied Jews the right to serve in office, either through a test oath requiring belief in Protestant or Christian creeds or through outright religious proscriptions. By November 1782 Mikveh Israel had established a committee working to "alter the Clause respecting the Jews," that is, to ask the state government to amend Pennsylvania's 1776 restriction of public office. The adjunta agreed "that we get it done immediately" and send a notarized petition to the state.[75] Seixas and the committee drafted a "memorial," which they presented to the general membership of Mikveh Israel.[76]

The memorial took issue with Pennsylvania's test oath, which required officeholders to acknowledge the New Testament as divine. At the same time, Seixas and the committee wrote, the constitution of Pennsylvania promised that "no man who acknowledges the being of a God can be justly deprived or abridged of any civil rights as a citizen on account of his religious sentiments." Yet the test oath itself "deprives the Jews of the most eminent rights of freemen."[77]

Not that the Jews *wanted* to run for office—the committee noted that they "cannot say that Jews are particularly fond of being representatives of the people in assembly"—but the restriction was "a stigma upon their nation and their religion." Pennsylvania's Jews had already become citizens by choice, the committee declared. "The conduct and behaviour of the Jews in this and the neighboring states, has always tallied with the great design of the Revolution" and "can count with any religious society whatsoever the Whigs among either of them." Sexias and his fellow memorialists mentioned specifically the cities under British siege whose patriots had fled to Philadelphia: Newport, Charleston, New York, "and their brethren at St. Eustatius," the tiny island whose Jewish community had defied the British and been expelled in retaliation. Jewish moral virtue reinforced Jewish patriotism: "In the religious books of the Jews . . . there are no such doctrines or principles as are inconsistent with the safety and happiness of the people of Pennsylvania."[78]

Jews were loyal, Jews were moral, and they were patriots. Mikveh Israel sent the petition to Pennsylvania's Council of Censors, the institution vested with the responsibility of ensuring that state laws conformed to the state's constitution, as soon as the censors met. The censors tabled the petition in December, but Philadelphia newspapers picked it up and printed it. The petition became a public declaration of the idea of American Judaism that Seixas had already explained to Shearith Israel: Jews were made of the same ideological stuff as their Christian fellow citizens. The *Independent Gazetteer* agreed, writing that the Jews "have been peculiarly firm and united in the great cause of America" and "therefore are, of right, entitled to all the privileges and immunities of her mild and equal government."[79]

This institutional restructuring and revolutionary politics spread throughout American Judaism. When Seixas returned to New York in 1784, Shearith Israel created a new "compact . . . constituted upon the principles of equal liberty." New York Jews could enjoy "every right and privilege belonging to this community," but only by subscribing to the compact. Anyone "professing to live as a Jew" could join at any time but did not have to; the synagogue community and the Jewish community were not the same thing.[80] In 1791, Savannah's synagogue circulated its constitution to the members and required a supermajority of votes (75 percent) for it to go into effect.[81]

Elsewhere in the British colonies the synagogue remained an institution that incorporated and ruled the Jewish community. Montreal's synagogue in 1768 made "membership practically compulsory," and when its leaders changed their laws during wartime (in 1778), they declared that "any Israelite that will not sign these our laws and regulations" within twenty days would be *forever* barred from any privilege or honor in the congregation.[82] In Barbados in 1819, synagogue Nidhe Israel petitioned the government to allow them to force Jews to pay taxes to the synagogue and for the synagogue to be made a parish vestry.[83]

In Barbados, that decision would have maintained the authority of the synagogue while giving some Jews the vote (through legal legerdemain).

In the United States, the synagogues had adjusted their authority in war, and political rights followed. By 1792 Jewish communities in Pennsylvania, South Carolina, and Georgia were all led by men who had been members of the new Mikveh Israel and returned home, and all three states had jettisoned their test oaths. When Charleston's Jews dedicated their new synagogue in 1794, the governor attended.[84] Even Jews who had supported the Crown in the Revolution subscribed to the new model. When Seixas returned to New York in 1784, Mikveh Israel hired Jacob Raphael Cohen, the loyalist hazzan of the Shearith Israel Tory congregation.[85] Meanwhile, New York's loyalist synagogue president, Abraham Zuntz, was invited to stay on as part of the adjunta of the republican Shearith Israel.[86]

Becoming an institution based on choice even led to calls for equality far beyond what Seixas had intended. In 1785 the three Judah sisters of Shearith Israel disagreed with a decision by synagogue functionaries to place them in assigned seats. They refused to accept the decision on the grounds that they were not subject to synagogue discipline: "When the gentlemen trustees can convince us that we are subject to any laws they choose to make which is to hinder us from attending Divine Worship, they may endeavor to exercise their authority." The women lost their battle, and they decided to leave the synagogue. The synagogue did not rule, and it did not have to negotiate. (They later rejoined, and Abigail Judah made an unsuccessful bid to become the world's first female *shamash*.)[87]

The Judah sisters were a bellwether. Divisions and separations became a natural part of an American synagogue structure that prioritized lay control and provided few means for silencing dissent. When Jacob Cohen wanted to marry Esther Whitlock Mordecai in 1782, Mikveh Israel had to convene a committee. Mordecai had converted, and Cohen, bearing the priestly title in his patronym, was not supposed to marry a convert. The committee voted 3–2 to forbid the marriage, but there was no enforcement. Prominent members of the community (including the patriot heavyweights Haym Saloman and Mordecai Sheftall) signed the Cohen-Mordecai *ketubah*, and the adjunta had to pass a resolution forbidding Seixas from officiating.[88]

After Cohen and Mordecai got married, they opened their own synagogue. In 1789 Cohen helped found Beth Shalome in Richmond, whose constitution truly put the power in the hands of the congregation. Any rule or regulation that a member objected to must be reviewed by "a meeting of all the members in toto," or at least two-thirds of them. Decision making was firmly in lay hands.[89]

Objections also subdivided American synagogues. In 1785, Charleston's synagogue split; they came back together in 1791 and split again in 1825.[90] In 1795, Mikveh Israel itself split in two; the new congregation, Rodeph Shalom, adopted a Yiddish model of worship and went even further on the road to democratization than its parent congregation, with no hazzan and members serving as their own readers. Mikveh Israel, with its powers delegated to the laity, could not keep all the Jews together. But neither could Rodeph Shalom: by 1810 they had to pass congregational rules concerning members attending minyan at both synagogues.[91]

The fissiparous nature of American Judaism would become its institutional model and remain so for the next fifty years.[92] Synagogues would possess relatively weak leadership and would split over divisions rather than seek to amalgamate all Jewish voices into one. Synagogues lost their bureaucratic function and became religious institutions—right alongside their Christian neighbors. This change directly affected the legal status of white Jewish Americans; if Jewish institutions worked like Protestant institutions, then the argument that Jews possessed the same moral capacity as Christians could secure them a place in the body politic, and the inability of the synagogue to act as an institution speaking on behalf of Jews helped obviate the European problem of Jewish classification.

Judaism became a choice, and each Jew a rabbi unto themselves, as the case of Abigail Judah shows. Such a positioning would necessitate new interpretations of Jewish law and practice; older forms of enforcement simply no longer applied. Yet this kind of assimilation was precisely what Seixas and the breakaway patriots of Shearith Israel and Mikveh Israel wanted, that is, the kind of synagogue they formed once the synagogue was no longer a singular institution. And to an extent, the ability of the synagogues to splinter helped secure Jewish rights in Revolutionary America. There was no rabbi in all of America, and the Jewish patriots wanted it that way.

Notes

1. Congregation Mikveh Israel, "Minutes and Correspondence of the Congregation, 1782–1790," Robert D. Farber University Archives and Special Collections, Brandeis University, entries for May 28, May 29, and June 2, 1782 (hereafter "Minutes and Correspondence").

2. Entry for 11 Tishri 5544 (October 7, 1783); Jonas Phillips to Parnass, June 5, 1786; Simon Nathans and Michael Gratz to Phillips, March 17, 1784, all in "Minutes and Correspondence."
3. Jacob Rader Marcus, ed., *American Jewry: Documents, Eighteenth Century* (Cincinnati, OH: Hebrew Union College Press, 1959), 193 (hereafter *AJD*).
4. Samuel Hays to Richea Gratz, November 27, 1793, *AJD*, 63, 67–68.
5. Rebecca Samuel to her parents, January 12, 1791, *AJD*, 52.
6. Deborah Dash Moore, foreword to Howard B. Rock, *Haven of Liberty: New York Jews in the New World, 1654–1865* (New York: New York University Press, 2012), xv. Zev Eleff traces the jeremiads over American assimilation to those European rabbis of the 1890s who portrayed America as a religious "wasteland" where laws of kashrut and intermarriage were neglected. Zev Eleff, "Rabbi Hayim of Volozhin, Rabbi Aharon Kotler, and the Remaking of an American Jewish Prophecy," *American Jewish Archives Journal* 72, no. 1–2 (2020): 88. Such notions of assimilation as betrayal rather than valid religious practice may persist in Jewish culture and historiography (more in the former than in the latter), but as Eleff points out, they were not the attitudes of early nineteenth-century Jews. The experience of Gershom Seixas and the Jewish patriots suggests that a loose institutional structure and assimilation were precisely what early American Jews wanted. Shari Rabin makes a similar argument about taking eclectic Jewish practices as a legitimate form of religion in later decades in *Jews on the Frontier: Religion and Mobility in Nineteenth-Century America* (New York: New York University Press, 2017).
7. Manuel Josephson to Moses Seixas, February 4, 1790, in *Jews in the Americas, 1776–1826*, ed. Michael Hoberman, Laura Leibman, and Hilit Surowitz-Israel (New York: Routledge, 2018), 211.
8. For assimilation as the primary challenge for American Jews of the eighteenth and nineteenth centuries, see Jonathan Sarna, *American Judaism: A History* (New Haven, CT: Yale University Press, 2004); Emily Bingham, *Mordecai: An Early American Family* (New York: Hill & Wang, 2003); and William Pencak, *Jews and Gentiles in Early America, 1654–1800* (Ann Arbor: University of Michigan Press, 2005).
9. See, e.g., Sarna, *American Judaism*, 45; and Howard M. Sachar, *A History of the Jews in America* (New York: Knopf, 1993), 37.
10. Samuel to her parents, January 12, 1791, in *AJD*, 52. Samuel noted that *galut* (rejection) occurred in New York and Philadelphia, where there were more Jews.
11. Manuel Josephson to Moses Seixas, February 4, 1790, in Hoberman, Leibman, and Surowitz-Israel, *Jews in the Americas*, 101.
12. Zev Eleff, *Who Rules the Synagogue? Religious Authority and the Formation of American Judaism* (New York: Oxford University Press, 2016), 4–6.

13. The historiography on democratization and American Protestantism is vast. Among many, see Nathan O. Hatch, *The Democratization of American Christianity* (New Haven, CT: Yale University Press, 1989); Catherine A. Brekus, *Strangers and Pilgrims: Female Preaching in America, 1740–1845* (Chapel Hill: University of North Carolina Press, 1998); and Jon Butler, *Awash in a Sea of Faith: Christianizing the American People* (Cambridge, MA: Harvard University Press, 1990). Leon Jick, Zev Eleff, and Jonathan Sarna have all mapped the rise of democratization in American Judaism after the Revolution. Some of this work actually preceded Hatch's work on the democratization of American Protestantism. My larger point here is not about the postwar democratization but that the ideological divisions of the Revolution and the exigencies of the war have a direct institutional and religious link to this democratization. The war changed Judaism; it did not happen independently of the Jews and drift back to them afterwards, nor were the changes due to demography.
14. Quoted in Jacob Rader Marcus, *Early American Jewry*, vol. 2, *The Jews of Pennsylvania and the South, 1655–1790* (Philadelphia: Jewish Publication Society of America, 1953), 158.
15. Fritz Hirschfeld, *George Washington and the Jews* (Newark: University of Delaware Press, 2005), 13.
16. 1665 January Petition of the Jewish Nation to the West India Company (Amsterdam), in Samuel Oppenheim, "The Early History of the Jews of New York, 1654–1664. Some New Matter on the Subject," *Publications of the American Jewish Historical Society* 18 (1909): 9–10.
17. Rock, *Haven of Liberty*, 12–16.
18. Rabin, *Jews on the Frontier*, 13–15.
19. Sarna, *American Judaism*, 12; Eleff, *Who Rules the Synagogue?*, 5.
20. C. S. Monaco, "Port Jews or a People of the Diaspora?," *Jewish Social Studies* 15, no. 2 (January 2009): 137–66; David Sorkin, "Port Jews and the Three Regions of Emancipation," *Jewish Culture and Identity* 4, no. 2 (2001): 31–46; Sorkin, *Jewish Emancipation: A History Across Five Centuries* (Princeton, NJ: Princeton University Press, 2019), 33.
21. Monaco, "Port Jews or a People of the Diaspora?," 138–39. Work on Judaism in the early modern Caribbean has exploded in recent years, raising pertinent questions as to whether the Caribbean experience was more emblematic of New World Judaism than the British North American experience in the eighteenth century. It may be that the wartime experiences of US Jews outlined here accounts for the division between the (smaller) Jewish communities in New York, Philadelphia, and Charleston and their coreligionists in Bridgetown, Curacao, etc. See among many Holly Snyder, "Rules, Rights, and Redemption: The Negotiation of Jewish Status in British Atlantic Port Towns, 1740–1831," *Jewish History* 20 (2006): 147–70;

Robert Cohen, *Jews in Another Environment: Suriname in the Second Half of the Eighteenth Century* (Leiden: Brill, 1999); and Stanley Mirvis, *Jews of Eighteenth-Century Jamaica* (New Haven, CT: Yale University Press, 2020).

22. Marcus, *Early American Jewry*, 2:166; Sorkin, *Jewish Emancipation*, 229–30.
23. Hoberman, Leibman, and Surowitz-Israel, *Jews in the Americas*, 195–96.
24. Rock, *Haven of Liberty*, 28.
25. Katherine Carté, *Religion and the American Revolution: An Imperial History* (Chapel Hill: University of North Carolina Press, 2021), 72.
26. Rock, *Haven of Liberty*, 52–53, 74; Pencak, *Jews and Gentiles in Early America*, 56–60.
27. Adam Jortner, *A Promised Land: Jewish Patriots, the American Revolution, and the Birth of Religious Freedom* (New York: Oxford University Press, 2024), 39.
28. Gershom Seixas to Hannah Adams, July 23, 1810, transcribed in Dan Judson, "The Mercies of a Benign Judge: A Letter from Gershom Seixas to Hannah Adams, 1810," *American Jewish Archives Journal* 56, no. 1–2 (2004): 186.
29. Jacob Rader Marcus, *The Handsome Priest in the Black Gown: The Personal World of Gershom Seixas* (Cincinnati, OH: American Jewish Archives, 1970), 64; *The Letters of Abigaill [sic] Levy Franks, 1733–1748*, ed. Edith B. Gelles (New Haven, CT: Yale University Press, 2004), 75n5.
30. Eleff, *Who Rules the Synagogue?*, 9.
31. Marcus, *Handsome Priest*, 16, 22.
32. Gersom Seixas to Sarah Kursheedt, January 29, 1814, Papers of the Seixas Family, Series III: Gershom Mendes Seixas and Descendants, Box 1, Folder 12, American Jewish Historical Society, New York (hereafter AJHS).
33. "Items Relating to Gershom M. Seixas," *Publications of the American Jewish Historical Society* 27 (1920): 129–30 (hereafter *PAJHS*); 1805 sermon, Sermons by Gershom Mendes Sexias, Jacques Judah Lyons Papers, Box 4, Folder 281, AJHS. On deist language for God, see David L. Holmes, *The Faiths of the Founding Fathers* (New York: Oxford University Press, 2005).
34. Gershom Seixas to Sarah Kursheedt, November 10, 1813, and January 29, 1814, Papers of the Seixas Family, Box 1, Folder 12, AJHS.
35. Undated sermons, Sermons by Gershom Mendes Sexias, AJHS.
36. 1799 sermon, Sermons by Gershom Mendes Sexias, AJHS.
37. Gershom Seixas to Moses Seixas, September 1, 1790, Papers of the Seixas Family, Box 1, Folder 11, AJHS.
38. Spencer McBride, *Pulpit and Nation: Clergymen and the Politics of Revolutionary America* (Charlottesville: University of Virginia Press, 2016), 17.
39. McBride, *Pulpit and Nation*, 19; U S Continental Congress, *In Congress, Saturday, March 16, 1776. In times of impending calamity and distress; when*

the liberties of America are immenently endangered . . . (Watertown, MA, 1776), Library of Congress, https://www.loc.gov/item/2020774946/.

40. Marcus, *Handsome Priest*, 14.
41. US Continental Congress, *In Congress, Saturday, March 16, 1776.*
42. John Witherspoon, *The Dominion of Providence over the Passions of Men* (Philadelphia: R. Aitken, 1776), 50–51.
43. Witherspoon, *Dominion of Providence*, 30, 46, 50–51, 60; "Order of Service observed in the Synagogue Shearith Israel, on a day of humiliation, fasting, & prayer, recommended by Congress," in "Items Relating to Congregation Shearith Israel, New York," *PAJHS* 27 (1920): 31–32.
44. Carté, *Religion and the American Revolution*, 169–75.
45. 1805 sermon, Sermons by Gershom Seixas, AJHS.
46. N. Taylor Phillips, "Reverend Gershom Mendes Seixas: The Patriot Jewish Minister of the American Revolution," in *The American Jewish Year Book*, vol. 6, ed. Cyrus Adler and Henrietta Szold (Philadelphia: Jewish Publication Society of America, 1904), 41; Phillips, "The Levy and Seixas Families of Newport and New York," *PAJHS* 4 (1896): 205.
47. Sermon, November 28, 1799, Sermons by Gershom Mendes Seixas, AJHS.
48. Final numbers are unavailable and would be unreliable. The "Tory synagogue" of New York, however, did hold sporadic services. Loyalist Jews from patriot-held locations sometimes migrated to Manhattan to join, as in the case of Isaac Touro, who briefly served as hazzan in New York after the Americans recaptured Newport. See Jortner, *Promised Land*, 62–63, 88–89.
49. Marcus, *Handsome Priest*, 14.
50. Jortner, *Promised Land*, 3.
51. Benjamin Rush, *A Memorial Containing Travels Through Life*, ed. Louis Alexander Biddle (Philadelphia: Biddle, 1905), 89.
52. Marcus Rezneck, *Unrecognized Patriots: The Jews in the American Revolution* (New York: Greenwood, 1975), 25.
53. Solomon Bush to Henry Lazarus, November 15, 1777, in Samuel Oppenheim, "Two Letters of Solomon Bush, a Revolutionary Soldier," *PAJHS* 23 (1915): 177–78.
54. Mark Twain, *Concerning the Jews* (New York: Harper, 1934), 17, first published in 1898.
55. "Items Relating to Congregation Shearith Israel," *PAJHS* 27 (1920): 252.
56. Rock, *Haven of Liberty*, 80; Jortner, *Promised Land*, 124.
57. Rock, *Haven of Liberty*, 79.
58. Jacob Rader Marcus, *The Colonial American Jew, 1492–1776*, 3 vols. (Detroit: Wayne State University Press, 1970), 3:1294.
59. Kenneth Libo and Abigail Kursheedt Hoffman, *The Seixas-Kursheedts and the Rise of Early American Jewry* (New York: Bloch & AJHS, 2001), 30.

60. Samson Mears to Aaron Lopez, July 30, 1779, in Hoberman, Leibman, and Surowitz-Israel, *Jews in the Americas*, 5.
61. Rebecca Mendes Seixas to Isaac Seixas, July 26, 1779, "Items Relating to the Seixas Family," *PAJHS* 27 (1920): 367–68.
62. Quoted in Michael Hoberman, "How It Will End, the Blessed God Knows: A Reading of Jewish Correspondence During the Revolutionary War Era," *American Jewish History* 99, no. 4 (October 2015): 298.
63. Pencak, *Jews and Gentiles in Early America*, 126.
64. Pencak, *Jews and Gentiles in Early America*, 211; Eli Faber, *A Time for Planting: The First Migration, 1654–1820* (Baltimore: Johns Hopkins University Press, 1992), 104; "Minutes and Correspondence," 73–74.
65. "Minutes and Correspondence," 13.
66. Minutes, Congregation Mikveh Israel, *AJD*, 116–17.
67. "Minutes and Correspondence," entries for March 17, March 25, and May 29, 1782.
68. First Philadelphia Synagogal Constitution, *AJD*, 95–96.
69. "Minutes and Correspondence," entry for March 24, 1782.
70. "Minutes and Correspondence," entry dated 17 Tishri 5543 (September 25, 1782).
71. "Prayer for Peace," Gershom Seixas Papers, Folder 6, American Jewish Archives, Cincinnati, OH.
72. Gershom Seixas, *A Religious Discourse Delivered in the Synagogue in This City* (New York: M'Lean, 1789), 13–14.
73. The Jews seeking rights in the United States were almost exclusively white, and race certainly played a factor in the Jewish transit to full citizenship rights. The classification of European Jews as white has been cited as a twentieth-century phenomenon, but as Rabin notes, "In the eyes of American law . . . Jews have been white from the beginning." Rabin, *Jews on the Frontier*, 13–14. See also Eric L. Goldstein, *The Price of Whiteness: Jews, Race, and American Identity* (Princeton, NJ: Princeton University Press, 2006); and Matthew Frye Jacobson, *Whiteness of a Different Color: European Immigrants and the Alchemy of Race* (Cambridge, MA: Harvard University Press, 2001).
74. Gershom Seixas to Hannah Adams, July 23, 1810, transcribed in Dan Judson, "The Mercies of a Benign Judge: A Letter from Gershom Seixas to Hannah Adams, 1810," *American Jewish Archives Journal* 56, no. 1–2 (2004): 187.
75. "Minutes and Correspondence," entry for November 17, 1783.
76. "Minutes and Correspondence," entry for November 20, 1783.
77. The memorial is reprinted in full in Marcus, *Early American Jewry*, 2:157–58.
78. Marcus, *Early American Jewry*, 2:157–58.

79. *Independent Gazetteer*, January 17, 1784.
80. Constitution and Bylaws of Congregation Shearith Israel, New York, 1790, *AJD*, 150.
81. Code of Laws for Congregation Mickva Israel, Savannah, 1791–1792, *AJD*, 179–80.
82. 1778 Montreal synagogue constitution, in Hoberman, Leibman, and Surowitz-Israel, *Jews in the Americas*, 254.
83. Laura Liebman and Sam May, "Making Jews: Race, Gender, and Identity in Barbados in the Age of Emancipation," *American Jewish History* 99, no. 1 (2015): 7.
84. David Ackerman, "The 1794 Dedication of Kahal Kadosh Beth Elohim of Charleston: Reconstructed and Reconsidered," *American Jewish History* 93, no. 2 (2007): 159.
85. Hays to Gratz, November 27, 1793, *AJD*, 63, 67–68.
86. Rock, *Haven of Liberty*, 93–94.
87. Rock, *Haven of Liberty*, 90–91.
88. "Minutes and Correspondence," entry dated 15 Elul 5542 (August 25, 1782), *AJD*, 78–79.
89. Sarna, "The Democratization of American Judaism," in *New Essays in American Jewish History: Commemorating the Sixtieth Anniversary of the Founding of the American Jewish Archives*, ed. Pamela Nadell, Jonathan Sarna, and Lance Sussman (Cincinnati: American Jewish Archives, 2010), 99.
90. Pencak, *Jews and Gentiles in Early America*, 134–35; Ackerman, "1794 Dedication," 172–73.
91. Edwin Wolf and Maxwell Whiteman, *History of the Jews of Philadelphia* (Philadelphia: Jewish Publication Society, 1975), 226–27.
92. Zev Eleff, in *Who Rules the Synagogue?*, argues that this model worked well through the Civil War, when again American politics shifted the synagogue. Rabbis took positions as chaplains in the military and used this new legitimacy to secure authority denied to them in previous decades.

Disrupting Religion

Universalist Print Networks and the American Revolution

MICHAEL BAYSA

★

IN THE BEGINNING of the 1780s, religious printing in Boston was just beginning to recover from the American Revolution's devastation of the print market. It was aided by a print debate brewing among Boston's clerical elite. News of the controversy reached the then diplomat John Adams in Europe, alerting him to "a religious dispute arising on Matters [that] do not tend to render Men wiser or better or more happy."[1] It began when the Universalist itinerant preachers Elhanan Winchester and John Murray began their 1780 circuit preaching the gospel of universal salvation throughout the New England countryside.[2] The Baptist minister Isaac Backus took the first initiative and published *The Doctrine of Universal Salvation Examined and Refuted* (1782) to combat the spread of universal salvation. Backus's text did not seem to gather much attention, but it elicited a response in an anonymously published pamphlet, *Salvation for All Men, illustrated and vindicated AS A Scripture Doctrine* (1782). The pamphlet's author called himself "One who wishes well to *all Mankind*" and argued, as did other Universalists, that God had predestined all humanity to eternal salvation and happiness in heaven. Charles Chauncy (1705–1787), who presided over the First Church of Boston, wrote the pamphlet and had been one of the most well respected and esteemed defenders of New England Congregationalist orthodoxy. He was famously known for his publication *Seasonable Thoughts on the State of Religion in New England* (1743), which rallied anti-revivalists against pro-revivalist itinerants like Northampton's Jonathan Edwards and the

Briton George Whitefield during the revivals of the 1740s.[3] Chauncy's success established him as the public defender of New England orthodoxy, a role he happily carried with him into the 1750s and 1760s, when he published against the Church of England for attempting to establish an Anglican bishop to govern over New England religious life. Backus praised the Boston minister as having "published more, for thirty years, to uphold the Congregational establishment in New England than any other man."[4] Despite Chauncy's publishing record, his print presence diminished from 1774 to 1782, when he would reemerge as a proponent of universal salvation preaching to a largely Calvinist reading public.

Using Chauncy's print absence throughout most of the 1770s and the subsequent difficulty of publishing a text on universal salvation in the 1780s, this essay posits a disruption thesis to explain continuities and discontinuities in eighteenth-century New England's religious public sphere. I argue that the American Revolution's disruptions of the domestic print industry created publishing barriers for Universalists to leverage print as a medium for gathering readers and followers. Figures like Chauncy and Winchester would have to rely on London publishers to print their works despite having established relations with American publishers. By contrast, critics of universal salvation from Backus to Timothy Dwight IV were able to easily flood the domestic public sphere with rebuttals and fuel readers' anxieties around Universalists and other emergent voices like deists, and their critiques would portend the revivals that would eventually be recognized as the Second Great Awakening.[5]

On this front, Chauncy makes for an important case study. He was a well-published minister who wrote extensively on some of the most important events of eighteenth-century religious and political life. His theological stances, as Backus noted, had reflected the consensus of the New England Congregationalist establishment for decades, and his turn to universal salvation, if not for the timing and publishing issues surround it, might have more cleanly facilitated the theological liberalism of the region into the next few decades.[6] Even during the publishing gaps of the Revolution, Chauncy's pro-Revolutionary stance represented the sentiments among his peers and the laity. The "patriot preacher," as Chauncy was known by King George III, loudly supported the revolutionaries during the 1760s by preaching fiery sermons alongside his friend Jonathan Mayhew, which earned him the scorn of the British troops occupying Boston. A 1774 handbill warned that if the residents of Boston were to attempt to rebel against the British occupying the city, the named men, which included Chauncy alongside famous revolutionaries like Samuel Adams and John Hancock, would be put "immediately to the sword," and the troops would "destroy their houses and plunder their effects" for "the mischiefs they have brought" upon the British.[7]

On the surface, Chauncy's print publication gap during the Revolution echoes a familiar declension or secularization narrative: the public had simply lost interest in religious matters as the American Revolution began to preoccupy the minds of writers and readers.[8] This distraction thesis was shared by Chauncy's friends and his biographers, who also believed that the political and economic events surrounding the colonies simply pulled his attention from matters pertaining to universal salvation.[9] However, such treatments of print improperly correlate publication with public interest and treat discourse as consisting of clearly demarcated boundaries between religious and political concerns, something Chauncy himself did not believe to be the case. On the contrary, gaps, absences, and silences in print records could be better accounted for through material and network infrastructures that undergird publishing itself. The events of the American Revolution had disrupted American publishers' ability to print for Universalists while still being able to readily publish opposition to it domestically. An understanding of the material difficulties faced by heterodox writers complicates narratives that have dismissed liberal religion as simply unpopular among or irrelevant to American readers compared with the success of newer Protestant denominations like Methodists and Baptists by the nineteenth century.[10]

More broadly, attention to the contingencies and nuances of print production grounds an amorphous, imagined "public" within the decisions, contestations, negotiations, relationships, and strategies of print networks to create the public sphere.[11] This focus on the production of print treats the medium as a human phenomenon shaped by the political, economic, social, and theological concerns of a print network made up of ministers, authors, printers, booksellers, and various other print intermediaries.[12] Therefore, if printed texts that we might consider to be in the genre "religion" weakened in impact, disappeared from pamphlets or newspapers, or ceded ground to more political, economic, or literary genres, then perhaps the answer lies in the shifting relationship between religious communities and the print networks that produced their texts. On this note, this essay tracks Chauncy's shifting relationship to publishers over the course of this period. The first section explores how Chauncy worked with the bookseller Thomas Leverett and the printer Samuel Kneeland, both of whom had facilitated his many publications against the establishment of Anglican bishops in the colonies. This relationship preserved his print presence in the years after the Boston Massacre in circumstances that otherwise made printing generally difficult. The second section contextualizes the proliferation of Chauncy's heterodox views about universal salvation within similar "publishing" strategies undertaken by Universalist communities across New England throughout the 1770s. Through widely distributed and circulating manuscripts, religious rhetoric continued to be published throughout New England without depending on printers and booksellers. The third section explores the transatlantic Universalist networks Chauncy had to leverage in order to print his views in London by 1783. Such attempts contrasted with the explosion in anti-Universalist materials published domestically. At a time when the new nation was establishing itself through institutions like the printing press, Universalists like Chauncy and Winchester had to rely on older connections for their theological innovations to reach an American audience.[13]

Publishing Heterodoxy During the Revolution

Chauncy was far from conservative in his rhetoric against the British soldiers occupying Boston. On a chilly March 5, 1770, evening, he heard that civilians had been wounded grievously when British soldiers fired into an angry crowd. A passerby yelled at Chauncy regarding the British captain Thomas Preston, the man who headed the soldiers charged with manslaughter: "If I was to be one of the Jury upon his Trial, I would bring him in guilty; *evidence or no Evidence*."[14] Two months later, Chauncy was approached by the Sons of Liberty to deliver a sermon to support their protest over the local courts' delaying the trial of the British soldiers. In *Trust in God, The Duty of a People in a Day of Trouble* (1770), Chauncy reminded the crowd, "Who the shedders of this blood were may possibly appear, upon the trial of those who are under confinement, as being supposed to be the guilty persons. We wish them as fair and equal trial as they themselves can desire."[15] While his sermon might seem conciliatory in its tone, it was not received as such. With the trial approaching, Justice of the Peace James Murray recounted that "after the pains taken by the Revd. Doctr. Chauncey and others to prejudice the People of Boston against Capt. Preston, there is too much room to suspect the Captain will pass his time but badly after his Trial."[16] *Trust in God* was rushed through the printing press. What ensured its speedy publication was not so much

Chauncy's consent or the efficiency of printer Daniel Kneeland but the timeliness of the text as perceived by the bookseller Thomas Leverett.

By 1770 Leverett and Kneeland had been publishing Chauncy's works for nearly a decade. Booksellers would generally be the primary purchasers for printers and negotiated the terms of publication with the author. Given that they took on the financial risks for carrying the books, they were also the ones most likely to make a hefty return.[17] Kneeland's own printing career was spent either operating the presses owned by booksellers like Leverett or depending on their patronage to finance his own business when printers finally owned their own press.[18] Leverett's initial business decision to print for Chauncy had paid off when he published Chauncy's *A Letter to a Friend, Containing Remarks on Certain Passages in a Sermon Preached by the Right Reverend Father in God, John Lord Bishop of Landaff* (1767) during the controversy over placing an Anglican bishop in the colonies. Chauncy's text was written as a response to the English bishop John Ewer, who had observed that the churches in the colonies would fare better if episcopal polity were established there. The idea of subjecting Congregationalist ministers to regional bishops incensed Boston ministers and warranted a response. In *A Letter to a Friend,* Chauncy accused Ewer of wanting to have "the Ecclesiastical state of things be inverted" so that the bishops arriving from England would threaten the colonists' "own mode of worship and discipline to that of the English church."[19] The text was likely a bestseller.[20] Over the next few years Chauncy would continue his battle with supporters of the episcopacy. The following year, he feuded with the Anglican priest Thomas Chandler. These exchanges resulted in numerous publications produced by Leverett and Kneeland: *An Appeal to the Public Answered* (1768), *A Reply to Dr. Chandler's "Appeal Defended": Wherein His Mistakes Are Rectified* (1770), and *A Compleat View of Episcopie* (1771). As a result of his flurry of attacks against the episcopacy, Chauncy became one of the most published colonial authors in the years 1761–70.[21]

Boston printing faced a major downturn in 1774 as the occupying general, Thomas Gage, and the British troops discouraged pro-Revolutionary booksellers and printers from operating their businesses. A British blockade made doing business in Boston even less profitable for the trade as colonial American currencies depreciated.[22] Chauncy's 1774 publication titled *A Letter to a Friend, Giving a Concise, but Just, Representation of the Hardships and Sufferings the Town of Boston Is Exposed to* described the plight of residents of Boston and neighboring towns as being reduced to a "starving desperate condition," with hundreds "starved to death" because the entirety of Boston's port-reliant economy depended heavily on trade as "the only means of their subsistence."[23] However, he did not have Leverett to assist him with its publication. By this time, Leverett had likely joined the exodus of printers and booksellers after toning down some of his Revolutionary publications. Leverett's last few productions consisted of reprints from London: *A New Version of the Psalm of David* (1773), a version of Psalms written by the chaplain N. Brady and the poet laureate N. Tate dedicated to the king of England; and *Reflections on Death* (1773), by William Dodd, which was reprinted with Nicholas Bowes and Henry Knox. With few established booksellers and printers available, Chauncy turned to the newcomer James Greenleaf to print his anonymously authored *Letter to a Friend*. Greenleaf had just started his print business in 1773, but as a supporter of the Revolutionary cause and someone already listed as a person of interest to the British if rebellion were to happen, he risked much to print for Chauncy. Perhaps it was his shared political views that encouraged the printer to take on this job as a last literary gasp before the city fell to British troops. Soon thereafter, Greenleaf abandoned his business to leave the city.[24] After colonial troops retook the city in 1776, loyalist booksellers and printers also left the city, leaving only the famous Fleet family of printers in Boston. The arrival of British troops and the subsequent American siege marked a precipitous decline in Boston printing, which originally boasted seven booksellers, four printers, ten printer-booksellers, and seven firms, all of whom sustained Boston's book trade in 1770.[25]

In the same way that pro-Revolutionary publishers left Boston's print market at the height of the imperial crisis, ministers like Chauncy also began abstaining from certain public roles. At a November 28, 1774, meeting with the Associated Pastors of Boston, Chauncy proposed that ministers abstain from reading any proclamations issued "by the Governour and council, for days of public thanksgiving," a function traditionally executed by New England clergy.[26] However, even with this withdrawal from public appearances and publishing incendiary thoughts through the printing press, Chauncy's Revolutionary rhetoric did not disappear in his writings. By circulating correspondences and conversations with sympathizers to the Revolutionary cause like Samuel Adams and Richard Price, Chauncy continued critiquing Britain. In many instances, Chauncy reserved his most scathing remarks about Britain for these non-print modes of communication.[27] Indeed, discreet modes of circulating information were not new to Chauncy, despite being a well-published figure.

For about two decades Chauncy had been circulating his views on universal salvation along similar channels, through conversations, correspondences, and other non-print forms that did not require negotiating with the world of booksellers and printers and their various political, financial, religious, and literary interests.

For most of the eighteenth century, heterodox religious communities like the New England Universalists had been "publishing" their views without the involvement of print intermediaries like booksellers, printers, and ministers.[28] From 1770 to 1775, Murray itinerated from Philadelphia to Boston, preaching his message of universal salvation and only halting his trip when he was appointed a chaplain of the Rhode Island Brigade.[29] When the war ended, Murray continued his itinerancy and even settled into leading the Universalists in Gloucester, Massachusetts. Correspondences of Universalist congregants and ministers also circulated widely so as to connect disparate communities of believers across New England. These efforts culminated in the first Universalist convention in 1785.[30] When Universalists eventually made their way to print, their earliest publications did not speak to a broader public but anticipated a mostly Universalist readership. Judith Sargent Stevens Murray's *Some Deductions from the System Promulgated in the Page of Divine Revelations* (1782) was the earliest domestically produced Universalist text. Understood as a catechism, the text summarized Murray's beliefs in a manner that could be taught to children. However, even before its circulation in print Sargent had been circulating copies of her work to Universalist networks for well over a year. Evidence that it was being published appeared in a letter whereby she recounted visiting Portsmouth, New Hampshire and was met with readers of her work whom she has never met before.[31] Sargent's husband, John Stevens, whom she described as "ever indulgent" of her works, purchased copies to distribute among their Universalist networks.[32] Even without formal print institutions and intermediaries, Universalists spread their works through correspondences and their own literary networks.

Chauncy's proliferation of his own views about universal salvation followed a similar trajectory. Even before the Revolution, Chauncy had been convinced of the tenets of universal salvation as early as the 1750s after a close and rigorous study of the book of Romans. He wrote the results of his study in a manuscript and invited family members to peruse his work. Shortly thereafter, he was packaging the text to correspondents like the minister Ezra Stiles and Richard Price with the hopes of gaining more converts to universal salvation.[33] During the episcopacy controversy and through the Boston Massacre, Chauncy and his readers debated endlessly about whether the manuscript should be sent to print or Chauncy should "order its being committed to the flames." As he relayed in a 1768 letter to Stiles, Chauncy eventually decided against destroying the work because of the years of study and writing he had poured into it.[34] From the time Washington retook Boston in 1776 to the print publication in 1783 of Chauncy's circulating manuscript, to which he gave the codename "pudding," the heterodox minister reached many audiences both in New England and across the Atlantic.

As the community of readers for Chauncy's work grew and ministers began talking amongst themselves about universal salvation, the contents of the manuscript also circulated outside his immediate circle. The Maine clergyman Moses Hemmenway caught wind of the manuscript and worried that "such a universal redemption of mankind as shall issue in universal salvation has been contended for by some, and has of late especially been favoured by numbers in different parts of this country."[35] Despite all his reservations about universal salvation, Hemmenway confessed that he was sympathetic to Universalists, sharing in their "hope that all will be finally happy and holy," but he struggled to be convinced until he "could reconcile it with the Scriptures."[36] Furthermore, ministers like John Eliot wrote to the New Hampshire minister Jeremy Belknap, who at that time had not yet read the manuscript, offering to write down any "passage you desired and anything else you may hereafter pursue."[37] Chauncy knew that circulating a manuscript risked leaking information about it to unintended recipients.[38] Most readers who encountered this growing Universalist-sympathizing public became self-professed Universalists or at the very least sympathetic to Chauncy's version of Universalism. Even without being printed, the manuscript gained converts, much in the manner of printed theological treatises shaping the minds of a reading public. After months of speculating and sharing his doubts, Eliot read the manuscript and believed. As he wrote to Belknap, "I think it unanswerable. Were I not of a sceptical turn of mind in things admitting much speculation, I should fall into it. Perhaps I may be said to believe it."[39] Through manuscript circulation, Chauncy changed the minds of New England clergymen. Hence, for his readers the question of print publication simply came down to whether they wanted to see a product of the movable-type press. For Chauncy, however, it came down to the logistics of who might be able to assist him with its publication.

Printing Heterodoxy After the Revolution

Even after the revolutionaries retook Boston, the printing business recovered slowly. Both patriot and loyalist printers and booksellers having left the city, there were only two to three newspapers from 1776 to 1783. Printing businesses would face a resurgence after the war formally ended, when printers from New York and Philadelphia reentered Boston, hoping to take advantage of new markets and connections.[40] Religious printing also saw some recovery, with news and publications about Universalism inviting controversy, which almost always sold.[41] The Connecticut printer John Trumbull stoked the flames of attacks on universal salvation by republishing Sargent's catechism and advertising it alongside Isaac Backus's *Doctrine of Universal Salvation Examined and Refuted*. Backus's text expressed concern over the growing number of Universalist congregations across New England as a result of Murray's itinerancy.[42] Put simply, ministers' perpetual concerns about heterodoxy promised a continuing market for religious controversy, in a way that assured new publishers that their business could thrive in a region previously dominated by a select number of printer-booksellers centered on Boston.

Chauncy sparked the Universalist controversy with the opportunistic timing of *Salvation for All Men Strictly Examined*, an abbreviated version of the manuscript he had been circulating that would eventually be published as *Mystery Hid from Ages and Generations* (1783). While Backus worried that Murray's itinerancy might invite further publications on universal salvation across New England, his publication became the very catalyst for Chauncy to attempt to reach readers with his own brand of Universalist principles through the printing press. Chauncy, who was not an ally of the Baptist minister's, saw enough flaws in *The Doctrine of Universal Salvation Examined and Refuted* that he pounced at the opportunity to kill several birds with one stone: to critique Murray Universalists for the shortcomings of their version of universal salvation, to attack Backus's unnuanced stance against all versions of universal salvation, and to provide a more traditional and scripturally informed account of universal salvation that might be amenable to the tastes and demands of New England clergy.[43] A few months after Backus's publication, the printers Thomas and John Fleet, the only printers whose Boston business survived the Revolution, printed *Salvation of All Men*. The printers' families had a history of working with Boston's established ministers, and their own religious inclinations made them amenable to printing for an esteemed minister like Chauncy. However, given the contents of what they were about to publish, it was understandable that even the author would desire it to be published anonymously.[44]

While Chauncy saw opportunity with Backus, *Salvation of All Men* was seen by those within his inner circle as a highly compromised work. Readers of the original circulating manuscript described it as a "meer castrated edition of the whole work" that may have harmed their long-term goals of publishing the manuscript itself.[45] Some, like Eliot, were thoroughly embarrassed by the entire affair, hoping to "run away from Boston" and "be content not to see the place for 7 years."[46] In other words, it did not publish his views in the same way that his circulating manuscript did. Their concerns revolved around whether such a view could be demonstrated as being supported by scripture, a recurring question voiced by those who had heard the rumors that some clergy were turning to universal salvation but had not yet seen the manuscript.[47] The manuscript itself demonstrated Chauncy's mastery of Hebrew and Greek in a way that persuaded readers of the text like Eliot and Belknap that scripture could support universal salvation. Printers had not had to print a text with as many Hebrew and Greek characters as Chauncy's since the Harvard instructor Judah Monis imported Hebrew types for his textbook. Unfortunately, those types were destroyed in a fire, making it difficult for Chauncy to work with domestic printers to publish his manuscript in full.[48] Chauncy proceeded with the less convenient option of printing it in London instead. However, with *Salvation of All Men* already in circulation, incensed ministers were ready to flood the public sphere with an assertion of orthodoxy. Some notable responses included the clergyman William Gordon's *Doctrine of Final Universal Salvation Examined and Shewn to Be Unscriptural* (1783), also published by Fleet; the minister Samuel Mather's *All Men Will Not Be Saved Forever* (1782), published by Edes & Sons, who retreated to Watertown, Massachusetts, because of the Revolutionary conflict; and Samuel Hopkins's *Inquiry Concerning the Future State of Those Who Die in Their Sins* (1783), published by Solomon Southwick in Providence, Rhode Island. Defenses for universal salvation similarly came from Murray's followers, even if the itinerant preacher himself was reluctant to engage against ministers in the presses. The layman Shippie Townsend published *Some Remarks on a Pamphlet Intituled All Men Will Not Be Saved for Ever* (1783), which attacked esteemed and established Congregationalist ministers. Murray himself read *Salvation of All Men* and saw "a great many good things" in Chauncy's pamphlet despite its attempts to maintain a veneer of "Puritan fire and brimstone."[49] The compromises Chauncy made and his decision to print overseas because of the limits of the domestic print market stifled timely and proper defenses of universal salvation.

Chauncy's decision to print across the Atlantic also meant relying on various intermediaries to facilitate the process of publication for the aging minister. With Boston printers busying themselves publishing attacks on universal salvation and the still recovering economy, Chauncy and his circle worried that they might "not obtain sufficient subscribers to make it worth to pursue the work [for the printers]."[50] Winchester made a similar observation after his tour of New England with Murray, writing in a letter: "It is likely that I have published more in the time that I have resided [in London] than I should have done my whole lifetime if I had remained in America."[51] Subscriptions had been the primary means by which printers could forecast some sort of market demand for religious works. Often, ministers had their own congregations and networks of peers to support their work. However, untested theological innovations such as Chauncy's and Winchester's often did not have the same access to subscribers as more established ones, making them risky products for an already struggling print industry. By contrast, however, Winchester observed the ease with which he obtained subscriptions for his works and the large number of printers willing to produce heterodox texts in London. Chauncy tasked Eliot with taking the manuscript to Price, who would mediate between the Boston minister and the London printer Charles Dilly. Unfortunately for Chauncy, Price refused to proceed with its publication. Upon reading the manuscript, Price grew "apprehensive of [the manuscript's] unpromising influence on the morals of the people," a conclusion he likely drew from the reputation of Universalists in London.[52] Although Chauncy had been subtly prodding Price toward universal salvation in their correspondence since the 1770s, reading the manuscript itself was a different matter altogether for the London minister.[53] Delays in publication worried the Boston Universalists, and Eliot's returning from the trip empty-handed further heightened anxieties. Fortunately for Chauncy, the Unitarian minister William Hazlitt intervened and ensured that the text would see print. Hazlitt wrote to Price about Murray's growing reputation in New England and that Chauncy's manuscript promised the appropriate correction. It was unlikely that the Boston minister anticipated the difficulty of printing a text in London and the continual dependence on intermediaries, who might doom a text to an unprinted form. Nevertheless, it was the connections he gathered with a circulating manuscript that would ensure that his manuscript could reach print.

When the published manuscript titled *Mystery Hid* arrived from London, it was received so positively by Boston elites that it somewhat eased some of the tensions around universal salvation. The text was described by Mary Cranch to her sister Abigail Adams as having "been much talk'd of [in New England]"; in the midst of the controversies around universal salvation, the publication had, Cranch wrote, "silenc'd every body."[54] John Adams himself was alerted to Chauncy's publication, being told that it "is likely to make a great noise in the World"; Price even directly forwarded a copy to him.[55] The ensuing discourse around the text reached John Quincy Adams who found the topic of universal salvation so much more riveting "more than cards, or dress or scandal."[56] In many ways, the overwhelming positive reception to the work complicated any notion that Chauncy would suffer consequences from the publication of his views. However, many of these figures were not avid critics or supporters through the printing press.

By contrast, the legitimizing effects of Chauncy's publication *Mystery Hid* worried his oldest opponents, the New Divinity. As theological inheritors of the revivalist group that Chauncy originally published against back in the 1740s, they continued the theological legacies of Whitefield and Edwards into the latter half of the eighteenth century. In the years after the revivals, figures like Jonathan Edwards and Joseph Bellamy were able to continue publishing through the printing press despite publishers' broader disinterest in the revivals, thanks in large part to sympathetic printers like Samuel Kneeland, who was himself a congregant of Old South Church under the minister Thomas Prince, and who was also a promoter of the revivals.[57] Others like Backus published their works with a wide array of printers in both Boston and Providence, which were not too far from his church in Middleborough, Massachusetts. This approach ensured that he would find publishers for his work in the years during and after the Revolution. Indeed, the Providence printer John Carter was the one who published *The Doctrine of Universal Salvation Examined and Refuted* for Backus, and it also helped that the Baptist minister had been working with the printer since Backus first published a commemoration sermon, *Gospel Comfort, Under Heavy Tidings*, in 1769 and *The Doctrine of Sovereign Grace* in 1771. With the devastation of the war, however, new printers helped ensure that New Divinity men would have new publishers for their critiques of universal salvation. Jonathan Edwards Jr.

published one of the earliest critiques in *The Salvation of All Men Strictly Examined* (1790) in New Haven, Connecticut, with the relative newcomer printer Abel Morse. In the same year, Morse cemented his stance against universal salvation by also publishing the anonymously authored text *Observations on Universal Salvation: Teach Not for Doctrine the Vain Traditions of Men.* In 1788 the Yale president Timothy Dwight IV published his poem *The Triumph of Infidelity*, famously targeting Chauncy's views on universal salvation.[58] The printer is not identified on the cover of the poem, but the fact that it was printed in Hartford, Connecticut, suggests that it was likely Thomas Green. Indeed, the famous Green family had long been printing for local ministers and governing bodies. But their shift toward printing for New Divinity men, after decades of promoting primarily the works of anti-revivalists like Chauncy, signaled an openness to different or new voices.[59] These opportunities for New Divinity men to publish during the Universalist controversy would only continue to help them establish themselves as public voices in the following decades.

By the close of the war, religious publications would begin to dominate the public sphere once again. In *The Democratization of American Christianity* (1989) the historian Nathan Hatch would write about this print explosion, whereby previously unpublished religious communities would begin to represent themselves in the public sphere.[60] This phenomenon was aided by the increasing availability of printers, facilitated by the creation of a distinctly American print infrastructure, including the establishment of the earliest type foundries, which provided some of the more expensive parts for printing. The appearance of these new religious movements in print was a product of the disruptive effects of the American Revolution print markets. Heterodox voices were confronted with a struggling publishing infrastructure that constrained the kinds of publications and scriptural citations they could deploy to support their theological innovations. Furthermore, a recovering economy made subscription concerns even more palpable for such novel ideas. Hence, figures like Chauncy preached, gathered followers, and circulated manuscripts independent of the struggling Revolutionary printing press but with the energy that shared in Revolutionary promises of the war. Ironically, as they aspired toward printing by turning to London, opposition to universal salvation found new opportunities in the domestic markets. Such dynamics suggest that any success or failure we attach to these groups as a product of their presence or absence from the public sphere may not actually have been a product of these groups' relevance or irrelevance to American society writ large. Material processes and publishing relations by which authors could have been made relevant was disrupted by something as devastating to the political economy of the British colonies as the American Revolution. Whatever discursive presences or absences scholars might claim about religion during the American Revolution, the history of Chauncy's manuscript suggests that these may have more to do with the state of print and manuscript circulation in this period than with the shifting demands and tastes of an imagined public.

Notes

1. Edmund Jennings to John Adams, July 22, 1783, Adams Papers Digital Edition, Massachusetts Historical Society (MHS), https://www.masshist.org/publications/adams-papers/index.php/view/ADMS-06-15-02-0071.
2. On Murray's itinerancy, see Kathryn Gin Lum, *Damned Nation: Hell in America from the Revolution to Reconstruction* (New York: Oxford University Press, 2014), 1–42. For more on the Great Awakening revivals, see Jon Butler, *Awash in a Sea of Faith: Christianizing the American People* (Cambridge, MA: Harvard University Press, 1990); Mark Noll, *The Rise of Evangelicalism: The Age of Edwards, Whitefield, and the Wesleys* (Downers Grove, IL: Intervarsity Press, 2003); Thomas Kidd, *The Great Awakening: The Roots of Evangelical Christianity in Colonial America* (New Haven, CT: Yale University Press, 2009); and most recently Doug Winiarski, *Darkness Falls on the Land of Light: Experiencing Religious Awakenings in Eighteenth-Century New England* (Chapel Hill: University of North Carolina Press, 2017).
3. Perry Miller, *Jonathan Edwards* (Lincoln: University of Nebraska Press, 1949). Miller declares that by 1743 "Edwards was beaten, an awesome but discredited figure. Harvard and Yale, infuriated by charges in Whitefield's journals, published testimonies that . . . they did not approve identifying the operations of the spirit with 'the swelling of their breasts and stomachs,' and condemned extravagance, which meant that they had no more to do with Edwards. When Whitefield returned in 1744, the opposition was organized and kept him out of most pulpits. . . . Chauncy was the great man" (176).
4. Isaac Backus, *A Church History of New England from 1620 to 1804* (Philadelphia: Baptist Tract Depository, 1839), 186.
5. On the contribution of Timothy Dwight IV and Isaac Backus to anti-deism and anti–universal salvation rhetoric, see Amanda Porterfield, *Conceived in Doubt: Religion and Politics in the New American Nation*

(Chicago: University of Chicago Press, 2012); and Christopher Grasso, *Skepticism and American Faith: From the Revolution to the Civil War* (Oxford: Oxford University Press, 2018).

6. I used the North American Imprints Program (NAIP) records. See *A History of the Book in America*, volume 1, *The Colonial Book in the Atlantic World*, ed. Hugh Amory and David Hall (Cambridge, MA: Cambridge University Press, 2000), app. 1, "Note on Statistics," 517–18. From 1741 to 1770 Chauncy ranked among the leading colonial authors. To further highlight Chauncy's strong publication career, ministers generally partner with only one or two printers or booksellers over the course of their lives if they ever proceeded with print. Throughout Chauncy's published career, however, he had works printed by Samuel Kneeland and Thomas Green in the 1730s; Rogers & Fowle, Green & Russell, and John Draper from the 1740s to the 1760s; and Daniel and John Kneeland in the 1770s. For more on the irregularity of New England minister publications that makes Chauncy an exceptional and perfect example for arguments about continuity and discontinuity, see George Selement, "Publication and the Puritan Ministers," *William and Mary Quarterly* 37, no. 2 (April 1980): 219–41. On the two public spheres, see Frank Lambert, *Inventing the "Great Awakening"* (Princeton, NJ: Princeton University Press, 2001); and Nathan Hatch, *The Democratization of American Christianity* (New Haven, CT: Yale University Press, 1989).
7. King George's mention of Chauncy appeared in a letter to Massachusetts Governor Thomas Hutchinson. See Charles Lippy, *Seasonable Revolutionary: The Mind of Charles Chauncy* (Chicago: Nelson-Hall, 1981), 100. On the handbill, see *Proceedings of the Massachusetts Historical Society*, 2d ser., vol. 16 (Boston: MHS, 1902), 92.
8. The earliest text to chart this secularist teleology was Perry Miller, *The New England Mind: From Colony to Province* (Cambridge, MA: Harvard University Press, 1953); and it appears in Miller's *Sources for the New England Mind: The Seventeenth Century*, ed. James Hoopes (Williamsburg, VA: Institute of Early American History and Culture, 1981). Harry Stout's 1986 work directly addresses the attention to print versus orality that informed these narratives. See Harry Stout, *The New England Soul: Preaching and Religious Culture in Colonial New England* (New York: Oxford University Press, 1986). Historians have long moved past these secularization narratives, identifying the persistent religiosity of the public sphere through sermons in the American Revolution. See Nathan Hatch, *The Sacred Cause of Liberty: Republican Thought and the Millennium in Revolutionary New England* (New Haven, CT: Yale University Press, 1977); Harry Stout, "Religion, Communications, and the Ideological Origins of the American Revolution," *William and Mary Quarterly* 34, no. 4 (October 1977);

Gordon Wood, "Religion and the American Revolution," in *New Directions in American Religious History*, ed. Harry S. Stout and D. G. Hart (New York: Oxford University Press, 1997); Mark Noll, *Christians in the American Revolution* (Vancouver, BC: Regent College Publishing, 2006); Thomas Kidd, *God of Liberty: A Religious History of the American Revolution* (New York: Basic Books, 2010); and James Byrd, *Sacred Scripture, Sacred War: The Bible and the American Revolution* (Oxford: Oxford University Press, 2013). However, literary scholars have continued to grapple with the transformations in religious thought from Jonathan Edwards to Benjamin Franklin. For a summary, see Sarah Rivett, "Early American Religion in a Postsecular Age," *Publications of the Modern Language Association* 128, no. 4 (2013): 989–96.

9. Chauncy's biographers argue that the war's timing likely conflicted with Chauncy's intent to publish the manuscript on universal salvation. See Edwards Griffin, *Old Brick: Charles Chauncy of Boston, 1705–1787* (Minneapolis: University of Minnesota Press, 1980); and Lippy, *Seasonable Revolutionary*. See also John Corrigan, *The Hidden Balance: Religion and the Social Theories of Charles Chauncy and Jonathan Mayhew* (New York: Cambridge University Press, 1987); and most recently John Oakes, *Conservative Revolutionaries: Transformation and Tradition in the Religious and Political Thought of Charles Chauncy and Jonathan Mayhew* (Cambridge: James Clarke, 2016).

10. The point about irrelevance also appears readily in Noll's *America's God: From Jonathan Edwards to Abraham Lincoln* (New York: Oxford University Press, 2005).

11. The starting point for the connection is Jürgen Habermas, *The Structural Transformation of the Public Sphere: An Inquiry into a Category of Bourgeois Society* (Cambridge, MA: MIT Press, 1991). This essay builds on critiques of the connection between print and democratization, most notably Michael Warner, *The Letters of the Republic: Publication and the Public Sphere in Eighteenth-Century America* (Cambridge, MA: Harvard University Press, 1992). Scholars of American religion continue to replicate the technological determinism of print as an abstracted social force that moves history toward more progressive ends. The most notable example is Nathan Hatch's *Democratization of American Christianity* (New Haven, CT: Yale University Press, 1989). Numerous scholars have troubled the democratization of American Christianity thesis, most notably Amanda Porterfield in *Conceived in Doubt* and, most recently, as it relates to readings of printed Bibles as a site for authority contestation in alignment with the democratization thesis, Seth Perry's *Bible Culture and Authority in the Early United States* (Princeton, NJ: Princeton University Press, 2018).

12. For works that have shown print's attachment to local institutions and reliance on printers' economic and political interests, as well as other explorations that challenge abstractions of print, see Jeffrey L. Pasley, *The Tyranny of Printers: Newspaper Politics in the Early American Republic* (Charlottesville: University of Virginia Press, 2002); Trish Loughran, *The Republic in Print: Print Culture in the Age of U.S. Nation Building, 1770–1870* (New York, Columbia University Press, 2007); Caroline Eastman, *A Nation of Speechifiers: Making an American Public After the Revolution* (Chicago: University of Chicago Press, 2010); and most recently Joseph Adelman, *Revolutionary Networks: The Business and Politics of Printing the News, 1763–1789* (Baltimore: John Hopkins University Press, 2019). It is also worth noting the various ways constraints on literacy, gender, racial, and other social inhibitions shaped what could and could not be published. See essays by Nancy Fraser, Michael Warner, and Seyla Bebhabib in *Habermas and the Public Sphere*, ed. Craig Calhoun (Cambridge, MA: MIT Press, 1992); Catherine Brekus, "Writing Religious Experience: Women's Authorship in Early America," *Journal of Religion* 92, no. 4 (October 2012); Joseph Rezek, "The Print Atlantic: Phillis Wheatley, Ignatius Sancho, and the Cultural Significance of the Book," in *Early African-American Print Culture*, ed. Lara Langer Cohen and Jordan Alexander Stein (Philadelphia: University of Pennsylvania Press, 2012); and Michael Millner, *Fever Reading: Affect and Reading Badly in the Early American Public Sphere* (Durham: University New Hampshire Press, 2012).
13. Hugh Amory contends that by 1790 "Boston's printer-booksellers had recovered their former prosperity or more." See Amory, "The New England Book Trade, 1713–1790," in Amory and Hall, *History of the Book in America*, 1:333. He also observed an opening up in which texts could be produced by non-urban printers, whose productions were "no longer restricted to sermons by local preachers, local institutional or governmental publications, and 'piracies' of Boston editions" and included reprints of "recent, belletristic, popular English properties" as well.
14. Peter Oliver, *Peter Oliver's "Origin and Progress of the American Rebellion": A Tory View*, ed. Douglass Adair and John A. Schutz (Stanford, CA: Stanford University Press, 1961), 91–92.
15. Charles Chauncy, *Trust in God, The Duty of a People in a Day of Trouble. A sermon preached May 30th. 1770* (Boston: Printed by Daniel Kneeland, for Thomas Leverett, 1770).
16. James Murray to Colonel Dalrymple, July 27, 1770, reprinted in Randolph G. Adams, "New Light on the Boston Massacre," *Proceedings of the American Antiquarian Society* 47, pt. 2 (October 1937): 324. For more on the sermon, see Griffin, *Old Brick*, 147–50.

17. Hugh Amory, "Reinventing the Colonial Book," in Amory and Hall, *History of the Book in America*, 1:45–46.
18. Isaiah Thomas, *The History of Printing in America with a Biography of Printers in Two Volumes*, 2d ed. (New York: Burt Franklin, 1810), 1:148–49.
19. Charles Chauncy, *A Letter to a Friend, Containing Remarks on Certain Passages in a Sermon Preached by the Right Reverend Father in God, John Lord Bishop of Landaff* (Boston: Printed by Kneeland and Adams in Milk-Street, for Thomas Leverett, 1782), 46, 53.
20. Griffin, *Old Brick*, 135. Griffin does not provide figures, but one could surmise from the number of Chauncy's publications after the fact that the speed with which Chauncy provided texts to print and sell only made such a partnership that much more profitable for all parties. It is also worth noting that by the 1760s Kneeland had specialized in religious print. See Amory, "New England Book Trade."
21. See Amory and Hall, *History of the Book in America*, app. 1, "Note on Statistics," 1:518. Chauncy ranked fourth in NAIP records, which is not necessarily an indicator of profitability on its own but is nevertheless helpful for discerning the relative value of Chauncy's publications compared with those of his peers.
22. See Rollo G. Silver, "Benjamin Edes, Trumpeter of Sedition," *Papers of the Bibliographical Society of America* 47, no. 3 (1953): 248–68.
23. Charles Chauncy, *A Letter to a Friend, Giving a Concise, but Just, Representation of the Hardships and Sufferings the Town of Boston Is Exposed to and Must Undergo in Consequence of the Late Act of the British-Parliament* (Boston: Greenleaf's, 1774), 9, 11, 5.
24. On Greenleaf, see Jeffrey L. Pasley, "Thomas Greenleaf: Printers and the Struggle for Democratic Politics and Freedom of the Press," in *Revolutionary Founders: Rebels, Radicals, and Reformers in the Making of the Nation*, ed. Alfred F. Young, Gary B. Nash, and Ray Raphael (New York: Vintage Books, 2011), 355–73. On Greenleaf being a person of interest, he was also named in the 1774 September royalist handbill that was printed in the *Boston Evening-Post* on September 19, 1774, 5. The handbill names: "Mess. Samuel Adams, James Bowdoin, Dr. Thomas Young, Dr. Benjamin Church, Capt. John Bradford, Josiah Quincy, Major Nathaniel Barber, William Mollineaux, John Hancock, Wm. Cooper, Dr. Chauncy, Dr. Cooper, Thomas Cushing, Joseph Greenleaf, and William Downing."
25. Amory, "New England Book Trade," 332–33.
26. MS Report of the Associated Pastors of Boston, November 28, 1774, Washburn Manuscripts, vol. XIV, 11, MHS.
27. See Chauncy to Samuel Adams, August 26, 1774, Samuel Adams Papers, New York Public Library; and "Reverend Doctor Charles Chauncy [the

Younger] to Doctor Richard Price, January 10, 1775," Electronic Enlightenment, University of Oxford, accessed February 1, 2026, https://doi.org/10.13051/ee:doc/pricriDU0010181a1c.

28. On uses of the word *publishing*, see David D. Hall, *Cultures of Print: Essays in the History of the Book* (Amherst: University of Massachusetts Press, 1996), 100–104; and Harold Love, *Scribal Publication in Seventeenth Century England* (Oxford: Clarendon Press, 1993). Love and Hall loosened the criteria for describing something as published by associating the manuscript with the text's relationship to the writer rather than the physical status of the text itself. Love defines manuscript publication as taking place when "the initiating agent knowingly relinquishes control of the future social use of that event" (36). Love's language of "relinquish[ing] control" and Hall and Amory's "surrendering" gesture toward this definition. For more on Chauncy's manuscript, see Michael Baysa, "Printing, Publics, and Pudding: Charles Chauncy's Universal Salvation and the Material Transformation of New England Orthodoxy," *Church History* 92, no. 2 (2023): 92–311.
29. Against accusations that universal salvation tainted the morals of the Continental Army while he served during the American Revolution, Nathaniel Greene produced a letter that vouched for his dutiful service as "an honest man and a good citizen." On Murray's connections, see Clarence Skinner and Alfred S. Cole, *Hell's Ramparts Fell, the Life of John Murray* (Boston: Universalist Publishing House, 1941), 88–94, 131.
30. For this network, see chapter 1 of Ann Lee Bressler, *The Universalist Movement in America, 1770–1880* (Oxford: Oxford University Press, 2001). Bressler names notable Universalist figures who lived in towns in New Hampshire, western Massachusetts, Connecticut, and Pennsylvania.
31. For more on these details, see Sheila Skemp, "Universal Salvation," in *First Lady of Letters: Judith Sargent Murray and the Struggle for Female Independence* (Philadelphia: University of Pennsylvania Press, 2009), 41–66.
32. Judith Stevens to Mr. Parker, June 9, 1782, quoted in Skemp, "Universal Salvation," 63.
33. William Chauncey Fowler, "President Charles Chauncy and His Ancestors and Descendants," in *The New England Historical and Genealogical Register*, vol. 10 (Boston, 1856), 335; Charles Chancy, "A Sketch of Eminent Men in New England," *Collections of the Massachusetts Historical Society, First Series*, vol. 10 (Boston: MHS, 1809), 163–65.
34. Chauncy, "Sketch of Eminent Men in New England," 158.
35. Moses Hemmenway to Jeremy Belknap, December 20, 1779, "Belknap Papers," *Collections of the Massachusetts Historical Society, Sixth Series*, vol. 4 (Boston: MHS, 1891), 160–61.

36. Hemmenway to Belknap, December 20, 1779, 173.
37. John Eliot to Belknap, January 26, 1780, "Belknap Papers," 174. Here, the Boston minister John Eliot (not to be confused with the seventeenth-century missionary and "author" of the Eliot Bible) offered to take notes for fellow minister and universalist sympathizer Jeremy Belknap. By this point in the "pudding"'s circulation, both ministers were close to agreeing with Chauncy on the tenets of universal salvation and only desired the ability to read it.
38. Hemmenway to Belknap, December 20, 1779, 160–61. On Hemmenway referring to Chauncy, his inclusive language in the following quote from this letter suggests that this theological shift may have been an internal development within the New England clergy and not an overseas heterodoxy breaking into New England orthodoxy: "The contrary doctrine (limited salvation), you know, has been received with so general a consent among us, that, amidst all the doctrinal disputes that have been moved, this seems scarce to have been called in question lately" (161).
39. Eliot to Belknap, April 14, 1780, "Belknap Papers," 183.
40. Amory, "New England Book Trade," 333.
41. Here I present two notable examples. The first is the case of Andrew Bradford, who was accused multiple times of publishing texts without the express consent of local Quakers and had liberally published about internal conflicts to outside readers in seventeenth-century colonial Philadelphia. While the degree to which he may have actually printed in support and opposition to Quakers is not clear, his financial woes from printing for the Philadelphia Quakers, the printers' continuing troubles with the community given his propensity to freely print, and his eventual departure for New York suggests a connection. For more on this, see James Green, "The Book Trade in the Middle Colonies, 1680–1720," in Amory and Hall, *History of the Book in America*, 1:201. A second example, closer to this period, involves the numerous printers printing texts for both revivalists and anti-revivalists, particularly as sermons by Whitefield were sure to be best-sellers. See Amory, "New England Book Trade."
42. For a brief overview of Trumbull's operations in Norwich, see Thomas, *History of Printing in America*, 1:192–93. It was not clear that Trumbull's gamble paid off, though there had been many precedents of colonial printers accused of playing both sides of a religious controversy for financial gain.
43. Chauncy's biographers have not yet picked up on this connection, often attributing his decision to external factors. Chauncy's *Salvation for All Men* playfully mirrors Backus's text in both style and content. Backus's text presents itself as universal salvation "examined and refuted," whereas Chauncy's title describes itself as "illustrated and vindicated." While Backus's *Doctrine of Universal Salvation Examined and Refuted* begins with a short history

of universalism in New England, Chauncy's starts with a long history of universalism dating back to Origen and Clement of Alexandria in the second century. Whereas Backus attempts to weaken the tenets of universal salvation by aligning it directly with Murray and the London Universalist James Relly, Chauncy spends much of his publication expanding the canon of known Universalists beyond these two infamous preachers.

44. Thomas and John Fleet were the sons of the famous printer Thomas Fleet, who had sided with the anti-revivalists during the Great Awakening revivals and printing for Chauncy himself. With regard to their religious life, Isaiah Thomas recounts a moment wherein the sons, upon inheriting their fathers' press, replaced a sign of the heart and crown, likely pointing to his English roots, with one depicting a Bible and heart. See Thomas, *History of Printing in America,* 1:99, 144–45.
45. Eliot to Belknap, August 14, 1782, "Belknap Papers," 234.
46. Eliot to Belknap, September 30, 1782, "Belknap Papers," 236.
47. In his letters, Eliot himself expressed such views. See Eliot to Belknap, January 26, 1780, 174–76. While Eliot was able to see the manuscript, Price and Hemenway, who were similarly worried, did not get a chance to see it prior to 1783.
48. The first set of Hebrew and Greek types was donated to Harvard College. The college's board would then import more types to complete the set for use in printing the Jew turned Protestant Judah Monis's textbook *Dickdook Leshon Gnebreet,* or *A Grammar of the Hebrew Tongue* (Boston: Jonas Green, 1735). According to the Hebrew scholar Shalom Goldman, the types were likely destroyed in a fire in January 1764. See Yosef Goldman, *Hebrew Printing in America, 1735–1926: A History and Annotated Bibliography,* ed. Ari Kinsberg, trans. Jeffrey Green, 2 vols. (Brooklyn: Goldman, 2006), 1:160. For a history of Hebrew printing in North America, see also Michael Baysa, "Protestant Hebrew: Performing Religious Authority Through Eighteenth-Century Language Production," *Religion and American Culture* 34, no. 2 (2025): 233–71.
49. John Murray, *Letters and Sketches of Sermons,* 3 vols. (Boston: Joshua Belcher, 1812–13), 2:94.
50. Eliot to Belknap, September 18, 1783, "Belknap Papers," 263. For more on subscription culture in Boston, see David D. Hall, "Learned Culture in the Eighteenth Century," in Amory and Hall, *History of the Book in America,* 1:427–28.
51. Elhanan Winchester to Benjamin Rush, July 27, 1792, MS 96, Rush Collection, Library Company of Philadelphia.
52. "William Hazlitt [the Elder] to Doctor Richard Price, Tuesday, 19 October 1784," Electronic Enlightenment, University of Oxford, accessed February 3, 2026, https://www.e-enlightenment.com/item/pricriDU0020238a1c/.

53. See "Reverend Doctor Charles Chauncy [the Younger] to Doctor Richard Price, Thursday, 22 March 1770," Electronic Enlightenment, University of Oxford, accessed February 3, 2026, https://www.e-enlightenment.com/item/pricriDU0010088a1c/. Chauncy had been teasing at universal salvation to Price in his letters. The March 22, 1770, letter read: "I could have greatly enlarged, especially upon the office of an ultimate restoration; but I would not be too tedious. I fear I have been too troublesome already."
54. Mary Cranch to Abigail Adams, April 25, 1785, Adams Papers Digital Edition, https://www.masshist.org/publications/adams-papers/index.php/view/ADMS-04-06-02-0033.
55. Cranch to Abigail Adams, April 25, 1785.
56. John Quincy Adams diary, entry for January 20, 1786, Adams Papers Digital Edition, https://www.masshist.org/publications/adams-papers/index.php/view/ADMS-03-01-02-0008-0001-0020.
57. For more on Edwards's relationship with printers both at home and overseas, see Jonathan Yeager, *Jonathan Edwards and Transatlantic Print Culture* (Oxford: Oxford University Press, 2016).
58. For a closer reading of Dwight's poem, see Colin Wells, *The Devil and Doctor Dwight: Satire and Theology in the Early American Republic* (Chapel Hill: University of North Carolina Press, 2002).
59. On the Green family, see Thomas, *History of Printing in America*. On the shift in Connecticut printing, see Christopher Grasso, *A Speaking Aristocracy: Transforming Public Discourse in Eighteenth-Century Connecticut* (Chapel Hill: University of North Carolina Press, 1999). Grasso narrates a kind of secularization of the printing press away from ministerial interests toward a broader array of voices, as evidenced by newspapers, essays, and other forms of orations. While he perhaps overstates what print itself signified (as demand or interest), his observation about the opening of the printing press to other voices seems validated by the theological openness of Connecticut printers to formerly delegitimized voices after the 1740s revivals.
60. Hatch argued for the importance of new religious groups in the broader project of American democracy and justified their inclusion in these intellectual histories on the basis of their appearance in print. In other words, because they were published, they could be deemed populist and thus seen as complicating the claims by intellectual historians like Richard Hofstadter, who otherwise argued that they were irrelevant or peripheral to the American project. See Richard Hofstadter, *Anti-Intellectualism in American Life* (New York: Knopf, 1962); and Sidney E. Mead, *The Lively Experiment: The Shaping of American Christianity in America* (New York: Harper & Row, 1963).

"Just Rights and Equal Laws"

Disestablishment and the Memory of the Revolution

ALYSSA PENICK

★

IN THE EARLY nineteenth century, Americans often described the downfall of colonial religious establishments as an essential and inevitable part of the Revolution. Looking back on independence in 1810, the Virginian Baptist minister Robert Semple recalled that as "republican principles had gained much ground . . . the leading men on that side, viewed the established clergy, and the established religion, as inseparable appendages of Monarchy."[1] In Semple's account, a revolution against the king was also a war against the established Anglican Church. A patriotic song published in Maryland for a Fourth of July celebration in 1804 likewise recalled that "in sev'nty-six, those men declared, Our Independence dear, Kingcraft and Priestcraft too they dared, Not knew, nor felt a fear." These lyrics celebrated the Revolution for ushering in "the objects so much prized, Just Rights and Equal Laws" and vanquishing the established Church of England.[2]

While Virginians and Marylanders agreed in hindsight that the Revolution had defeated Anglican establishment in the Chesapeake, such a prospect was not foreordained at the outset of independence nor clear even by the conclusion of the war. The standard nineteenth-century account of the war compressed the Revolution and disestablishment into a single event, but in the early 1780s many non-Anglicans had looked on with dismay at the lack of progress made toward securing religious liberty. Soon, though, popular memory would elide this period of apprehension in favor of a triumphant narrative that made disestablishment and revolution inseparable. How did the story change?

Both Chesapeake states left the establishment of religion in an ambiguous position from 1776 to 1783. Their legislatures rescinded the taxing power of the established church during the war, but many other elements of religious establishment remained intact. Only after the fighting ended did reformers succeed in dismantling the legal scaffolding of establishment more comprehensively. The postwar campaign to reform church and state offered a glorious retelling of the Revolution to combat the practical ambivalence of the laws passed during the conflict.

Advocates for disestablishment changed the story of 1776 in two key ways. First, reformers argued for more expansive readings of their 1776 state constitutions, framing these Revolutionary charters as mandates for radical change, far beyond wartime legislators' initial interpretations. Virginians and Marylanders contended that the Revolutionary values of liberty and equality were the bedrock of their 1776 state constitutions, and they used this claim to assert sweeping constitutional guarantees of religious freedom. Second, non-Anglicans invoked the war as a moment of collective sacrifice. Their heroism and dedication to the patriot cause had earned them not just liberty of conscience but full religious equality. By recasting religious freedom as fundamental to the spirit of 1776, advocates for disestablishment overcame the legal hurdles that the Revolution had left in place.

There is a significant analytical payoff to considering disestablishment in Maryland and Virginia side by side. Scholars have discussed church and state in Virginia at length, while events in Maryland have been studied far less often. This unevenness in the literature reflects a common tendency among scholars of disestablishment to focus on particular religious groups or a single state.[3] There were important differences between the two Chesapeake states' Revolutionary constitutions, wartime laws, and postwar reforms, yet very little of the historiography draws out these distinctions. A comparative approach both elaborates upon and enriches our understanding of disestablishment as a highly localized and contingent process that varied from one state to another. Indeed, the flattening of disestablishment in Virginia and Maryland into a single narrative underscores how effectively reformers constructed a universalizing discourse. Disestablishmentarians cemented a new, more radical narrative of the war that framed religious liberty as a broad condition of American independence. The Revolution became the most powerful symbol in their campaign for expanded and equal rights. These efforts created a lasting precedent for the expansion of civil rights by invoking the memory of the Revolution and arguing that its essential promises had yet to be fulfilled.[4]

The Church Established by Law

When historians of the colonial Chesapeake refer to the church "established by law" or the "legal establishment of religion," they are recognizing that numerous parliamentary statutes, colonial laws, and common law made the Church of England an arm of the state and penalized dissent from its ranks. Under this framework, public morality, social harmony, and political order were inseparable, and the established church worked hand in hand with the state to promote all three.

Both Maryland and Virginia established the Anglican Church in the seventeenth century, Virginia at its founding in 1607 and Maryland in 1692 after decades of turmoil between the colony's Catholics and Protestants. Both colonies technically fell within the Diocese of London, but the bishop of London had little to do with running the colonial church. Instead, colonial governments carried out the traditional duties of the episcopacy. The governors appointed clergymen, and the assemblies created new parishes, dissolved vestries, and oversaw the acquisition and sale of church property. For the most part, though, the colonial church was highly decentralized, and its power was exercised locally at the level of the parish. Overseen by groups of laymen called vestries, Anglican parishes were essential bodies of local government and carried out many civic responsibilities. The interwoven nature of church and state was deeply ingrained in the Chesapeake by the mid-eighteenth century.

A limited form of religious toleration existed in Anglo-American law. Following the Glorious Revolution, the Crown embraced toleration as the best means of maintaining peace. Freedom of conscience was divorced from the public exercise of religion. This policy recognized the power of the state to dole out privileges or restrict religious liberty in the interest of the public good.[5] While belief could not be compelled or curtailed by the state, freedom of worship certainly could be. The rights of dissenting Protestants remained a gift from the Crown and were always vulnerable to retraction or revision. Any public profession of Catholicism was tantamount to treason, and Catholics lost their civil liberties.

In the Chesapeake, non-Anglicans faced a variety of penalties and restrictions. In both Maryland and Virginia, all colonists were required to pay annual parish levies that went toward the salary of the parish rector, the construction of new worship spaces, and other parish expenses.[6] Protestant dissenters and Catholics supported their own churches, as well as paying these taxes to fund the established church. In Virginia, Quakers were unable to give evidence in criminal cases, serve on a jury, vote, or hold government offices. After 1747, Virginia did begin granting licenses to some dissenting Protestant ministers, but even then county courts had the authority to grant or deny these privileges as they saw fit. Catholics in Maryland faced even harsher penalties. By the second decade of the eighteenth century, they could neither vote nor hold office. They could not worship publicly or legally be married by a priest of their own faith. During the Seven Years' War, Catholic landholders were forced to pay a double tax on their property. The laws of the Chesapeake colonies dealt numerous disadvantages to those outside the Anglican fold.

Beginning in the mid-eighteenth century, the Great Awakening spurred numerous conversions to evangelicalism in the region. The rapid growth of dissenting denominations posed a fundamental challenge to the power of the establishment. A writer in Maryland lamented "the apparent decay of the established religion" and blamed "the growth of popery and superstition, and an increase of sects, dissenting from the established church."[7] On the eve of the Revolution, popular anger toward the established church seemed close to a breaking point.

The 1776 State Constitutions

Upon declaring independence in 1776, both Virginia and Maryland ratified new state constitutions, which included Declarations of Rights. In the realm of religion, both documents carved out new protections for individual religious liberty, a concession to dissenters, whose support mattered dearly to the patriot cause. On the whole, however, these state constitutions took very different approaches to religion. Four extended articles in the Maryland Declaration of Rights—articles 33–36, running to 779 words—dealt with religion. The Virginia Declaration of Rights, on the other hand, limited its consideration of religion to article 16, a pithy provision that addressed religion in just 68 words. This disparity in length epitomized the vast differences between the ways in which the two constitutions attended to questions of church and state.

Article 16 of Virginia's 1776 Declaration of Rights declared "that religion, or the duty which we owe to our Creator, and the manner of discharging it, can be directed only by reason and conviction, not by force or violence; and therefore all men are equally entitled to the free exercise of religion, according to the dictates of conscience."[8] No longer would Virginia coerce adherence to the established church, nor would it restrict free exercise. However, the text also asserted the "mutual duty of all to practice Christian forbearance, love, and charity toward each other." By characterizing a citizen's responsibilities as "Christian," the text seemed to retain a special relationship between the state and Christianity and left the door open to some forms of state action in the realm of religion.[9] The Virginia Declaration's abstract language included no mention of the established church, and the legislature was not given a clear constitutional directive about how to proceed with disestablishment. This broad language left the specifics open to interpretation.

The very first clause of Maryland's article 33 asserted the freedom of conscience in the broadest possible terms, stating that "it is the duty of every man to worship God in such manner as he thinks most acceptable to him" and promising that "no person ought by any law to be molested in his person or estate on account of his religious persuasion or profession, or for his religious practice." However, the text then narrowed the protection of "religious liberty" to "all persons, professing the Christian religion." With this qualification, Maryland's Declaration distinguished freedom of conscience from free exercise, and only Christians were granted the latter. In articles 35 and 36, the state ended the system of religious tests that had barred Catholics from voting and officeholding; however, it still required "a declaration of a belief in the Christian religion" for "admission to any office of trust or profit."[10] Together, Articles 33, 35, and 36 set out a highly qualified version of free exercise.[11]

The use of the ecumenical term *Christian* in the Maryland Declaration of Rights seemed like a panacea to Catholics, Quakers, and other Nonconformists, who had long been denied equal rights. The Marylander and Jesuit priest John Carroll, who would later become the first Catholic bishop in America, proclaimed in 1784 that "by the Constitution, our Religion has acquired equal Rights & privileges with that of other Christians."[12] Interestingly, a year later Carroll worded his summary of Maryland's constitutional protections without mentioning Christianity at all, instead writing that "in our new Constitution, it is fixed as a matter of natural justice, that every person has a right to worship Alm. God in that religious mode or form which his conscience dictates." He added that the legislature could "oblige all persons to contribute to the support of that particular Religion."[13] Carroll easily swung between references to Christianity and to "religion" without remarking upon the distinction. Carroll saw equality between Catholics and Protestants as the great religious victory of the new Declaration of Rights. This slippage in his language obscured the plight of non-Christians, who were explicitly left out of Maryland's constitutional protections.[14]

Furthermore, article 33 permitted the legislature to "lay a general and equal tax for the support of the Christian religion" and also went to significant lengths to secure the property of the Church of England.[15] It laid out a detailed plan for preserving "the churches, chapels, glebes, and all other property now belonging to the church of England." The provision also guaranteed every parish minister "who hath remained in his parish, and performed his duty" his state-supported salary for the year 1776. Article 34 limited the amount of property a religious society could hold without receiving legislative permission, which left the legislature in a position to supervise religious denominations.[16] Maryland's 1776 constitution sought to put all Christians on equal footing and maintained close ties between religion and government but did not lay out explicit terms for the future of the established church.[17]

While the Revolutionary constitutions signaled the end of the traditional Anglican establishment, their terms were ambiguous and did not chart a clear path for reforming the church-state relationship in either Chesapeake state.

Revolutionary Legislation

Acting under the authority of these new constitutions, the republican legislatures in Maryland and Virginia undertook the task of governing. Both states took steps to curb the legal powers of the established church and extend greater rights to non-Anglicans during the war. New statutes exempted Nonconformists from having to pay parish levies, stripped parishes of the power to raise taxes for the church, and altered some aspects of the vestry system.[18] As much as this Revolutionary legislation was framed as a concession toward religious pluralism, many of its terms reflected the ongoing entrenchment of Anglicanism in the Revolutionary Chesapeake.

The initial changes made to marriage laws in both states during the war exemplified the limitations of wartime reforms. In the colonial Chesapeake, marriage had been not only a holy sacrament to be performed before God but also a civic institution essential to "every well-regulated Government."[19] Anglican parishes closely regulated marriage, and non-Anglicans in both colonies struggled to be legally married by their own clergymen.[20] In 1777, Maryland passed a new law declaring that the rite of matrimony could be performed by "ministers of the church of England, ministers dissenting from that church, or Roman priests" who had been licensed.[21] Virginia likewise overhauled its marriage statute in 1780 by outlining a new process for "dissenting ministers" to gain licenses to perform marriages.[22] While these acts sought to remedy a long-standing grievance among evangelical Protestants and Catholics in the Chesapeake, practical inequities lingered. Under Virginia's new system, non-Anglican ministers still had to apply for licenses from the counties where they resided, whereas Anglican parish rectors were automatically afforded the legal power to officiate marriage by right of their office. In Maryland, Anglican parish clerks were empowered to solemnize marriage by reading the banns, while laymen of other denominations were never granted this civic power. These statutes also continued to refer to "dissenting" faiths, suggesting that there was a state religion in place from which some citizens dissented. Ultimately, the limited scale of these legislative reforms revealed the continuity of religious establishment during the war as much as its dismantling. Of course, religion was only one of numerous topics requiring legislators' attention in the midst of the conflict. But the lackluster record of disestablishment during the Revolution underscored that the 1776 constitutions had neither ushered in religious freedom in absolute terms nor laid out a clear plan to dismantle the public powers of the Church of England.

Considering these shortcomings, many non-Anglican observers vacillated between optimism and wariness at the close of the war. In 1783, John Carroll famously declared that "in these United States our Religious system has undergone a revolution, if possible, more extraordinary, than our political one."[23] He explained that Maryland's Catholics had been granted not only "free toleration" but "all civil rights, without distinction or diminution." Despite these exuberant statements, in the same letter Carroll warned that Catholics had to heed "the temper of Congress, of our assemblies and the people at large" to "preserve" these newly won rights. Carroll worried that Catholics' religious liberty would be subject to popular whims and majoritarian politics.[24] In the following years, Carroll continued to sound the alarm, reporting in 1785 that "many of our people, especially in Maryland, fear that there is a desire among non-Catholics to exclude us altogether from holding office."[25] He worried that his flock had been granted mere "toleration," not a "common right" to the free exercise of their faith.[26] Carroll warned Maryland's Catholics that until they received assurance that their rights were fundamental, they had to rely on the continued goodwill of the state to protect their religious freedom. Catholics across the Anglo-American world understood all too well that toleration offered them no certainty: what the state giveth, the state taketh away. Sounding crestfallen, Carroll preached caution as the best way forward following the war.

While Carroll framed religious freedom as vulnerable, Virginia's Baptists described the task as altogether unfinished. In the early 1780s, they lobbied the Virginia legislature in a raft of petitions sent by local communities and the statewide General Association. Baptists awaited "the completion of religious liberty" and complained that equality was still elusive.[27] Their pleas framed religious liberty as a stalled project, and they urged the assembly to "remove every just cause of Offence" immediately. Whether they characterized disestablishment as incomplete, contingent, or vulnerable, non-Anglicans expressed dissatisfaction with the church-state relationship at the end of the war.

Within a matter of decades, however, the halting legislative progress made during the war and widespread anxiety in the early 1780s would be forgotten. Instead, the Revolution would be celebrated as the glorious advent of religious liberty. The juxtaposition between the situation in 1783 and the popular narrative by 1803 is striking. This shift in memory reflected non-Anglicans' success in winning greater protections from their legislatures and moving the needle decisively toward disestablishment.

The "Republican Spirit"

Reformers successfully pursued disestablishmentarian legislation in the mid-1780s and enshrined far more radical readings of their state constitutions in the process. After the war, proposed laws concerning the clergy, governance, and property of the former established church, as well as proposals for a general assessment, all sparked intense public debate. Reformers in Maryland and Virginia criticized these measures by invoking the "spirit" of the states' 1776 constitutions. Proclaiming that the values of liberty and equality underwrote these charters, they argued that the Revolutionary Declarations of Rights were radical decrees for religious freedom. In both states, campaigners wielded nearly identical arguments, which is particularly noteworthy given the dissimilar terms of the two state constitutions.

In Maryland, the Reverend Patrick Allison of Baltimore's First Presbyterian Church remained wary after the Revolution. In May 1783 the American branch of the Anglican Church reorganized as the Protestant Episcopal Church and petitioned Maryland's state legislature for a law recognizing its legal standing and outlining the church's internal governance, which became known as the Clergy Bill.[28] Allison viewed the Clergy Bill as a dangerous threat to the 1776 state constitution, and he published a scathing critique under the pseudonym Vindex. By asking for permission to alter their liturgy and rites of ordination, the Episcopal Church had invested the state with the "authority . . . to grant or refuse" those rights that all Christians assuredly had under the Declaration of Rights.[29] Allison quoted part of article 33 and then paraphrased its core principle as "unequivocal and universal equality." He argued that the charter had already ushered in "perfect freedom," and thus he denounced ambivalent Revolutionary-era legislation as a betrayal of Marylanders' constitutional rights rather than an expression of the limits of the constitution itself.[30]

But Allison's arguments employed a highly selective approach to the state constitution. Allison omitted article 33's lengthy discussion of the property and clergy of the Church of England when condemning the clergy's petition. This cherry-picking of the constitution reflected the minister's disquiet about these provisions, which he elsewhere condemned as neither "fair" nor "equitable."[31] Allison was careful in his ideological gloss of the constitution and treated it as an unconditional assertion of religious liberty and equality. Allison's protest was widely read and prompted numerous responses in Maryland's newspapers.[32] The legislature balked and did not pass the Clergy Bill.

In much the same way that Allison extracted ideals from the constitution without necessarily attending to the entirety of its text, evangelicals in Virginia also celebrated that "Republican Spirit which breathes in our Constitution and Bill of Rights."[33] Virginia's Declaration of Rights lent itself to a variety of interpretations because of its brevity. For conservatives, the ambiguity of the text left the door open to government action and the possibility of retaining some form of government support for and supervision of religion. But for radicals, the constitution's abstract bent illustrated its breadth in guaranteeing religious freedom. The meaning of the constitution stood at the center of debates over a wide variety of laws touching religion in the following decades.

During the 1780s, Evangelicals in Virginia inundated the legislature with demands for the state to revise past laws and objections to proposed bills. Of particular significance was the fight over a general assessment. Episcopalians hoped to restore some sort of state funding for religion and threw their weight behind a 1784 bill for "establishing a provision for teachers of the Christian religion." Introduced by Patrick Henry, a longtime ally of dissenters, the bill proposed a tax on every individual, who could choose which "society of Christians" to support. The taxes of those who did not elect a denomination would be used to fund public education.[34] The proposal was framed as an ecumenical compromise that would ensure some state support for Christianity without contravening any individuals' liberty of conscience.

The bill proved immediately divisive. Debates over the passage of the law revealed widespread disagreement about what Virginia's 1776 constitution had promised and whether any form of religious tax was permissible. James Madison circulated his *Memorial and Remonstrance* to argue that the bill violated numerous parts of the Declaration of Rights. To Madison, article 16 meant that "in matters of Religion, no mans right is abridged by the institution of Civil Society and that Religion is wholly exempt from its cognizance. . . . [I]f Religion be exempt from the authority of the Society at large, still less can it be subject to that of the Legislative Body." Furthermore, such an act violated the free exercise of religion because it would "deny an equal freedom to those whose minds have not yet yielded to the evidence which has convinced us."[35] Madison's constitutional arguments fleshed out an expansive reading that firmly separated church and state and safeguarded personal liberty with remarkable clarity.

While Madison offered a detailed exegesis of the constitution, many petitioners invoked the constitution in abstracted terms to make arguments for and against assessment. Episcopalians who supported an ecumenical tax argued that it would not be "in any respect inconsistent with the principles of our free Constitution . . . no violation is offered to the rights of private Judgement, but Men are left, free as air in the choice of their own Religion."[36] Opponents of the bill likewise advanced sweeping constitutional assertions. One petition declared that the bill was "contrary to the Spirit of the Gospel and the Bill of Rights," while another insisted that any such tax would violate "the spirit and meaning of" the constitution's guarantees.[37] Across these varied arguments, petitioners followed a similar strategy of citing the dictates of the constitution in the broadest terms to bolster their claims. These more general invocations supplemented textualist arguments and offered another mode of constitutional interpretation in which Virginians extrapolated and explicated their understanding of the constitution's promises.

Opposition toward the law proved strong enough to defeat the bill. In 1786 the legislature passed the Statute for Religious Freedom, which cemented Madison's interpretation in law. While Madison's careful analysis has gone down in history, it is essential to remember that popular constitutional arguments also invoked the state constitution's principles. These debates over the general assessment in Virginia refined the meaning of the 1776 constitution and gave weight to its legal protections.

Maryland also considered a general assessment for religion in 1785. Maryland's article 33 had expressly granted the legislature the power to "lay a general and equal tax for the support of the Christian religion." Despite the radically different language of the two state constitutions, the public condemnation of assessment was nearly identical in both states. As in Virginia, reformers in Maryland asserted that constitutional principles nullified the proposed tax.

In light of this explicit grant of power in the text of the constitution, Marylanders had to get creative to explain why the proposed tax nonetheless violated its terms. A petition printed in the *Baltimore Gazette* claimed that only an assessment approved by every religious denomination could be constitutional. Because several religious denominations opposed any state funding for churches, the proposed bill violated the constitutional protection for the freedom of conscience.[38] Another opposition piece admitted that the legislature's right to impose a general tax "is expressly declared by the 33d section of the Bill of Rights" but argued that any actual assessment lacked the "equity" and "expediency" embodied in the constitution. This author predicted that the proposed assessment would "trample or impair the civil or Religious Rights" of Marylanders and soon "subvert all order and good government."[39] These popular arguments identified equality and freedom of conscience as core principles of Maryland's constitution. Any law that betrayed these tenets thus violated the constitution itself, even if it appeared textually permissible at first glance.

John Carroll regarded the general assessment bill as a thinly veiled attempt to reestablish the Episcopal Church. He explained in 1785 that the legislature had the power to impose a tax "on all persons to contribute to the support of that particular Religion, and minister, which each one prefers." If the proposal had been "truly formed upon the principle of the Constitution, we R.C. should have no very great objection to it: but from certain clauses in it, and other circumstances, we, as well as the Presbyterians, Methodists, Quakers, and Anabaptists are induced to believe, that it is calculated to create a predominant and irresistible influence in favour of the Protestant Episcopal Church."[40] To Carroll, the proposal may have sounded constitutional, but its actual terms reflected a pernicious favoritism. Carroll's comments suggested that equality and impartiality were at the heart of the constitution and thus formed a standard against which any proposed bill must be measured. A constitutional avenue to religious taxation might exist, but it had to accord with the true principles of the Declaration of Rights.

The united opposition of non-Episcopalians defeated the bill, but more importantly, this debate sharpened the constitutional protection of religious freedom well beyond the specific terms of article 33. Opponents of the bill succeeded in arguing that the general assessment would unavoidably violate the "principles" of Maryland's constitution. Equality and equity became the standing interpretation, no matter the express terms of the document. Maryland would amend its constitution in 1810 to formally remove the clause empowering the legislature to impose a tax for the Christian religion.

While debating a general assessment, Marylanders and Virginians adopted radical readings of their state constitutions. They offered sweeping ideological interpretations to augment textualist arguments, and in so doing they made guarantees of rights far more expansive.

Common Blood

Calls for a more radical disestablishment rested not only upon the 1776 state constitutions but also on the memory of the war itself. Disestablishmentarian appeals drew on several themes embedded in the rhetoric of the patriot movement: tyranny, slavery, and sacrifice. Religious reformers borrowed this language to insist that the Revolution had already promised religious freedom in the pantheon of republican liberty. They argued that the war had made way for religious pluralism, and they called upon state legislatures to protect this legacy in their laws.

Advocates for disestablishment in the 1780s painted Revolutionary-era state legislation as an insidious return of tyranny. In Virginia, the Baptist General Association proclaimed that the state's wartime laws had been a "foundation for Ecclesiastical Tyranny."[41] Similarly, Rev. Patrick Allison argued that "ecclesiastical tyranny had already commenced her intolerant reign" in Maryland when the legislature passed its 1777 marriage law and later when it considered the Clergy Bill.[42] Reformers deployed the familiar rhetoric of liberty and tyranny to make the postwar fight over religion an extension of the Revolution itself. These critics rebuked the people for yielding to the reappearance of tyranny and warned that the very legacy of the war was in jeopardy.

Reformers also relied on the allegory of slavery to make their case. Throughout the war, white Americans heard calls to cast off "those chains which the British ministry have been so long forging" and reminders that peace was "purchased at the price of chains and slavery."[43] By using this same language of enslavement, reformers made their fight over religious liberty in the 1780s a direct continuation of the American struggle for political independence. Allusions to enslavement were particularly resonant in the Chesapeake, where the violence of slavery was woven into daily life. John Carroll described the movement against a general assessment in 1785 in the brutal terms of bondage, noting that everyone outside the Church of England had "smarted heretofore under the lash of an established church" and would fight with "might and main" against its return.[44] Patrick Allison referred to Maryland as a "recently liberated land" that faced the return of a "civil and religious slavery."[45] Of course, these comments ignored the actual enslavement of African Americans in the state, who had not been liberated by the Revolution. The petition of Virginia's Baptist General Association in 1783 similarly combined the themes of tyranny and slavery, declaring that "while we were opposing our enemies in the field, we were petitioning our rulers, at the helm of legislation, to set us free from the yoke of religious oppression, which we long groaned under."[46] Their retelling of the war likened Virginia's republican legislature to king and Parliament; just as the Crown had oppressed and enslaved the American people, the state legislature continued to do the same to non-Episcopalians. Once again, white religious petitioners drew on slavery as a convenient allegory without condemning the actual institution of racial slavery.

Finally, disestablishmentarian campaigners frequently emphasized the lives and property risked and lost during the Revolution. In 1787 John Carroll proclaimed that "freedom and independence, acquired by the united efforts, and cemented with the mingled blood of Protestant and Catholic fellow-citizens, should be enjoyed equally by all."[47] Carroll and others portrayed the war as a victory accomplished through shared sacrifice. Allison remembered the "bloody war, waged to vindicate the essential rights of humanity," and specifically called attention to the "blood of numerous heroes, shed for equal impartial liberty."[48] Both placed emphasis on the carnage of war, which had made all American patriots into Christian martyrs. Their bloodshed had been a willing sacrifice that entitled them to equal rights.

This specific line of argument was also widespread in Virginia's disestablishmentarian debates. A petition in favor of confiscating the property of the Episcopal Church retold the story of the Revolution: "During the Common Struggle with Great Britain, Your Petitioners were encouraged to sacrifice the tender ties of Blood and Treasure, under the Expectation of Equal and impartial liberty given to all the free Citizens of this Commonwealth indiscriminately, and without Distinction."[49] Another petition declared that "Political Equality . . . is the indoubted Privilege of every Christian in the Federal Union as the reward of the common blood and Treasure so freely spent by all" but accused the state of reneging on its promises "before the wounds we received in our Country's Cause had ceased to bleed."[50] These invocations of violence and destruction emphasized the painful losses suffered together by Americans. It was not a far leap from the invocation of common sacrifice to demanding equality in the laws. The language of "blood and treasure" appeared time and again in Maryland and Virginia, and reformers used this expression to illustrate their willingness to risk their property and their lives for American independence. There was frequent slippage between "religion" and "Christian" in these demands for equality. In the early 1780s, evangelical and Catholic reformers did not make it a priority to consider whether their calls for equality included non-Christians.

In their efforts to broaden the promises of the 1776 constitutions and overturn Revolutionary-era legislation, reformers reminded the public of their contributions to the war. They framed disestablishment as an extension of the Revolution's fight for freedom against tyranny. These arguments fashioned a new narrative of the Revolution and insisted that laws had to embrace individual liberty and guarantee citizens' equality to fulfill the true spirit of the war and make good on its promises. These two claims proved powerful for later generations.

In the 1820s, the Jewish community in Baltimore protested Maryland's long-standing restrictions on their civil and religious rights. Legislators seeking to expand the civil rights of Maryland's Jewish community followed the same rhetorical strategy used by Catholics, Presbyterians, and Baptists four decades earlier.[51] The 1776 Maryland constitution required "a declaration of a belief in the Christian religion" for "admission to any office of trust or profit," which meant that Jewish citizens were unable to hold office, serve on juries, practice law, or hold commissions in the militia.[52] In a series of debates in 1824, state representatives speaking on behalf of the Jewish community claimed that the "spirit" of the 1776 constitution was synonymous with liberty and equality. Said one legislator, "I will ask, whether the religious test in the constitution of this state, can stand for a moment, when construed by the spirit of this declaration? No, sir, they are utterly incompatible."[53] He invoked the overriding principles of the state constitution to undermine its specific prohibitions on Jewish rights, in effect deeming parts of the 1776 constitution unconstitutional. In addition, supporters recalled that "Israelites had gallantly fought for freedom" during the American Revolution and called attention to the "wounds received" in that "bloody conflict."[54] Another speech blasted the antebellum legislature for ignoring the "men who, and their forefathers, have fought with Washington for the very liberty you now enjoy, and yet you refuse them a full and equal participation."[55] Ultimately, the reform bill passed, granting Jews greater rights in the state.[56] These debates underscored that the narrative of the Revolution fashioned during disestablishment had not only taken root in popular memory but proved to be a powerful avenue for legal change.

NARROWING OUR discussion of disestablishment to simply a question of state funding for churches misses the significance of this process to American national identity and memory. It was not clear in 1776 to what extent independence would disrupt traditional religious establishments. Indeed, even in 1783 many of the other traditional legal privileges and disadvantages of establishment persisted in the Chesapeake, as did the possibility of new forms of multi-establishment. Reformers ultimately changed the meaning of the war by arguing that ambivalent laws and new proposals were a betrayal of the Revolution.

By every measure, the campaign for disestablishment in the Chesapeake was highly successful in the 1780s. In Maryland, Catholics and evangelicals prevented the passage of the Clergy Bill, rallied to avert a general assessment, and insisted on an expansive reading of the 1776 constitution. In Virginia, evangelicals likewise defeated a general assessment and enshrined a radical interpretation of their Revolutionary constitution into state law. Across the Chesapeake, reformers effectively made disestablishment an extension of the Revolutionary fight for liberty and a mandate for legal equality. Their calls reverberated beyond state borders because they appealed to the universal nature of the war and narrated the Revolution as an arduous, collective undertaking that delivered equality to all who had participated. For the legislatures to deny religious equality in their laws was to betray the spirit of every Revolutionary state constitution and the patriot cause. This universalizing strategy had a far-reaching resonance. In reformers' hands, the legacy of the Revolution became a powerful tool for mounting future rights claims.

Notes

1. Robert Baylor Semple, *A History of the Rise and Progress of the Baptists in Virginia* (Richmond, 1810), 26–27.
2. *Maryland Herald and Hagers Town Weekly Advertiser*, July 4, 1804.
3. The body of scholarship about disestablishment in Virginia is much larger than that about disestablishment in Maryland, and scholars rarely discuss events in the two states together. Many works focus on particular religious groups and closely trace state legislation. Both approaches are important but tend to narrow the scope and reinforce a siloed view of the topic. Thomas Curry provides one of the best comparative accounts of the two states' disestablishments. Curry, *The First Freedoms: Church and State in America to the Passage of the First Amendment* (New York: Oxford University Press, 1986), 134–58. The classic work on Virginia's disestablishment is Thomas Buckley, *Church and State in Revolutionary Virginia, 1776–1787* (Charlottesville: University Press of Virginia, 1977). See also Carl H. Esbeck, "Disestablishment in Virginia, 1776–1802," and Michael D. Breidenbach, "Church and State in Maryland: Religious Liberty, Religious Tests, and Church Disestablishment," in *Disestablishment and Religious Dissent: Church-State Relations in the New American States, 1776–1833*, ed. Carl H. Esbeck and Jonathan Den Hartog (Columbia: University of Missouri Press, 2019), 139–80 and 309–26; John A. Ragosta, *Wellspring of Liberty: How Virginia's Religious Dissenters Helped Win the American Revolution and Secured Religious Liberty* (New York: Oxford University Press, 2010); and Thomas J. Hanley, *The American Revolution and Religion; Maryland 1770–1800* (Washington, DC: Catholic University of America Press, 1971).
4. For a discussion of Virginia's Declaration of Rights and constitution, see Daniel L. Dreisbach, "George Mason's Pursuit of Religious Liberty in Revolutionary Virginia," *Virginia Magazine of History and Biography* 108,

no. 1 (2000): 2+5–44. On Maryland's constitution, see Kenneth Lasson, "Free Exercise in the Free State: Maryland's Role in Religious Liberty and the First Amendment," *Journal of Church and State* 31 (1989): 419, 423–34; and Breidenbach, "Church and State in Maryland Religious Liberty."

5. For a thorough and wide-ranging consideration of toleration in early America, see Chris Beneke and Christopher S. Grenda, eds., *The First Prejudice: Religious Tolerance and Intolerance in Early America* (Philadelphia: University of Pennsylvania Press, 2011).
6. John K. Nelson, *A Blessed Company: Parishes, Parsons, and Parishioners in Anglican Virginia* (Chapel Hill: University of North Carolina Press, 2001), 28; Dell Upton, *Holy Things and Profane: Anglican Parish Churches in Colonial Virginia* (Cambridge, MA: MIT Press, 1986), xx–xxvi, 183–91.
7. "By the committee of aggrievances and courts of justice," June 22, 1768, Archives of Maryland Online, vol. 61, p. 411, https://msa.maryland.gov/megafile/msa/speccol/sc2900/sc2908/000001/000061/html/am61--411.html.
8. Virginia Declaration of Rights of 1776, section 16.
9. Virginia Declaration of Rights of 1776, section 16. For a discussion of the drafting of the Virginia Declaration of Rights, see Dreisbach, "George Mason's Pursuit of Religious Liberty in Revolutionary Virginia."
10. Maryland Declaration of Rights, articles 33, 35, 36.
11. Scholars typically credit Charles Carroll, the Barrister; Charles Carroll of Carrollton; or Samuel Chase with authorship of the state constitution. Dan Friedman, *The History of the Maryland Constitution* (New York: Oxford University Press, 2011), 5n4.
12. John Carroll to Ferdinand Farmer, December 1784, in *The John Carroll Papers*, ed. Thomas O'Brien Hanley, 3 vols. (Notre Dame, IN: University of Notre Dame Press, 1976), 1:156.
13. Carroll to Charles Plowden, February 27, 1785, in *John Carroll Papers*, 1:168.
14. Edward Eitches, "Maryland's 'Jew Bill,'" *American Jewish Historical Quarterly* 60 (1971): 258–79.
15. Maryland Declaration of Rights, article 33. Scholarly discussions of the Maryland constitution do not discuss the second half of article 33. Breidenbach, "Church and State in Maryland."
16. Numerous states restricted the amount of property held by religious societies. See Sarah Barringer Gordon, "The First Disestablishment: Limits on Church Power and Property Before the Civil War," *University of Pennsylvania Law Review* 162, no. 3 (2014): 312, 323.
17. See Eitches, "Maryland's 'Jew Bill,'" 260–61.
18. William Waller Hening, ed., *The Statutes at Large; Being a Collection of All the Laws of Virginia from the First Session of the Legislature in the Year 1619*

(Richmond: J. & G. Cochran, 1821), 1:68–69, 9:165–66, 10:288–89; Maryland Declaration of Rights, article 33; Hening, *Statutes at Large*, 10:288–90; "An Act for the Establishment of Select Vestries," *Archives of Maryland Online*, 203:207, https://msa.maryland.gov/megafile/msa/speccol/sc2900/sc2908/000001/000203/html/am203--207.html.

19. "Forasmuch as divine institutions . . . ," *Archives of Maryland Online*, 52:503, https://msa.maryland.gov/megafile/msa/speccol/sc2900/sc2908/000001/000052/html/am52--503.html.
20. Hening, *Statutes at Large*, 6:84; "Marriage," *Archives of Maryland Online*, 75:686, https://msa.maryland.gov/megafile/msa/speccol/sc2900/sc2908/000001/000075/html/am75--686.html.
21. "An Act Concerning Marriages," *Archives of Maryland Online*, 203:165, https://msa.maryland.gov/megafile/msa/speccol/sc2900/sc2908/000001/000203/html/am203--165.html.
22. Hening, *Statutes at Large*, 10:362.
23. Carroll to Vitaliano Borromeo, November 10, 1783, in *John Carroll Papers*, 1:80.
24. Carroll to Borromeo, November 10, 1783, 1:81.
25. Carroll to Cardinal Antonelli, February 27, 1785, in *John Carroll Papers*, 1:170–71.
26. Carroll to Antonelli, February 27, 1785, 1:170.
27. Baptist Association: Petition, November 11, 1780, Legislative Petitions, Digital Collection, Library of Virginia, https://lva.primo.exlibrisgroup.com/discovery/collectionDiscovery?vid=01LVA_INST:01LVA&collectionId=81114009740005756&lang=en, hereafter LPDC.
28. "The Memorial and Petition of the Subscribers, in behalf of themselves and others the Clergy of the Episcopal Churches," in *Journals of General Conventions of the Protestant Episcopal Church, in the United States, 1785–1835*, ed. William Stevens Perry, vol. 3 (Claremont, NH: Claremont Manufacturing Company, 1874), 20.
29. Vindex [Patrick Allison], *Candid Animadversions on a Petition*, 2d ed. (Baltimore: Goddard & Angell, 1793), 5.
30. Vindex, *Candid Animadversions*, 3.
31. Vindex, *Candid Animadversions*, 11.
32. Curry, *First Freedoms*, 154–58.
33. Baptist Association: Petition, November 8, 1780, LPDC.
34. Virginia General Assembly, House of Delegates, *In the House of Delegates, Friday, the 24th of December, 1784* (Richmond: s.n., [1784 or 1785]), *Early American Imprints, Series I: Evans* (no. 44619), https://infoweb.newsbank.com/apps/readex/doc?p=EVAN&docref=image/v2%3A0F2B1FCB879B099B%40EAIX-0F2F81FDD7BED798%40-101EBEE876675A58%400.

35. James Madison, "Memorial and Remonstrance Against Religious Assessments, [ca. 20 June] 1785," *Founders Online*, National Archives, https://founders.archives.gov/documents/Madison/01-08-02-0163.
36. Inhabitants: Petition, Surry County, November 14, 1785, LPDC.
37. Inhabitants: Petition, Westmoreland County, November 2, 1785, and Inhabitants: Petition, Southampton County, November 29, 1785, LPDC.
38. "Copy of a Petition, now Signing," *Baltimore Advertizer*, March 25, 1785, quoted in Curry, *First Freedoms*, 156.
39. "For the Maryland Journal, &c. to All Christians within the State of Maryland," *Maryland Journal* (Baltimore), February 8, 1785.
40. Carroll to Plowden, February 27, 1785.
41. Representatives of Several Baptist Associations: Petition, November 11, 1786, LPDC.
42. Vindex, *Candid Animadversions*, 11.
43. Patrick Henry, "Give Me Liberty or Give Me Death," March 23, 1775, The Avalon Project: Documents in Law, History, and Diplomacy, Lillian Goldman Law Library, Yale University, last modified 2008, https://avalon.law.yale.edu/18th_century/patrick.asp. See also Bernard Bailyn, *Ideological Origins of the American Revolution* (Cambridge, MA: Harvard University Press, 1992), 231–32; Edmund Morgan, *American Slavery, American Freedom: The Ordeal of Colonial Virginia* (New York: Norton, 1975), 376; Peter A. Dorsey, "To 'Corroborate Our Own Claims': Public Positioning and the Slavery Metaphor in Revolutionary America," *American Quarterly* 55 (2003): 353–86; and David Brion Davis, *The Problem of Slavery in the Age of Revolution, 1770–1823* (Ithaca, N.Y.: Cornell Univ. Press, 1975), 39–40, 263, 560–64; Okoye argued that it was not only a familiar institution but horrifying prospect and the worst "nightmare" of white Americans. F. Nwabueze Okoye, "Chattel Slavery as the Nightmare of the American Revolutionaries," *William and Mary Quarterly*, 3d ser., 37 (1980): 12.
44. Carroll to Plowden, February 27, 1785.
45. Vindex, *Candid Animadversions*, 10.
46. Baptist Association: Petition, November 6, 1783, LPDC.
47. Carroll to the editor of *Columbian Magazine*, September 1, 1787, in *John Carroll Papers*, 1:259.
48. Vindex, *Candid Animadversions*, 9, 16.
49. Baptist Association: Petition, November 6, 1783.
50. Freemen: Petition, Rockbridge County, December 1, 1784, LPDC.
51. The debates were informed by other political developments in the early republic, particularly the rise of Unitarianism and the rural-urban divisions in Maryland politics. See Eric Eisner, "'Suffer Not the Evil One': Unitarianism and the 1826 Maryland Jew Bill," *Journal of Religious History* 44 (2020): 338–55; and Eitches, "Maryland's 'Jew Bill,'" 262–65.

52. Maryland Declaration of Rights, article 35. While Maryland formally prohibited Jews from all positions of public trust, Eisner argues that, in practice, Jewish Marylanders did occasionally serve on juries. Eisner, 339, 341.
53. H. M. Brackenridge, *Speeches on the Jew Bill, in the House of delegates of Maryland* (Philadelphia: J. Dobson, 1829), 135.
54. Brackenridge, *Speeches on the Jew Bill,* 115, 113, 98.
55. Brackenridge, *Speeches on the Jew Bill,* 116.
56. The law weakened but did not fully repeal the religious test in Maryland's constitution. For more, see Alyssa Penick, *A Great Revolution in Church and State: Religion, Government, and Property in the Chesapeake, 1700–1830* (Charlottesville: University of Virginia Press, 2026), chap. 6.

"That Liberty, Wherewith God Has So Strangely Made Them Free"

Methodist Expansion and Division in the Revolutionary Atlantic World

CHRISTOPHER CANNON JONES

★

On September 10, 1784, the Anglican cleric John Wesley penned a letter attempting to articulate his efforts to make sense of the recently concluded Revolutionary War, which had severed ties between Britain and thirteen of her American colonies. "By a very uncommon train of providences," wrote Wesley, "many of the provinces of North America are totally disjoined from the British empire, and erected into Independent States." Wesley, who had opposed independence and withdrawn the English preachers he had sent to North America before the war, now wondered what to do with "our American brethren," who "are now totally disengaged from" Britain. While he remained firmly attached to the Church of England, he "dare[d] not entangle" American Methodists with the languishing Anglican community in the United States and pronounced them "now at full liberty, simply to follow the scriptures and the primitive church." "We judge it best," Wesley concluded, "that they should stand fast in that liberty, wherewith God has so strangely made them free."[1]

What it meant to "stand fast in that liberty" remained to be seen. Shortly after writing his letter, Wesley dispatched Thomas Coke, Richard Whatcoat, and Thomas Vasey to America with instructions to ordain Francis Asbury and organize the first independent Methodist church. The English-born Asbury was the only Wesleyan preacher who remained in North America during the war, and he emerged as the leader of a band of American-born itinerants during the conflict, helping to keep the scattered movement united amid the violence of war and a threatened schism among the preachers. In December 1784, Asbury and Coke were elected and ordained to superintend the Methodist Episcopal Church (MEC). Together, they organized the church, agreeing upon a form of church government, affirming core theological doctrines, and instituting policies regulating the lives of its members. Relying on a band of itinerant preachers who took the Methodist message to the furthest reaches of the American frontier and helped pioneer new methods and modes of worship, Asbury and Coke oversaw a period of unprecedented church growth, with the Methodist Episcopal Church soon becoming the largest Protestant body in the United States.

Historians have long debated the sources of Methodism's success in early America, with explanations ranging from the idea that early American revivals served as a program of social control, to Methodism embodying a democratized and voluntaristic Christianity uniquely well suited to the early republic, to the movement's growth instead being fueled by broader fears over free thought, partisan politics, and public morality.[2] The majority of scholarship, however, has focused on Methodist growth within the United States and the social, cultural, and political environment of the early republic. But Methodism's expansion during the Revolutionary era did not stop at national borders. Methodists were among the first American colonizers to traverse North America's Western frontier. During and after the war, they also fled the thirteen colonies turned states, journeying to Britain's Maritime and Canadian colonies, the West Indies, and even across the Atlantic Ocean to Africa.

These migrations further spread the Methodist faith, as lay men and women (and the itinerant preachers that followed) established classes, congregations, and societies wherever they went. But they also introduced new tensions that threatened to divide Methodists from one another. When John Wesley authorized the ordination of Francis Asbury and the formation of the Methodist Episcopal Church, he encouraged his followers "to follow the scriptures and the primitive church" as their guide. But the Bible was silent on the questions the new church faced or offered contradictory answers. Who, for example, was responsible for ministering to Methodists in Nova Scotia or Quebec? British missionaries, who shared a common subjecthood, or American preachers, who lived much closer? Did "that liberty, wherewith God has so strangely made [Americans] free" extend to enslaved Africans too? Methodists, both Black and white, joined in these conversations and asserted their own freedom in various ways.

In this essay, I analyze the migrations of three groups of Methodists during the final decades of the eighteenth century: the first a group of formerly enslaved people who escaped from bondage, took up arms for the British, and spent most of the war in English-occupied New York City before continuing on to Nova Scotia and Sierra Leone; the second, their white loyalist coreligionists who left their homes in the thirteen colonies and settled in Britain's Maritime and Canadian colonies; and the final group, a community of antislavery Methodists from Virginia who set out for Ohio in the 1780s and 1790s. Each group sought their own land of liberty, where they would be free to live their Methodist faith and pursue holiness amid the ongoing disruptions of the American Revolution and its aftermath.

The American Revolution emerges here as a profoundly disruptive event for religionists in the Revolutionary Atlantic world. The liberty "wherewith God [had] so strangely made [American Methodists] free" was not only religious but political and social as well. It held implications for Methodist attitudes toward slavery, raised questions about the relationships between—and ministerial authority for—Methodists in the US-Canadian borderlands, and helped spur Black Methodists to pursue their own ecclesiastical independence in the United States and abroad. If the American Revolution signaled an opportunity for new beginnings, it also underscored existing tensions and introduced new ruptures within the Methodist movement. As early American Methodism expanded, new expressions of Methodism emerged. And in the process, each of these divisions helped shape and define early American Methodism.

The formation of the Methodist Episcopal Church in December 1784 was justified on the grounds that in the United States "no one either exercises or claims any ecclesiastical authority" from the state. The disestablishment of the Church of England had left Methodists there with "none either to baptize or to administer the Lord's supper." In Wesley's mind, the new church was simply the most "rational and scriptural way of feeding and guiding those poor sheep in the [American] wilderness."[3] From its inception, however, the MEC's jurisdiction extended beyond the borders of the new nation. Among the fifteen elders "elected, and solemnly set apart to serve our societies" at the organizing conference were one sent to Antigua "and two for Nova Scotia."[4] The Methodist Episcopal Church would soon send preachers to British Canada as well.

These efforts were spurred by the migrations of Methodists during the Revolutionary War. As Black and white Methodists moved to Britain's Maritime and Canadian colonies, they took their faith with them, organizing new classes, building new chapels, and soliciting new preachers to minister to their societies. As preachers arrived from the United States in the 1780s and 1790s, those regions of British North America emerged as sorts of ecclesiastical borderlands, where American and British Methodists interacted, ostensibly in cooperation but just as often in conflict. The scars of the Revolutionary War ran too deep. Black Methodists, meanwhile, struggled under the sometimes heavy hand of white church leaders and the retreat from the Methodist Episcopal Church's initial antislavery measures to accommodate slaveowners in both the United States and Britain's American colonies. In response, many antislavery Methodists, both Black and white, migrated yet again in protest of ecclesiastical policies and in the hope of finally finding their long-sought land of liberty.

In the spring of 1778, patriot forces seized the recently vacated farm of Paul and Barbara Heck in Charlotte County, New York. The Hecks had first arrived in North America nearly two decades earlier from Ireland, where they had been converted under the preaching of John Wesley. In 1765, Barbara and her cousin Philip Embury had organized the first Methodist class meeting in New York City before moving upstate in 1770, settling on a large tract of land in New York's Camden Valley along with several other Irish Methodist families. Descended from German Palatines, the Irish Methodist community was fiercely loyal to the British Empire, which had provided their ancestors refuge. In 1777, Paul Heck had joined the loyalist Corps of Volunteers in Canada, following the example of his close friend and coreligionist John Dulmage. Barbara and her children had migrated north across the Saint Lawrence River the following year, making their home in Montreal, where Paul joined them following his discharge in 1778. Heck had supported his family as a carpenter, dockhand, and bateauman until the end of the war, when the Hecks, the Emburys, and other Camden Valley Methodists had moved yet again, this time onto grants of land in what would soon become Upper Canada.

In both Montreal and Augusta Township, where the Hecks settled, the migrants "carried on their Methodist testimony." Philip Embury's widow, Margaret, and her new husband, John Lawrence, organized the region's first Methodist class meeting in their home, with Margaret's son Samuel Embury assuming his late father's former post as leader of the small society.[5]

Other Methodists soon followed, settling on the Niagara Peninsula and in the Bay of Quinte. In 1792, the first Methodist church building in Upper Canada was constructed in Adolphustown.[6] Paul Heck died in 1795. Barbara followed in 1804. By the time of her death, the region had become a Methodist stronghold, earning her the unique distinction of being the "mother of Methodism" in two separate North American British colonies turned countries.[7]

Another group of Methodists, meanwhile, migrated further east, to the Maritime province of Nova Scotia. Like their counterparts who settled in Canada, they were loyalist exiles. They were a considerably more diverse lot than the Camden Valley Methodists, with more single men and women and proportionally fewer families. Their number included John Mann, a class leader, trustee, and treasurer of New York City's John Street congregation during the war, and Robert Barry, a wealthy merchant. The group also included several hundred formerly enslaved African Americans from Tidewater Virginia and coastal Carolina, including popular lay preachers like Moses, an enslaved man formerly owned by the Suffolk County, Virginia, merchant Mills Wilkinson.

One month after Lord Dunmore issued his 1775 proclamation declaring martial law in Virginia and promising freedom to "all indentured Servants, Negroes, and others (appertaining to Rebels) . . . that are able and willing to bear Arms" and joined "His Majesty's Troops," Moses fled Wilkinson's home.[8] Three years earlier, Moses had been converted to Methodism by the first Wesleyan preachers to reach Tidewater Virginia, and he had soon gained a reputation as a charismatic preacher, exhorting his enslaved fellows to Christian holiness at clandestine meetings held late at night in the isolated confines of the Great Dismal Swamp.

Moses did not escape alone. By the end of November, between two hundred and three hundred enslaved men and women had joined Dunmore's forces. The following spring, that number grew to nearly fifteen hundred. Over the course of the entire war, some twenty thousand enslaved Africans throughout British North America safely escaped to British lines.[9] Among their number were dozens, perhaps hundreds, of

Black Methodists from Tidewater Virginia who looked to individuals like Moses as spiritual guides. During the war, these Black loyalists were sustained by their Methodist ties, as they served in Dunmore's Ethiopian Regiment, suffered an outbreak of smallpox that left many in the company dead or disabled, and spent the remainder of the war in British-occupied New York City, constantly on the lookout for former owners coming to reclaim lost property.[10]

Following the war, the closely knit band of Black Methodists, whose numbers had grown during their time in New York, joined other loyalists, Black and white, in setting sail for Nova Scotia, where they arrived in October 1783. There, Moses and other preachers, including Boston King and Luke Jordan, went to work organizing Methodist meetings in Birchtown, the hastily organized and overcrowded settlement just south of Shelburne set aside for Black immigrants to the colony. At Birchtown they met William Black, a 22-year-old lay preacher who had arrived in the province in 1775 and written John Wesley requesting that preachers be sent to Nova Scotia. At Wesley's urging, Black set off for the United States in September 1784, arriving in Baltimore in time to attend the famed Christmas Conference, at which Francis Asbury and Thomas Coke were set apart to superintend the newly formed Methodist Episcopal Church. In early 1785, Black returned to Nova Scotia, accompanied by Freeborn Garrettson and James Cromwell, each now an ordained Methodist minister.[11] Garrettson, Cromwell, Black, and another lay preacher named John Mann set out to organize the hundreds of recently arrived Methodists in the province. Their efforts met with some success, and official membership in Nova Scotia grew to over one thousand by the early 1790s, with thousands more regularly attending Methodist meetings.

A sizeable portion of Methodism's membership in the Maritimes was Black, including an expansive congregation in Birchtown. When William Black visited in 1785, he reported preaching "to about two hundred negroes" and was pleased to find some "deeply affected, and others greatly comforted." He noted with satisfaction that the Black Methodists were led by Moses, whom Black described as "a poor negro, who can neither see, walk, nor stand." Moses and other Black preachers had organized fourteen classes in the community, all of which, according to Black, were "in a prosperous state."[12] Other Black classes were soon established in Shelburne, Halifax, Brindleytown, Preston, and Liverpool, all led by lay Black preachers. The successful partnership between white and

Black Methodists there made Nova Scotia an unexpected stronghold in the Methodist Episcopal Church's early years.

The decisions to send US-based preachers to those regions of British North America and the Caribbean were practical decisions determined by proximity, but they were intentional and consequential. In the MEC's first *Discipline,* Coke and Asbury amended John Wesley's earlier declaration that "God's Design in raising up the Preachers called Methodists" was to "reform the Nation" and "spread scriptural holiness over the land" to reflect new realities. In their version, the Methodist mission was "to reform the *Continent,* and to spread scriptural Holiness over these *Lands*"—the English *nation* and its *land* becoming the *lands* of the American *Continent.* More than a US church, then, the MEC aimed to be transnational in its outlook, the North American expression of an emerging global faith.[13]

But while an independent Methodist church made sense in the United States, with its lack of an established church, its presence in post-Revolutionary British North America proved more problematic. In Nova Scotia and New Brunswick, Methodists were not "totally disentangled" from the Church of England. And while Wesley urged American leaders to send preachers to those provinces, he continued to operate as if they were under his own oversight.

Wesley was explicit in his directions to Methodists in the Maritimes not to cause conflict with the established church: "Wherever there is any [Anglican] church service, I do not approve of any appointment the same hour," he wrote Freeborn Garrettson in 1786, "because I love the Church of England, and would assist, not oppose it, all I can."[14] Wesley's views, however, were not shared by either Garrettson or local Anglicans, who expressed little interest in nurturing ties between their two groups. In Garrettson's mind, the Church of England represented a withering branch of Christianity. Anglicans were "enemies to the life and power of religion."[15] For their part, Anglicans viewed Methodists not as fellow laborers in the project of imperial Protestantism but as religious rivals. As Methodists made further inroads throughout the 1780s, Anglican clerics became increasingly concerned.

The most vocal critic was Jacob Bailey, an Anglican minister who had been forced from his Maine home in 1779 to Cornwallis, Nova Scotia. To Bailey, Methodists represented not only a religious threat to Anglican hegemony in the Maritimes but a political threat to British sovereignty. Over the course of the 1780s, Bailey penned a thirty-one-book satirical poem titled *The Adventures of Jack Ramble, the Methodist Preacher.* Written over a ten-year period beginning in the 1780s, it chronicles the life and (mis)adventures of Jack Ramble, a Revolutionary War drummer turned itinerant preacher sent to Nova Scotia. Directly inverting charges of Toryism preachers like Garrettson had faced in Maryland and Virginia during the war, Bailey portrayed Jack Ramble as an agent of American imperialism, at one point quoting him admitting that "tis our intention, first to command / New Brunswick and the Acadian land," and "with enthusiastic ire / set both the provinces on fire." More than spiritual metaphor, Ramble and the Methodists intended to instigate US rule in the Maritimes. In Bailey's verse, Methodist leaders disclosed to Ramble those goals when ordaining him for his mission to Nova Scotia:

> The parson vers'd in all the tricks
> Of state reveal'd his politicks:
> "By right the congress ought to reign
> "O'er Britains proud usurped domain.
> "And, to extend its mighty power
> "Thro' all the vast Columbian shore."

They intended "to drive the Britons forth / From the cast regions of the north," and "To make our states wide as our souls / To grasp in all between the poles."[16] Real-life Methodists like Freeborn Garrettson, then, represented the dangers of both religious and political enthusiasm.

Garrettson initially accepted the assignment to Nova Scotia "with reluctance," and in spite of the growth he oversaw during his two years there, he became increasingly convinced that American preachers would never be openly welcome. In a 1786 letter to Francis Asbury, he revealed that "a number of people would prefer an Englishman to an American," admitting that "many have refused hearing me on this account." While he expressed confidence that "this prejudice would soon wear away," the opposition Garrettson and the other Methodist preachers encountered only increased.[17]

William Black, who succeeded Garrettson in superintending the work in eastern British North America, echoed his predecessor's views. In 1792, he wrote to Asbury that "put[ting] ourselves under the direction of the American bishops . . . would excite the jealousies of our Civil Governors."[18] But with Wesley's continued refusal to send English preachers to North America, Black remained reliant upon the Methodist Episcopal

Church for missionaries. At the 1792 MEC Annual Conference in Baltimore, "it was mentioned . . . that preachers were wanting as misaneries for several places," including "espesialy" Nova Scotia. Black "spacke very pressive to Conference for preachers," succeeding in recruiting a few, though "with great reluctance."[19] Nova Scotia's harsh climate and remote location discouraged American preachers from volunteering for the station. So, too, did ongoing international conflict.

As early as 1786, John Wesley expressed his fears of "another American revolution," wondering in a letter to Freeborn Garrettson how it might affect Methodists in Nova Scotia.[20] Those worries accelerated with the outbreak of war between Britain and France in 1793. Isaac Lunsford, one of the American preachers who, "after a fiew Hours consideration & deliberation," agreed to go to Nova Scotia, wrote in his journal on April 13 of that year of "certin news today by a packit from Urope, that war is declared between France & Ingland." He was especially concerned with rumors of a potential "war, between Great Britain and The United States." If that occurred, he confided to his diary, "I cannot stay heare unless They put me like The People of old, did Jeramiah in Prison." Worse still in Lunsford's mind was the threat of being impressed into the British Navy. "Some friends advised me to be carful in how I walked The streats," he wrote, "for Thare was avery hot press gang going about town."[21]

Lunsford safely returned to the United States in 1795, avoiding both imprisonment and impressment. He was one of the last American Methodist preachers to undertake an assignment to Nova Scotia. The scarcity of preachers willing to follow in his footsteps led William Black to appeal to British church leaders once more for assistance. This time he was successful, and in 1799 the first English preachers arrived, bringing Nova Scotian Methodism under the umbrella of the British Wesleyan Methodist Church and ending its formal ties with the MEC and American Methodism.

As Methodism's strength in Nova Scotia waned in the 1790s, its presence in Upper Canada was beginning to take off. There, William Losee, Nathan Bangs, and other American preachers ministered to societies composed almost entirely of loyalist migrants. This arrangement at first worked with few problems; Upper and Lower Canada were logical extensions of the thriving circuits in upstate New York, Vermont, Pennsylvania, and Ohio, all strongholds of the Methodist Episcopal Church. But Methodist growth in Upper and Lower Canada coincided with increasingly fraught relations between the American and British governments.

Taking a cue from civil leaders, lay Methodists in Kingston, Ottawa, and Montreal viewed American preachers in the province with suspicion. Writing to church leaders in England, they lamented that the American preachers judged them to be "Strangers & Foreigners" living in "a miserable Country . . . under a Despotic government amongst poor people." They petitioned for missionaries to be sent from London, as had been done in Nova Scotia. American Methodists, they complained in making their case, "are in general bitter Enemies to our good old King & Government, and . . . zealous admirers of the Democratic Republican form of Government established amongst themselves." Such overt political preaching caused problems with neighbors and local authorities, "defil[ing] and corrupting" their reputation in the region. They pointed to a law "expressly forbid[ding] any Majistys subjects in Canada to receive or even to acknowledge the Ministers belonging to or sent out by any Preacher who is a foreigner" and worried that things would only get worse "as the United States Government are now so very much opposed to Britain & her dependancies, and are manifestly bent to favor our enemies." In a show of defiance and an expression of loyalty to local and imperial governments, Methodists in Canada insisted that American preachers "pray for . . . His Magisty King George by Name." But they feared that they might soon find themselves trapped "in the Serbonian Bog of Democracy which we abhor." "On these accounts," they concluded, "we have long wished, and most affectionately desire an Union with you who are our Fathers & Brothers, who dwell in a Country we are united to by every sacred tie of love and Gratitude as well as by an union of sentiment and pious regard for that blessed Constitution & Government under which we both live."[22]

As relations between American and British Methodists in the Maritime and Canadian colonies soured, so, too, did those between white and Black Methodists in the region. Upon their arrival in Nova Scotia in 1783, Black Methodists were hopeful that they had reached their long-promised land of liberty. But land in Nova Scotia was not as plentiful as expected, and lots originally designated for Black settlers were given to (or sometimes *taken by*) white neighbors. The timing of their arrival made conditions worse. After arriving in late summer, the formerly enslaved migrants scrambled to find work and were forced to make do with scarce provisions in preparing for the winter months ahead. Their experience in Nova Scotia was worsened by the steadily increasing number of still-enslaved individuals being brought to Nova Scotia and New Brunswick. Others, though legally free, were forced by their indigence into "temporary bondage to white masters," accepting terms of indenture that resembled their former experience as enslaved laborers. A society with slaves, they reasoned, could not also be a land of liberty.[23]

Struggling under the weight of these circumstances, Black Methodists sought solace in their faith. But there, too, they encountered difficulties. Among Nova Scotia's slave-owning population were several prominent Methodists, signaling to those formerly enslaved that antislavery was far from the default position within the church. Moreover, weekly worship in Methodist chapels was segregated. When Freeborn Garrettson first encountered the large community of Black Methodists in Shelburne, he encouraged them to build "a little house at the north end of town" so that he could preach "to them separately, in order to have more room for the whites."[24] While some of that separation was preferred by Black Methodists, as it was in Philadelphia, New York, and Baltimore, that preference came in response to the second-class status they occupied in the white-led church. No Black Methodists were ordained in Nova Scotia; they remained subservient to Garrettson, Black, and other white ministers.

The political, economic, and religious discrimination that defined the Black loyalists' lives helped persuade them that their journey was not yet through, and when the British naval lieutenant and abolitionist John Clarkson arrived in Birchtown in 1791 with an invitation to Nova Scotia's free Blacks to resettle in Sierra Leone, the majority of Methodists eagerly accepted his offer, including the congregations led by Moses Wilkinson, Luke Jordan, and Boston King, who opened their chapels to Clarkson.

In Sierra Leone the Methodists hoped they would find their long-sought promised land, and in John Clarkson they believed they had found their Moses. Setting sail in January 1792, the Black loyalists arrived at their destination a little less than two months later, singing upon sight of land the popular refrain "The day of Jubilee is come! / Return ye, ransomed sinners, home."[25] But instead of a land flowing with milk and honey, the migrants discovered the shoddy remains of the recently razed Granville Town, located just upriver from the notorious slave-trading fort on Bunce Island. Plots of land and political rights proved nearly as hard to come by in Freetown as they had been in Nova Scotia, and their appeals for redress fell on deaf ears, especially after the replacement of Clarkson as colonial governor in 1794 with Zachary Macaulay, a former slave manager on a West Indian plantation only recently converted to the cause of abolition and still evidently skeptical of the abilities of people of color to govern themselves in a free society. Macaulay not only failed to deliver on earlier promises made to the Black settlers but also attempted to impose new regulations on their religious activities, mandating catechism classes in the Anglican church and refusing to recognize the assumed authority of Methodist and Baptist preachers. He mocked their pretensions to be ministers of God, decrying Moses Wilkinson's congregation as "mad Methodists" and criticizing their church government as "pure democracy, without subordination to anyone."[26]

Unsure where else to turn, the Methodists of Freetown wrote a series of letters to John Clarkson and petitioned the Sierra Leone Company's board to reappoint him as governor. "You should be our leader as Mosis and Joshua was in bringing the Children of Esaral to the promise land," begged James Liaster in 1796. James Hutcherson and Moses Murray went a step further, identifying not only Clarkson as their Moses but also Macaulay as Pharaoh, comparing their oppression at his hands to that of "King Pharoah Where With [He] Oppressed the Egyptians." Urging Clarkson to "leve us Not in the Wilderness to Opressing Masters," they begged him to "be Amongst us . . . Until the End."[27]

When it became clear that Clarkson was not returning, the Methodists took matters into their own hands, choosing from among themselves individuals to assume the role of Moses and Joshua leading them to liberty and salvation. Nathaniel Snowball, a member of Moses Wilkinson's congregation from their time in enslavement in Tidewater Virginia, announced in a letter to Clarkson that "I am Chosin out of the head of A Number of people to take my Departure as the Ezerlites did" so that "we may be no longer in bondage to this tyranious Crew." The company, led by Snowball, James Liaster, and Luke Jordan, negotiated with local Koya Temne rulers for the acquisition of "a piece of ground" called Pirate Bay, located about four miles west of Freetown. By 1797, "six or nine Family" had left "the Colony," with "many other Familys . . . thinking of going," perhaps as many as "one half of the Colony."[28] Although nowhere near half the settlers joined the company, Snowball and Jordan did successful recruit thirty families to their new colony, where Snowball was elected governor.[29]

The majority of Methodists remained in Freetown, though, continuing their struggle against Macaulay and his successors in the colonial government. In July 1796 a group of 128 individuals signed their names to a petition announcing the establishment of "The Independent Methodist Church of Freetown," declaring themselves "a perfect church" with "no need of the assistance of any worldly power to appoint or perform religious ceremonies for us."[30] Predictably, Macaulay refused to recognize their right to form any such independent church and threatened to try them for treason, punishable by hanging. But this early effort at establishing an independent Methodist church signaled the start of a broader move toward ecclesiastical independence in Sierra Leone that mirrors in striking ways the beginnings of the African Methodist Episcopal Church in the United States at almost the exact same time.

Racial division, then, posed an additional threat to the transatlantic Methodist community in the wake of the Revolutionary War. The shadow of slavery loomed large in the experiences of Black Methodists in both the United States and Britain's North American and West African colonies. Their push for independence from white ecclesiastical rule was understood as an additional step in their ongoing pursuit of freedom from bondage.

SHORTLY AFTER Nova Scotia's Black Methodists sailed across the Atlantic Ocean and settled in Freetown, a group of their coreligionists followed in their initial footsteps by fleeing Virginia to escape slavery. Instead of moving north to the Maritimes and then sailing east across the Atlantic Ocean, however, this second group of antislavery Methodists looked west, toward the newly opened Northwest Territory, settling in the Scioto River Valley in present-day Ohio. From 1790 to 1810, more than one hundred Methodist migrants left the Old Dominion to settle in the region, in protest of both the state and their church's acquiescence to slavery.

Like the Black loyalists who set sail for Nova Scotia and then Sierra Leone in search of a land of liberty, the first Methodist settlers to Ohio were firmly opposed to slavery and drew upon similar Old Testament tropes in describing their migration. Unlike their Black counterparts, however, these white Methodist migrants from southern Virginia were proud patriots of the new United States, and their conception of liberty combined Methodist notions of religious freedom with Jeffersonian understandings of political and economic opportunity.

In 1785, Philip Gatch, a recently retired Methodist preacher, moved with his family to Buckingham County, Virginia. He purchased a 1,000-acre plot of land, "reduced 500 acres of it to cultivation, and made such other improvements as were calculated to render my family comfortable." Gatch had been instrumental in sustaining and growing the nascent American Methodist community during the disruptive years of the Revolutionary War. From 1774 to 1785, he had traveled circuits and fulfilled preaching assignments all along the Eastern Seaboard, from New Jersey to North Carolina. Seeking now to settle down with his wife, Elizabeth, and their two youngest children, Gatch planned to take up farming and assume an active role in the local Methodist congregation. He "had in view a settlement for life," he later recalled. Buckingham County, home "to a flourishing society of Methodists," was a seemingly ideal location.[31]

But the Gatch family's stay in Buckingham County lasted little more than a decade. Thirteen years after their arrival, Philip, Elizabeth, their eight children, and four Black servants (all recently manumitted from enslavement, still the legal responsibility of the Gatches) joined a group of several dozen others, left their homes in southern Virginia, and set out for the newly opened Northwest Territory. Although Virginia had provided them with almost "all the advantages and privileges we could expect in a fallen world," one particular nagging issue finally prompted the group to set out for the Ohio Country. "I could not feel reconciled to die and leave my posterity in a land of slavery," Gatch explained.[32]

The Northwest Territory, formally opened to settlement in 1787, provided the frustrated Methodists with a seemingly ideal outlet. To the migrants who made the journey, it was a providential opportunity. Frederick Bonner wrote with confidence that "the Lord provided for the Vertuous sons of the Eastern States in the liberty of [the] State of Ohio—the thing speaks for its self."[33] The liberty of which Bonner spoke encompassed political, economic, and religious freedom, all of which were linked in the minds of the Methodists. Free from the harmful effects of a slaveholding society and its corrupting influence on both civil and ecclesiastical matters, they hoped to receive God's blessing. As Bonner explained further, "The Legislature of Va has determined against liberty," and Methodists there were "purchasing Slavs without a prospect of liberating them." "Whats worse," he continued, "they take protection under General Conference. Lord have Mercy on the Methodists cause and fix it on a firm basis." Concerned about "the condition of the church in the state when slavery is encouraged & liberty supprest," Bonner and his family joined the Gatches in Ohio.[34]

Like their Black coreligionists, the white Methodist migrants to Ohio were concerned about their children's welfare. In an 1802 letter, Philip Gatch explained that he "felt unwilling" to "leave my Children whom I tenderly loved in a land of slavery not knowin what the Evils there of would amount to in there [*sic*] time." "The Lord," he gratefully concluded, "has conducted us safely to this New Countrey." Unlike their Black counterparts, these white Methodist migrants described "no red Sea in the way . . . no pharos host to pursue us while traveling to the American Canaan." Even better, as Peter Pelham explained in an 1807 letter, "our Jordon (I mean the Ohio [River]) is easy to cross." In Ohio, he concluded, "our children are saved from the harmfull practice of trading on their fellow creatures."[35]

Lurking beneath this spirited antislavery rhetoric, however, was sometimes a noticeable lack of sympathy for the enslaved. White Methodists' opposition to slavery was, at its core, intensely concerned with their own personal righteousness and that of their families.[36] Frederick Bonner thus expressed his relief that his children would grow up in "a land where they are not to be troubled with slaves," while Peter Pelham explained that his family "frequently mention how much better [it was] to do their family business of Cooking &c themselves, than to have any black ones about them."[37] Sometimes the enslaved were cast as not merely burdensome but dangerous. James Tawler called those held in bondage the "most dangerous & formidable enemy she has under heaven, I sincerely believe, the *slaves*," a view shaped in response to Gabriel's Rebellion in 1800.[38] In 1802, Philip Gatch responded to a friend's inquiry concerning the threat of Indigenous attacks in Ohio by assuring him that "we feel no more affraid of them than you do there. . . . We have been more affraid of the Negroes in Virginia than I have ever been in this Country of Poor Indians."[39]

But it was not only the enslaved over whom the Methodist migrants expressed concern. Free people of color were unwelcome too. Peter Pelham noted, with apparent approval, that "our assembly appear to be much against colourd people settling in this State," a reference to the Black Laws passed by Ohio's legislature in 1804 and 1807. The first iteration of the Black Laws required all free people of color in the state to produce a certificate of freedom and forbade anyone from employing those who could not. Ohio's first governor, the Methodist Edward Tiffin, signed it into law in 1804.[40]

The land of liberty sought (and created) by white Methodists in Ohio was one not just free from slavery but almost entirely free from people of color. While Black people occasionally attended Methodist revivals there, they resisted joining the Methodist Episcopal Church. In Ohio as in other regions, Black Methodists were relegated to segregated seating in chapel galleries or formed into separate congregations. The limits of Methodist antislavery increasingly made MEC churches unwelcome places for free Black people.

THE POLITICS of race, slavery, and nation inherited from the Revolution introduced and intensified pressures that threatened to divide Methodism, even as it continued its rapid growth. Those tensions reached their climax in the second decade of the nineteenth century. On June 18, 1812, just three weeks after Methodists in Montreal wrote to church leaders complaining about American preachers and requesting missionaries from England instead, the United States declared war on Great Britain. Word "that there is a war between our people and the English people" first reached Francis Asbury as he presided over the proceedings of the New England Annual Conference in Lynn, Massachusetts. Asbury's initial response was short and to the point: "My trust is in the living God."[41] But such platitudes did little to resolve the realities the war wrought for the Methodist movement.

The Methodist Episcopal Church's Genesee Conference was forced to relocate its annual meeting in July from Niagara, Upper Canada, to Lyons, New York, with the "brethren of Canada . . . all absent."[42] Most American-born preachers returned to the United States, and after the war they were replaced by missionaries from England. While Francis Asbury staked out an official policy of neutrality, other US preachers embraced nationalism. Although the preacher David Lewis believed war was "antagonistic to the gospel," he nevertheless invoked God's support on behalf of the American armies. Referencing "the noble blood of patriot martyrs" that "consecrated this whole land of freedom," Lewis prayed that "the God of power, who sustained our fathers in the Revolutionary struggle, would give us the victory."[43] Over the course of the conflict, at least fourteen Methodist preachers served as chaplains in volunteer militias, and Jesse Lee accepted an invitation to serve as chaplain in the United States House of Representatives (1812–14) and then in the Senate (1814–15).[44] White Methodists were more at home in the United States than ever before.

Meanwhile, Black Methodists in Sierra Leone continued to resist the encroachment of white British government and ecclesiastical leaders into their affairs. Like did their better-known counterparts in Philadelphia, Baltimore, and New York, Black Methodists in Sierra Leone battled over legal possession of church property for nearly a decade, asserted their right to regulate their own associations, and finally, in 1821, organized themselves into the West African Methodist Society.[45] For most of the original settlers, ecclesiastical independence marked a fulfillment of their hope that their children would not "be in bondage after us."[46] For the formerly enslaved women and men who journeyed from Norfolk to Nova Scotia and then Sierra Leone, slavery encompassed much more than forced servitude on Southern plantations. It was seen in every broken promise from government officials and every effort (real and imagined) to regulate and restrict their social, economic, political, and religious rights as British subjects. The land of liberty they sought, then, was one where they hoped to enjoy not only freedom from bondage but also freedom from interference in their everyday lives, including especially their spiritual and religious lives.

And back in the United States, white Methodists witnessed the exodus of thousands of their coreligionists into the African Methodist Episcopal and African Methodist Episcopal Zion Churches in the second and third decades of the nineteenth century. Of the 20,000-plus Methodists in the MEC's Ohio Conference in 1812, only 561 were not white, and most non-whites lived on the other side of the Ohio River, in slaveholding Kentucky. The Miami district, where the Virginia migrants were concentrated, counted only 50 people of color among its members. By the 1820s, Black congregations in both Cincinnati and Chillicothe had voted to leave the Methodist Episcopal Church and unite with Richard Allen's independent African Methodist Episcopal Church instead.[47]

It is perhaps inaccurate, then, to speak of a singular early American Method*ism*. The American Revolution gave birth to not only the Methodist Episcopal Church but ultimately many Methodist organizations, each in pursuit of "that liberty" unleashed by the Revolution. As Methodist migrants set out in search of their own land of liberty, they not only expanded the movement's geographical reach but set the stage for future divisions. Nation, race, and slavery were the fault lines that eventually ruptured Methodist unity. There was no *united* Methodist movement by the early nineteenth century.

The separations of British and American Methodists in Canada from one another and the establishment of independent African Methodist churches on both sides of the Atlantic were, however, instrumental in shaping early American Methodism. In 1830 the Methodist Episcopal Church was the largest Protestant church in the United States. It was also an institution increasingly at home there. By retreating from Canada, American church leaders redefined the scope of the Methodist Episcopal

Church's mission, which had abandoned efforts at transnational connection and now focused largely on westward expansion. The withdrawal of free Blacks from the MEC, meanwhile, left that church without important antislavery voices, allowing proslavery compromises to continue and setting the stage for the 1844 division of the MEC into Northern and Southern institutions. That division, like those that preceded it, both revealed the existence of multiple Methodisms and affirmed the Americanness of the church. In order to understand the early stages of that process, though, it is necessary to look beyond the borders of the United States.

Notes

1. John Wesley to Dr. Coke, Mr. Asbury, and our Brethren in North America, September 10, 1784, in *Minutes of the Methodist Conferences, Annually Held in America, from 1773 to 1794, Inclusive* (Philadelphia: Henry Tuckniss, 1795), 75–77.
2. On revivals as a form of social control, see Paul E. Johnson, *A Shopkeeper's Millennium: Society and Revivals in Rochester, New York, 1815–1837* (1978; reprint, New York: Hill & Wang, 2004). Compare Nathan O. Hatch, *The Democratization of American Christianity* (New Haven, CT: Yale University Press, 1989). For a sampling of the several studies that followed, see Russell E. Richey, *Early American Methodism* (Bloomington: Indiana University Press, 1991); A. Gregory Schneider, *The Way of the Cross Leads Home: The Domestication of American Methodism* (Bloomington: Indiana University Press, 1993); Christine Leigh Herman, *Southern Cross: The Beginnings of the Bible Belt* (New York: Knopf, 1997); Cynthia Lynn Lyerly, *Methodism and the Southern Mind, 1770–1810* (New York: Oxford University Press, 1998); John H. Wigger, *Taking Heaven by Storm: Methodism and the Rise of Popular Christianity in America* (New York: Oxford University Press, 1998); and Dee E. Andrews, *The Methodists and Revolutionary America, 1760–1800: The Shaping of an Evangelical Culture* (Princeton, NJ: Princeton University Press, 2000). More recent contributions have begun to push the study of early American Methodism in new directions, even as they retain a focus on the movement's growth and its place within the political, religious, and cultural landscape of the early American republic. See Jeffrey Williams, *Religion and Violence in Early American Methodism: Taking the Kingdom by Force* (Bloomington: Indiana University Press, 2010); Amanda Porterfield, *Conceived in Doubt: Religion and Politics in the New American Nation* (Chicago: University of Chicago Press, 2012); Kyle T. Bulthuis, *Four Steeples over the City Streets: Religion and Society in New York's Early Republic Congregations* (New York: New York University Press, 2014); Russell E.

Richey, *Methodism in the American Forest* (New York: Oxford University Press, 2015); and Hunter Price, *Sacred Capital: Methodism and Settler Colonialism in the Empire of Liberty* (Charlottesville: University of Virginia Press, 2024).

3. Wesley to Dr. Coke, Mr. Asbury, and our Brethren in North America, September 10, 1784.
4. Francis Asbury Journal, December 18, 1784, in *The Journal and Letters of Francis Asbury, in Three Volumes,* ed. Elmer T. Clark, J. Manning Potts, and Jacob S. Payton (London and Nashville: Epworth Press and Abingdon Press, 1958), 1:474.
5. G. G. Findlay and W. W. Holdsworth, *The History of the Wesleyan Methodist Missionary Society,* 5 vols. (London: Epworth Press, 1921–24), 1:354–55; Abel Stevens, *The Women of Methodism: Its Three Foundresses, Susanna Wesley, the Countess of Huntingdon, and Barbara Heck; with Sketches of their Female Associates and Successors in the Early History of the Denomination* (New York: Carlton & Porter, 1866), 193–94.
6. See Neil Semple, *The Lord's Dominion: The History of Canadian Methodism* (Montreal: McGill-Queen's University Press, 1996), 42–43; and J. William Lamb, *The Founders: The Twenty-two Persons Who Established Old Hay Bay Church in 1792* (Kingston, ON: Hay Bay Books, 2005).
7. Dee Andrews, "Barbara Heck," *American National Biography Online,* February 2000, http://www.anb.org/articles/01/01-00393.html.
8. *Virginia Gazette,* November 24, 1775. For more on Moses Wilkinson, see Cassandra Pybus, "Mary Perth, Harry Washington, and Moses Wilkinson: Black Methodists Who Escaped from Slavery and Founded a Nation," in *Revolutionary Founders: Rebels, Radicals, and Reformers in the Making of the Nation,* ed. Alfred F. Young, Gary B. Nash, and Ray Raphael (New York: Knopf, 2011), 155–68.
9. Cassandra Pybus, "Jefferson's Faulty Math: The Question of Slave Defections in the American Revolution," *William and Mary Quarterly* 62, no. 2 (April 2005): 243–64.
10. Gary Sellick, "'Undistinguished Destruction': The Effects of Smallpox on British Emancipation Policy in the Revolutionary War," *Journal of American Studies* 51, no. 3 (August 2017): 865–85.
11. William Black, "The Life of Mr. William Black, Written by Himself," in *The Lives of Early Methodist Preachers, Chiefly Written by Themselves, Edited, with an Introductory Essay, by Thomas Jackson, Third Edition, with Additional Lives,* 3d ed., 6 vols. (London: Wesleyan Conference Office, 1866), 5:284
12. Matthew Richey, *A Memoir of the Late Rev. William Black, Wesleyan Minister, Including an Account of the Rise and Progress of Methodism in Nova Scotia* (Halifax: William Cunnabell, 1839), 128–29.

13. *Minutes of Several Conversations Between The Rev. Thomas Coke, LL.D., The Rev. Francis Asbury and Others, at a Conference, Begun in Baltimore, in the State of Maryland, on Monday, the 27th. of December, in the Year 1784, Composing a Form of Discipline for the Ministers, Preachers and Other Members of the Methodist Episcopal Church in America* (Philadelphia: Charles Cist, 1785), 3. See also Richey, *Early American Methodism*, 35–36.
14. Wesley to Freeborn Garrettson, November 30, 1786, in *Letters of the Rev. John Wesley, A.M.*, ed. John Telford, 8 vols. (London: Epworth Press, 1931), 7:354.
15. Freeborn Garrettson, *American Methodist Pioneer: The Life and Journals of the Rev. Freeborn Garrettson, 1752–1827*, ed. Robert Drew Simpson (Rutland, VT: Academy Books, 1984), 94.
16. Jacob Bailey, *The Adventures of Jack Ramble, the Methodist Preacher*, Book 1, Jacob Bailey Papers, Nova Scotia Archives and Records Management, Halifax. On Bailey, see James S. Leamon, *The Reverend Jacob Bailey, Maine Loyalist: For God, King, Country, and for Self* (Amherst: University of Massachusetts Press, 2010); and Thomas B. Vincent, *Narrative Verse Satire in Maritime Canada, 1779–1814* (Ottawa: Tecumseh Press, 1978), which includes a transcription of the first seven books of *Jack Ramble*.
17. Garrettson to Asbury, 1786, Garrettson Family Papers, General Commission on Archives and History, United Methodist Church, Drew University Library, Madison, NJ, reprinted in Garrettson, *American Methodist Pioneer*, 251.
18. Richey, *Memoir of the Late Rev. William Black*, 309–10.
19. Isaac Lunsford Journal, entry for November 1, 1792, Microfilm MS, Swem Library, The College of William and Mary, Williamsburg, VA.
20. Wesley to Garrettson, November 30, 1786.
21. Lunsford Journal, entries for November 1, 1792; April 13 and 25, 1793; March 30, 1794.
22. Montreal Methodists to Wesleyan Methodist Missionary Society, May 26, 1812, Microfilm Roll A-258, Methodist Missionary Society Fonds, Library and Archives Canada, Ottawa. "Serbonian bog" is a literary allusion to ancient Lake Serbonis in Egypt, used first by John Milton in *Paradise Lost* to refer to a "situation or predicament from which it is difficult to extricate onseself." See *Oxford English Dictionary*, 3d ed. (1989), under "Serbonian"; also available at http://www.oed.com.
23. Maya Jasanoff, *Liberty's Exiles: American Loyalists in the Revolutionary World* (New York: Knopf, 2011), 281.
24. Garrettson, *American Methodist Pioneer*, 127.
25. J. B. Elliott, *Lady Huntingdon's Connexion in Sierra Leone* (London, 1851), 15.
26. Zachary Macaulay Journal, September 13, 1793, November 26, 1794, Zachary Macaulay Papers, Huntington Library, San Marino, CA.

27. James Liaster to John Clarkson, March 30, 1796, and James Hutcherson and Moses Murray to Clarkson, May 24, 1796, in Christopher Fyfe, *Our Children Free and Happy: Letters from Black Settlers in Africa in the 1790s* (Edinburgh: Edinburgh University Press, 1991), 49–50, 51.
28. Nathaniel Snowball and Hutcherson to Clarkson, May 24, 1796, and Boston King to Clarkson, June 1, 1797, in Fyfe, *Our Children Free and Happy*, 52, 54.
29. Cassandra Pybus, *Epic Journeys of Freedom: Runaway Slaves of the American Revolution and Their Global Quest for Liberty* (Boston: Beacon, 2006), 185.
30. "The Independent Methodist Church in Freetown to the Governor and Council (11 July 1796)," in Viscountess Knutsford, *Life and Letters of Zachary Macaulay* (London: Edward Arnold, 1900), 145–46.
31. John M'Lean, *Sketch of Rev. Philip Gatch* (Cincinnati: Swormstead & Poe, 1854), 95.
32. M'Lean, *Sketch of Rev. Philip Gatch*, 94.
33. Frederick Bonner to Edward Dromgoole, July 19, 1807, Dromgoole Papers, Southern Historical Collection—University of North Carolina, reprinted in William Warren Sweet, *Religion on the American Frontier, 1783–1840*, volume 4, *The Methodists* (Chicago: University of Chicago Press, 1946), 170–71.
34. Bonner to Dromgoole, July 19, 1807.
35. Philip Gatch to Dromgoole, February 11, 1802, and Peter Pelham to Dromgoole, [1807], both in Dromgoole Papers.
36. Bennett Maxey to Dromgoole, July 27, 1807, Dromgoole Papers, reprinted in Sweet, 175.
37. Bonner to Dromgoole, July 19, 1807; Pelham to Dromgoole, July 27, 1807, Dromgoole Papers.
38. James Tawler to Dromgoole, September 11, 1809, Dromgoole Papers.
39. Gatch to Dromgoole, February 11, 1802.
40. Pelham to Dromgoole, [1807].
41. Asbury, *Journal and Letters of Francis Asbury*, 2:701.
42. Minutes of the Genesee Conference, 1810–1824, 23, General Commission on Archives and History, United Methodist Church, Drew University Library, Madison, NJ; Asbury, *Journal and Letters of Francis Asbury*, 2:703, 705.
43. David Lewis, *Recollections of a Superannuate: Or, Sketches of Life, Labor, and Experience in the Methodist Itinerancy*, ed. Rev. S. M. Merrill (Cincinnati: Methodist Book Concern, 1857), 76, 99. For a fuller analysis of Lewis's writings on the war, see Williams, *Religion and Violence*, 102–4.
44. Lee was initially appointed chaplain to the US House of Representatives on May 22, 1809, and he was reappointed shortly after the outbreak of war, in November 1812. He was appointed chaplain of the US Senate on

September 27, 1814. Lee was the first Methodist to serve as US Senate chaplain and the second to serve as House chaplain. Thomas Lyell had served in that position from 1800 to 1801. See "Chaplains of the House," http://history.house.gov/People/Office/Chaplains/; and "Senate Chaplains," http://www.senate.gov/artandhistory/history/common/briefing/Senate_Chaplain.htm, both accessed April 15, 2016.

45. James W. St. G. Walker, *The Black Loyalists: The Search for a Promised Land in Nova Scotia and Sierra Leone, 1783–1870* (Toronto: University of Toronto Press, 1992), 293–95.

46. Settlers' Petition, n.d., in Fyfe, *Our Children Free and Happy*, 36–37.

47. *Minutes of the Annual Conferences of the Methodist Episcopal Church, for the Years 1773–1828* (New York: Thomas Mason and George Lane, 1840), 1:227–29; Lyle S. Evans, ed., *A Standard History of Ross County, Ohio: An Authentic Narrative of the Past, with Particular Attention to the Modern Era in the Commercial, Industrial, Civic and Social Development*, vol. 1 (Chicago: Lewis Publishing, 1917), 334–36.

The Rise and Fall of Evangelical Abolition in the Age of Revolution

PETER Y. CHOI

★

EVANGELICALS' SUPPORT for the abolition of slavery was tentative and fragmented throughout the eighteenth century. Their vacillation throughout the Age of Revolution reveals patterns of cultural entanglement that conflicted with their lofty religious rhetoric. To make such an observation is to contradict the humanitarian argument, also known as the Clarkson Thesis, named after Thomas Clarkson, a member of the Clapham Sect, whose influential history of his evangelical peers and their abolitionist activities long shaped the historical understanding of evangelical contributions to the cause of abolition. For proponents of evangelicalism's humanitarian impulse, later interventions and forays into antislavery causes made amends for earlier, admittedly misguided involvement in slavery. While modern scholarship has moved past Clarkson to more complex and more nuanced assessments of the relationship between evangelicals and abolition, the humanitarian argument remains deep in the bones of our historical imagination, especially in popular works of evangelical history.[1] This essay interrogates the relationship between religion and abolition through a survey of the rise and fall of evangelical abolition in the Age of Revolution.[2]

The evangelicals in this study represent mostly white Protestants, who enthusiastically joined the revival movements of the eighteenth century by trumpeting the message of Christianity as good news for all who repented and committed to live in conformity with their interpretation of true Christianity. Yet, as they prioritized spiritual salvation over physical liberation, they not only made Christianity and slavery compatible but bolstered what one historian has called "Christian slavery."[3] These efforts contributed to the formation of racial hierarchies, so much so that it may not be far-fetched to see religion and race as "conjoined twins."[4]

The disruption of revolution at long last jolted religious sentiment toward liberty for the enslaved. Indeed, the American Revolution forced devout Christians to reckon with what many in their ranks began to call the sin of slavery. Breaking from the pattern of previous decades, abolitionist sentiment among evangelicals surged in the mid-1770s, with significant numbers of leading evangelical voices venturing to decry the evils of slavery. Despite these signs of change, evangelical zeal for emancipation waned in the early years of the new republic as rapidly as it had surged only a few years before. The arc of evangelical history follows a pattern from clarion proslavery to zealous antislavery to vexed ambiguity on the slavery question. This overview shows an inherent flexibility within evangelical thought that, by way of cultural accommodations, bends toward racial hierarchy.

To make sense of evangelicals' changing positions, this essay details four evangelical responses to slavery in the eighteenth century: rationalization, amelioration, abolition, and reparation. Although these attitudes were not mutually exclusive, they reveal distinct emphases that amounted to divergent paths of action. For some, these viewpoints represented four different developmental stages, marking a process that moved from proslavery accommodation to antislavery activism; others located their convictions firmly in one position, evincing little to no movement over time. These four responses to slavery present a porous typology as well as a rough chronology. For if there was forward movement and progress in the course of time from rationalization to reparation, there were also plentiful examples of backsliding. For evangelicals confronting slavery, there was no ineluctable progress toward freedom.

Far from a simple narrative of good triumphing over evil with evangelicals leading the charge toward antislavery sentiment, the facts on the ground reveal a more complicated story. The truth of the matter is that evangelical responses to slavery were uneven and fluid and changed over time. New birth Christians, preoccupied with revival, first tried to live with slavery before they adopted antislavery positions. They found it easier to denounce the harsh conditions of enslavement and the cruelties of the slave trade than to stake out a more confrontational position against slavery in general. In other words, an evangelical history of slavery ought to begin not with John Wesley's 1776 treatise against slavery, as it often does, but rather with the longer prehistory of Wesley's and other evangelicals' accommodation of slavery and resistance to the call of abolition. Historians have provided rich documentation for evangelical retreat from abolitionist positions in the post-Revolutionary period leading up to the Civil War, and this study builds on their significant body of contributions.[5] A broader survey that reaches further back in time, as attempted here, builds on an early republic historiography to demonstrate how evangelicalism's embrace of compassionate slavery during the colonial period can be understood alongside the Revolutionary surge of abolitionist sentiment. Evangelicals' slide into uneasy ambiguity in the years following the Revolution is also part of their distinctive contribution to Christian rapprochement with slavery in America. The protracted détente between evangelicalism and slavery over a long ambiguous history of abolitionist engagement is a distinguishing theological feature of religious history in America.

Not by coincidence did evangelical abolition peak alongside Revolutionary ferment. Theological emphasis on the new birth set up a hierarchy of beliefs that made it easy to overlook the cause of abolition when other matters took precedence. Indeed, the struggle for political freedom often played second fiddle to spiritual salvation in the evangelical imagination. But during the Revolutionary period, these two priorities that ran along parallel tracks converged, at least for a time. When Revolutionary fervor died down, however, so did the energy that fired abolition among evangelicals. If the focus shifted once again toward accommodation, the evangelical position on slavery was more fractured and divided. In these ways, the rise and fall of evangelical abolition represented a pivotal turning point, from unitary consensus to multivocal ambiguity.

Rationalization

At the beginning of the eighteenth century and before the dawn of the evangelical era, most Christian masters harbored ambivalence toward the salvation of their enslaved laborers. With widespread anxiety over the incompatibility of slavery and Christian identity, many British slaveholders placed conversion beyond the reach of Africans. To take one example, an ideology of "hereditary heathenism" prevailed in Virginia, where slaveowners put forth legal, economic, and religious justifications for the implausibility of slave conversions.[6] Withholding the gospel of salvation became untenable, however, as revival preachers crisscrossing the Atlantic world exhorted spiritual awakening with fever-pitched urgency. The incongruity of subjecting fellow human beings to a cruel system of forced labor became increasingly problematic if there was no hope of spiritual redemption. As they made experiential new birth the centerpiece of "true" spirituality, revival-seeking evangelists recovered an old but increasingly rare belief in the gospel's appeal to all peoples. The emboldened spiritual call that resulted ironically had the effect of hardening theological rationalization for the acceptance of slavery.

To slaveholders anxious about the implications of conversion for enslaved labor, a variety of religious arguments highlighted the benefit of greater docility and obedience that resulted from the Christianization of slaves. According to the historian Charles Irons, to any who feared that evangelical efforts to convert the enslaved risked upsetting the social order, preachers "explained that—far from destabilizing slavery—evangelical conversion changed the heart and made better slaves, a seminal moment in the evolution of proslavery."[7] This argument for the compatibility of Christianity and slavery provided a forceful apologetic for the justification of slavery. When revivalist zeal intensified, evangelicals, more than other British and American Protestants, came to prioritize conversion in their attitudes toward racial slavery. In the process, however, they also made the fateful decision to separate the spiritual needs of enslaved persons from their physical well-being. Without wading into highly nuanced internal matters of doctrine, it may still be fruitful to examine the problematic outward implications of the doctrine of *felix culpa*. The propagation of a "fortunate fall" provided a way to gloss over the horrors of slavery by glorying in the Christianization of enslaved persons. This belief in the positive good of slavery brooked no dissent for evangelicals, who carefully cultivated a rhetoric of prizing spiritual salvation over earthly treasures as well as torments. If the bitter cup of slavery was a necessary evil that accompanied the bread of new life, then there could be no just or moral opposition to slavery.

Put one way, rationalization was an early evangelical response to slavery that sought to provide theological answers to a moral as well as economic dilemma. Talk of a fortunate fall enabled evangelicals to acknowledge the dark side of slavery while simultaneously promulgating its redemptive qualities. If the horrors of slavery were regrettable, went the argument, it was far better for enslaved persons to suffer in the New World than to face the eternal doom that would have been their inevitable lot in Africa. The doctrine of *felix culpa* held broad appeal for British Christians in search of justification for the cruelties of chattel slavery because it used theological language to provide spiritual sanction. These Christians received not only permission for slavery but a profound call to action and mission fueling their endeavors in the New World.

Consequently, leading evangelical figures promoted racial slavery and thereby buttressed ideas of racial difference. And they stretched theological reasoning to align countervailing realities. Even their efforts to lessen the cruelty of slavery led to paternalistic attitudes that perpetuated the lower status of Africans in colonial society. According to one historian, "Evangelicals like George Whitefield and Samuel Davies admitted that slavery had its objectionable features, but they sought to eradicate those features by converting both the master and the slave."[8] Use of the fortunate-fall thesis was especially common among pro-revival Christians because of their emphasis on the new birth. The rationalization of slavery resulted from evangelical emphasis on conversion but found support in a biblical hermeneutic that assumed the ability of Christians to rightly discern God's will for the minutiae of human affairs. With supreme confidence in their spiritual knowledge, evangelicals claimed access to divine authority in ordering human life. They knew what was best for themselves, society, and the church; and they presumed to know what enslaved Africans needed for their progress. By conferring moral obligation on themselves, they could continue their righteous cause with confidence.

Evangelicals believed that when it came to one's eternal destiny there was no cross too heavy, no sacrifice too high. In the case of slavery, because physical suffering led to spiritual salvation, there was lasting redemptive good to be found under the yoke of injustice. Whatever harm slavery caused, they argued, the conversion of primitive and benighted souls outweighed the worldly suffering they endured in their temporal existence. This theological rationalization of racial slavery had profound consequences that went beyond matters of religious doctrine. In the evangelical mind, theological justification gave rise to an emerging racial logic according to which Black suffering eventually led to Black salvation and thereby justified Black slavery. The problem was made worse by the fact that white masters who benefited financially from Black slaves were making these arguments. Efforts to rationalize slavery give credence to Rebecca Goetz's argument that throughout "the English colonial adventure in North America, Christian baptism was a tool of conquest."[9]

Amelioration

Another common evangelical response to slavery, amelioration, faced the uphill task of trying to make an inherently inhuman system more humane. Evangelicals hoped that benevolence and proselytization would help offset the pain and suffering inflicted. Recognizing the enormity of slavery as an economic system, moreover, many focused their criticism on the slave trade, preferring to decry the cruelty of a traumatic and dehumanizing sea voyage. Ultimately, ameliorationism found solace in the vision of a more munificent institution. It was also the option of ease, as it avoided the frontal attack on slavery that more vocal abolitionists sought. Whereas some accommodationists emphasized the redemptive good of slavery, ameliorationists sought to minimize the harm done by slavery. Importantly, amelioration envisioned the continuation of slavery, albeit in kinder and gentler form. The difficulty of an effort to make the living hell of slavery more habitable notwithstanding, this approach allowed evangelicals to stand for justice in ways that minimized risk to themselves and avoided disruption to the status quo. Concern for the destiny of enslaved souls emerged with gathering force during the period of evangelical origins, when the new birth took center stage. This spiritual priority, particularly when it presented no interference to slave productivity, further bifurcated the world into spiritual and physical realms. The appeal to spiritual concerns that enabled neglect of physical enslavement nevertheless required a baseline of physical stability and relief (or amelioration) for bruised bodies.

Racial slavery in the British Empire meant that the enslaved were invariably Africans and Indians. Although whites were capable of heathenish behavior, the remedy of slavery as a kind of reforming tool was exclusively reserved for non-whites.[10] Proslavery arguments were common in the broader British context, such as in Edward Long's *History of Jamaica in Three Volumes* (1774), which described the experience of Blacks on the plantations as near "perfect freedom."[11] Gordon Turnbull's *Apology for Negro Slavery* (1786) argued, "Negro slavery appears, then, to be, as far as reason can judge, one of those indispensable and necessary links, in the great chain of causes and events, which cannot, and indeed ought not to be broken."[12] Turnbull was not alone in making the case that cultural advancement required slavery. Evangelicals added to the accumulating body of cultural sentiments by presenting theological explanations couched in a language of benevolence. In the pursuit of providential purposes, it was important to lessen the harsh extremes of a necessarily coercive institution like slavery. Amelioration thus provided guardrails against taking divine blessing too far.

In practical terms, amelioration laid bare not only the worldly compromises but also the otherworldly dualism of early evangelicals. Christianity that elevated spiritual concerns by divorcing religious goals from earthly conditions and needs exemplified the kind of rigorous asceticism that marked the spirituality of the Holy Club at Oxford, where evangelical leaders like Whitefield and the Wesley brothers first met. It would not be the last time evangelicals elevated spiritual matters at the expense of physical needs. A logical extension of the fortunate-fall thesis, the drive for amelioration dealt with the practicalities of Christian mission. At the heart of evangelical arguments for amelioration, and crucial for its justification, was a prioritization of spiritual goals, especially conversion. Evangelicals sought better physical conditions for enslaved persons so that they might be more receptive to hearing the good news of salvation. This response went beyond rationalization, however, by repudiating the more extreme, harsher versions of slavery. The desire to ameliorate the conditions of enslavement could sometimes even attach to a gradualist approach to abolition. It is significant, however, that not all ameliorationists were abolitionists.

George Whitefield's public letter to slaveholders in 1740 was an early evangelical plea for amelioration.[13] Carving out a position on benevolent, or "compassionate," slavery without reaching abolitionist conclusions, Whitefield spelled out the rationale for Christian forbearance with an imperfect institution. The paradoxical tension for this position was that amelioration expressed both antislavery sentiments and proslavery strategies. In Whitefield's case, his ameliorationist posture eventually hardened into a stridently proslavery position. To put it another way, Whitefield was careful to point out the abusive excesses of slave owners without directly criticizing the validity or viability of slavery as an institution. His call for a gentler, milder form of Christianity envisioned a more humane, and therefore more Christian, approach to slavery.

Alongside and after Whitefield, Samuel Davies worked out theological support for slavery by presenting forceful arguments for evangelizing Africans. In a sermon titled "The Duty of Christians to Propagate Their Religion Among Heathens," he argued for the humanity of enslaved persons and the universal call of faith: "Christianity, in its own Nature, is calculated to be a *catholic*, or *universal* Religion, and is equally the concern of *all* the Sons of Men. It proposes *one* God, as the Object of *universal* Adoration to White and Black, Bond and Free: *one* Lord Jesus Christ, as a *common* Saviour for Britons, Africans, and Americans."[14] Davies appealed to the Christian consciences of slaveholders, describing the conversion of Africans in bondage as a moral duty. He also shrewdly pointed out their economic interests: "Your own Interest inclines you to wish, they would become good Servants; faithful, honest, diligent and laborious."[15] According to this logic, slavery was an institution designed for the spiritual good of Africans and the economic benefit of Britons. Importantly, therefore, Davies decried harsh treatment of enslaved persons and admonished fellow believers "to not treat them with Barbarity, as if they were Dogs."[16] His reasoning was clear: their common humanity and potential to advance culturally through conversion.

In the latter half of the eighteenth century, as movements for liberty and Revolutionary upheaval reshaped European activity across the world, the need for Christians to minimize the misery of slavery took on greater urgency. More than unadulterated altruism, however, lay at the heart of amelioration. As Christopher Brown has written, "Support for slavery could become an embarrassment if and when the virtue of imperial rule became a public question. At the same time, moral capital might be accrued by framing antislavery initiatives as an emblem of the national character."[17] Brown's point that motivation for the accrual of "moral capital" lay at the heart of antislavery sentiment helps to us to understand ameliorationism as a proslavery stance that responded to the same social concerns as abolitionism, albeit with different goals. If abolitionists sought to dismantle the evils of slavery, ameliorationists wanted to minimize harm and simultaneously find ways to eke out what benefits they could.

Through the alleviation of slavery's brutality, evangelicals not only managed the feat of accommodating enslaved labor for economic profit but also manipulated the problem of slavery to advance their religious goals. Brown's analysis of evangelical motivation is illuminating: "It matters a great deal, then, that the first impulses toward reform were ameliorationist rather than abolitionist or emancipationist, that activists often aimed to make slavery more humane or more Christian, not to liberate the enslaved." In stark terms, according to Brown, to make slavery "more Christian" was the goal. Far less than a temporary compromise, many reform-minded evangelicals found no reason to dismantle slavery so long as it proved benevolent and provided opportunities for spiritual improvement. In their desire not to be distracted by worldly motives, they eschewed political factors. As Brown has argued, "The Evangelicals . . . did not set out to become abolitionists. They were concerned about slavery, but not, initially, with promoting abolition or emancipation."[18] With their concerns for the souls of the enslaved front and center, abolition became a belated goal. In the meantime, racial slavery provided a vehicle for evangelizing Africans and Native Americans, and amelioration supplied further evidence that slavery could be deployed in ways that were useful for moral respectability as well as spiritual fruit, not to mention worldly riches.

The hierarchy of values at work in amelioration becomes more comprehensible in light of the evangelical tendency to privilege spiritual aspirations over physical rewards. For many decades, winning souls had been the overriding concern, far more important than repealing slavery. According to Brown, "Only with the establishment of the Society for Effecting the Abolition of the Slave Trade in 1787, and not before, did the Wesleyans lobby actively for antislavery measures. The Wesleyans, like other Evangelicals, aimed to save souls, not change laws."[19] For early evangelicals, saving souls was not the penultimate goal but rather the crowning achievement. It is little wonder that the antislavery cause had little traction among evangelicals, when slavery provided so many spiritual blessings as well as material benefits. As George Boulukos has observed, "Amelioration seems to recognize slavery as a problem, but seeks to solve this problem through reform rather than more extreme measures such as emancipation."[20] Even if the long view of amelioration could sometimes aspire to abolition, it is hard to deny that in the short term amelioration represented a proslavery position. It envisioned the continuation of slavery in order to achieve other, more spiritual goals.

Although amelioration proved to be a stepping-stone to abolition for some evangelicals, for others the movement was in the opposite direction. The historian of slavery Ira Berlin notes this abrupt shift from antislavery to proslavery sentiment on the part of the Revolutionary generations by pointing to their worldly accommodations: "The evangelicals' antislavery moment soon passed. The preachers' opposition to slavery faltered under pressure from planters and from their own quest for respectability."[21] Not only did the proportion of Blacks enjoying freedom decline over the course of the eighteenth century but the prospects for abolition also dwindled as the exigencies of revolution and early national life took precedence. Indeed, it appears that evangelical positions toward slavery during this period were often more subject to social and political expediency and less beholden to religious conviction. At the same time, for evangelicals, who saw the world through a providential lens, there was often a hierarchy of theological values operating in the background to support these decisions and processes. In other words, evangelicals often exercised theological discernment when they made social and political accommodations for slavery.

Two prominent Methodist examples are Thomas Coke and Francis Asbury, who sought immediate abolition in the early phase of their American ministry in the late eighteenth century only to backtrack later. When they met with vociferous opposition, they relented by retreating to the ameliorationist position. Thomas Coke, in a 1795 letter to Ezekiel Cooper, wrote: "My dear brother, have great compassion for the poor Negroes, and do all you can to convert them. If they have religious liberty their temporal slavery will be comparatively but a small thing."[22] His colleague Asbury voiced a similar sentiment: "Would not an amelioration in the condition and treatment of slaves have produced more practical good to the poor Africans, than any attempt at their emancipation?"[23] In both Coke's and Asbury's letters, not only is the language of racial slavery a fundamental assumption but there is the equation of terms like *negro*, *African*, and *slave*, with the words functioning as interchangeable synonyms. In addition, perpetual racial slavery could be justified as long as these human captives experienced spiritual salvation. Their temporal slavery, insofar as it was attended by humane treatment, was a matter of minor or negligible inconvenience. Amelioration made the evangelical accommodation to slavery not only tolerable but a mark of virtue when it showcased pious restraint and generous compassion for the plight of the enslaved African.

Another example of the strident slaveholder defiance leading to an evangelical shift to ameliorationist position can be found in the Baptist leader John Leland. While some historians point to Leland as an example of an evangelical who held antislavery views, over time he came to take a neutral stance in order to avoid the sharp ecclesiastical battles that were sure to erupt. In 1789 he declared without ambivalence: "Slavery is the violent deprivation of the rights of nature, and inconsistent with republican government." By 1839 he was describing slavery as "humane, just and benevolent," advocating for the right of slave owners and government noninterference.[24] In Leland's case, as in so many other instances, the combustibility of slavery as a social and political issue forced the Baptist to take a more gradualist, nuanced position that had the effect of upholding slavery.

A respectable approach to the problem of slavery, amelioration was often a means of expressing moral outrage but also a way of avoiding the far-reaching horrors of slavery, as if alleviating some outward suffering could provide adequate compensation in the longer term. It provided a rhetorical device that enabled some white Christians to claim the moral high ground while simultaneously turning a blind eye to the tragic plight of slavery. As a position white Christians generally advocated for Black slaves, it was especially prone to paternalism, and its prescribed spiritual as well as material solutions for enduring a life in bondage was problematic. The trope of the grateful slave demonstrates the deleterious effects of amelioration. By creating conditions of enslavement that could only be construed as an improvement, white ameliorationists found positive virtue in their cautious restraint. At the same time, this work of advocacy created a greater rift between racial categories of white and Black. As Boulukos noted about this trope, "Once gratitude makes certain forms of slavery acceptable, deeper differences between master and slave begin to be implied."[25] And as we have seen with Coke, Asbury, and Leland, some evangelical leaders staked out an abolitionist position before retreating to the compromise of amelioration. They could take this backward step without legitimizing the most brutal features of slavery. Too often, evangelicals spiritualized the matter as a choice between pagan freedom and Christian slavery. With such a clear fork in the road, the moral necessity, however imperfect, of bondage in Christianity became a rallying point for some and a more pragmatic compromise for many others.

Abolition

Amelioration was not a durable position in the Age of Revolution, and evangelicals eventually came around to the cause of abolition, if for a fleeting moment. Far from a straight line of logical development, however, the actual progress toward emancipation raises numerous questions about the theological complicity of evangelicals and their relationship to racial slavery.[26] Evangelicals frequently acquiesced to forces fueled by economic, social, and political exigency.[27] As a consequence, the movement toward abolition was uneven and filled with setbacks, especially when racial thinking influenced competing priorities such as Protestant security over against slave manumission. Although some evangelicals eventually came around to the cause of abolition, only a beleaguered minority remained steadfast.

The argument that economic factors, and not humanitarian motivations, gave rise to abolition, advanced by Eric Williams in *Capitalism and Slavery* (1944), had a profound historiographical impact even if Williams's argument has enjoyed uneven reception.[28] *Capitalism and Slavery* irrevocably opened the door to a long debate among historians about the variety of factors that animated abolition by critiquing an overemphasis on "the humanitarian attack on Negro slavery."[29] Williams debunked the humanitarian narrative through an anti-imperialist lens by demonstrating how capitalism aided abolition in Britain while prolonging slavery in America. Despite his critiques of Williams and his nod to the moral force of evangelical views on slavery, David Brion Davis also saw class interests motivating evangelicals alongside moral obligation and spiritual conviction.[30] And in his book *Moral Capital,* Christopher Brown pointed out the rather negligible role of evangelicals: "Historians of antislavery, by contrast, tend now to treat the Evangelicals as of marginal interest and limited consequence."[31] Evangelical abolitionists in their time, moreover, prevaricated over the best strategy for effecting emancipation and frequently settled for half measures. When opposition grew fierce or other causes presented distractions and detours, evangelicals often shelved the issue of slavery for what they deemed to be more urgent concerns.

Put simply, evangelicalism's vexed relationship to abolition was marked by hesitancy and indecision. With an early preference for amelioration, evangelicals arrived late to abolitionism and focused much of their energy in the last decades of the eighteenth century on abolition of the slave trade, not slavery itself. This provisional and limited effectiveness of evangelical activism against slavery is often neglected in favor of a heroic narrative centering on figures like Granville Sharp and William Wilberforce. With the evidence before us, it becomes increasingly difficult to argue that evangelicals were trailblazers of antislavery reform. What Manisha Sinha has observed about leaders of the republic could be said of evangelical theologians: "Antislavery sentiment among the founding fathers may have been widespread, but committed abolitionists were few and far between."[32]

While the most influential evangelical leaders made peace with slavery, those who criticized slavery were few and largely ignored by their coreligionists for much of the eighteenth century.[33] To be sure, there were outspoken Protestants adjacent to evangelicals, Quakers like Anthony Benezet and John Woolman, who began writing public protests in the middle of the eighteenth century. Both published their first antislavery publications in 1754. Benezet's essay *An Epistle of Caution and Advice Concerning the Buying and Keeping of Slaves* inaugurated a thirty-year career of writing and lobbying against slavery. His epistolary activism began during the 1740s in correspondence with Christian leaders like George Whitefield; Selina Hastings, the Countess of Huntingdon; and others. Despite many years of disappointing fruits, Benezet sharpened and expanded his argument. He chronicled the inhumane conditions of enslaved life in the colonies, describing it as unchristian and savage. He conducted extensive research on African societies and extolled the virtues of their political, economic, and social systems. He quoted Enlightenment philosophers like Frances Hutcheson, Arthur Lee, and George Wallace and deployed natural-law arguments. This rejection of racial difference leading to racial hierarchy was rare and limited to figures like Benezet and Woolman.

John Woolman first wrote *Some Considerations on the Keeping of Negroes* in 1746 but did not publish the piece until six years later for fear that it was too controversial.[34] In this pamphlet, he condemned the hierarchy of racial difference that resulted from slavery: "Placing on men the ignominious title SLAVE, dressing them in uncomely garments, keeping them to servile labor, in which they are often dirty, tends gradually to fix a notion in the mind, that they are a sort of people below us in nature, and leads us to consider them as such in all our conclusions about them." Although Woolman articulated a clear and forceful position condemning the evils of slavery, his was a minority position and one largely ignored by fellow Christians. While evangelicals like Whitefield, Edwards, and the Countess of Huntingdon certainly knew about the tireless efforts of Quakers like Benezet and Woolman to fight the ignoble practice of slavery, their persistence made little to no difference in the public position of influential evangelicals. They remained, for much of the eighteenth century, marginalized and neglected voices in the wilderness, until the Revolutionary era.

It was a pattern that matched broader trends in the social and political climate of waging war for liberty. As Matthew Lockwood put it, "Before the American War, abolition was not merely unpromising and unlikely; one could hardly even speak of a coherent abolition movement."[35] With the outbreak of a war for independence, abolition became a much more formidable idea and even a movement. According to Seymour Drescher, the Declaration of Independence may not have explicitly named slavery and African Americans, but it "unequivocally embraced principles of individual rights to equality and liberty that were implicitly subversive of the institution of slavery."[36] In fact, Thomas Jefferson's original draft of the declaration contained an excoriating critique of Britain and George III for their guilt in "captivating and carrying [Africans] into slavery in another hemisphere, or to incur miserable death in their transportation thither."[37] The colonists could not easily avoid the contradiction of their struggle for liberty with their enslavement of Africans. As Samuel Johnson famously quipped, "If slavery be thus fatally contagious, how is it that we hear the loudest yelps for liberty among the drivers of Negroes?"[38] At the height of Revolutionary fervor, those with the least to lose ventured into abolitionist activism. Drescher has notably pointed out that states with the smallest number of slaves, such as Vermont, New Hampshire, Massachusetts, Connecticut, and Rhode Island, led the way in abolishing slavery by way of constitutional articles or judicial decisions. In broader public discourse, agitation for abolitionism quickly diminished when war came to an end. In the aftermath of the Revolution, "the United States imported far more new enslaved Africans between 1783 and 1808 than the estimated net loss of escaped and emancipated slaves during the revolutionary conflict."[39]

Evangelical engagement with abolition followed a pattern strikingly similar to that of the broader political culture. After the Quakers' long toil in the wilderness, a sudden surge in abolitionist sentiment among evangelicals occurred during the 1770s, in the period of Revolutionary fervor. Tentative forays into abolition followed the rhetoric of liberty growing ever louder during the American War of Independence. When Jonathan Edwards Jr. published several newspaper articles arguing against slavery in the fall of 1773, because of hesitancy among many Christians he decided to do so anonymously. This move is likely indicative of evangelical resistance to antislavery sentiments even on the eve of the Revolution. Finally, in 1774, after many decades of persistent encouragement from Benezet, John Wesley lent his influential voice to the antislavery movement with *Thoughts upon Slavery*. He used explicitly racial language to criticize "white" supporters of slavery, flipping the civility argument: "Whites, not Blacks, are without natural affection!"[40] His treatise mainly recapitulated arguments Benezet had been making for decades. A gratified Benezet appreciated Wesley's effort but saw room for improvement. For the American publication of Wesley's work, Benezet added five extensive footnotes as well as an afterword. If expectations for Wesley's intervention ran high, the reality was less than underwhelming. As we have already seen, Thomas Coke and Francis Asbury, his deputies in America, found it difficult to implement Wesley's belated and lofty ideals into pragmatic action in their spheres of influence in the South.

In 1775, Levi Hart (1738–1808), a New Divinity pastor in Prescot, Connecticut, published a notable sermon, "Liberty Described and Recommended," in which he not only condemned the evils of slavery but called for emancipation. In the following year, Samuel Hopkins, a key leader in the New Divinity movement, published *A Dialogue Concerning the Slavery of the Africans* (1776). In this pamphlet, he highlighted "the inconsistence of promoting the slavery of the Africans, at the same time we are asserting our own civil liberty."[41] Hopkins' theological arguments confronted the racial prejudice of his white coreligionists. He insisted on the importance of seeing Blacks as "by nature and by right, on a level with our brethren and children, and . . . our neighbors."[42]

The newfound vigor of evangelical abolitionist sentiment in the 1770s—evinced in these three prominent missives dispatched in quick succession, appearing as they did after a veritable decades-long drought—warrants closer scrutiny, especially for the ways social pressures and political exigency influenced the leading evangelical voices. Joseph Conforti's study of the New Divinity movement is helpful when he reminds readers how contextual factors shaped Hopkins's antislavery position: "The importance of Hopkins's antislavery stand, then, does not stem from a heroic solitariness. Rather, it originates in the comprehensiveness of his arguments against the slave trade and slavery, their derivation from New Divinity theology and social criticism, and their linkage to the republican political thought of the Revolution."[43] Conforti's assessment helpfully identifies both theological and political reasons for the gathering strength of Protestant support for abolition in the 1770s. The synergistic connection also limited the long-term viability of evangelical abolitionism in the North American context. When political interest in abolition died down, so did religious support.

The concurrence of evangelical involvement and Revolutionary rhetoric came as a result of evangelicals sensing not only divine leading but also social and political pressure to speak out on slavery. It is worth pointing out that the most concentrated burst of evangelical abolition in the eighteenth century came not at the height of revival fervor but amid Revolutionary ferment, at a time when many public voices were pointing out the inconsistency of the agitation for liberty in the context of a slave society. The moral weight of indictments against Christian hypocrisy regarding slavery were real and difficult to avoid in the Age of Revolution.

At the same time, any study of early evangelical support for abolition must recognize that in the early years of the new republic, evangelical zeal for emancipation witnessed an abrupt about-face. It was not long before the cause of antislavery gave way to proslavery sentiment once more. As one explanation for this trajectory, in a study that sought to reintroduce the role of the Edwardseans in the New Divinity in antislavery debates, Kenneth Minkema and Harry Stout pointed out that "most white Edwardseans were racists. They were disgusted by the prospect of a mixed-race society, feared 'amalgamation,' and so favored colonization, for which New England Congregationalism was a seedbed."[44] Rather than treating this racism as an extraneous feature of evangelicalism in the eighteenth century, it is important to consider the possibility that the idea of racial hierarchy was deeply embedded in the spiritual and theological heart of early evangelicals. When we identify racial thinking actively at work in both proslavery and antislavery sentiments of early evangelicalism, it is easier to make sense of the ebbs and flows in evangelical abolitionism.

Meanwhile, the cause of abolition in Britain advanced steadily, and while some evangelicals participated, they were not the primary figures. In America, despite the three-fifths compromise of the Constitutional Convention, abolition met significant legal success in the Northern states. Vermont was the first state to abolish slavery, in 1777, to be followed by the remaining New England states within the following seven years. Following suit, Rhode Island and Connecticut also abolished slavery in 1784.[45] Enslaved persons, moreover, were not passive onlookers in the fight for abolition despite the severe obstacles they faced. The variety of options available to them included flight, lawsuits against their owners, nonviolent resistance, inciting riots, engaging in scientific and philosophical debates, and presenting arguments based on faith and theology. As Manisha Sinha has shown, "African Americans were not silent spectators to (the many) controversies" that surrounded slave resistance.[46] The activism of enslaved and free Black persons like Elizabeth Freeman, Ottobah Cugoano, Olaudah Equiano, Phillis Wheatley, James Mars, and countless others was crucial. Jupiter Hammon turned the tables on white slave owners and questioned their Christianity.[47] Peter Hanson, a free Black man, highlighted the moral problem of slavery in a novel way when he sought to divorce his enslaved wife, Venus. By seeking separation from a system that would trap his children in slavery, Hanson forced white lawmakers to face the difficult moral conundrums precipitated by slavery. The choice, clear for Hanson, was much more complicated for white slaveholders. Black abolitionists were "steeped in the idioms and ideas of their times" but also "developed alternative and oppositional understandings of Christianity and revolutionary republicanism to criticize both slavery and racism."[48] In other words, sometimes Africans Christians could not help reinscribing racial categories, while at other times they found ways to resist and transcend the chains of bondage, both physical and spiritual.

In addition to the limited work of white evangelicals in the slave's cause for abolition, it is important to foreground evangelicals of color and their efforts for reform. Moreover, it is unhelpful to assert that Christianity was intrinsically antislavery in the period of early evangelicalism, when theological arguments remained unresolved into the middle of the nineteenth century in North America. As David Brion Davis has argued, "A fortunate convergence of economic, political, and ideological circumstances" helped the cause of abolition.[49] Attempts to uncritically link abolition with evangelicalism's innate theological virtue must therefore contend with multiple mitigating factors. Further study is needed to understand how and why early evangelicals worked for abolition, but we also need to remember the ways in which they set their hearts against emancipation. When evangelicals belatedly rallied around second-wave abolitionism in greater numbers, the theological rationale was one, arguably minor, factor among others. David Brion Davis, for instance, has highlighted the impulse toward ennobling labor as the most important driving factor behind abolition. In Davis's words, "By the late eighteenth century there was a pressing need felt by both skilled workers and employers to dignify and even ennoble wage labor, which for ages had been regarded with contempt."[50] For our purposes, it is important to note that with the exception of a few solitary voices in the wilderness who went neglected and sometimes derided, abolition arose late, and faltered almost immediately, in the world of early evangelicalism.

Reparation

Finally, for those who spoke of emancipation, merely abolishing slavery was far from sufficient, as emancipation would bring a fresh set of challenges. Abolitionists faced the anxiety of those who wondered how a large, free Black population would disrupt and endanger the social order. Recognizing the far-reaching devastation of slavery, some began casting about for ways to provide practical aid to emancipated persons. Too often, emancipation segued into a new kind of suffering, merely illustrating the profound effects of slavery's harm. Whereas Quakers in the mid-eighteenth century wanted to think creatively about incorporating free Africans into American life, it became more common for evangelicals in the last decades of the century to explore possibilities of sending free Black people to Africa. This turn toward colonization schemes presented practical as well as theoretical challenges. The disjointed, often dysfunctional early initiatives toward reparation can help us understand the state of disarray in which antislavery advocates labored in the period of early evangelicalism.

Samuel Hopkins is often hailed as a man ahead of his times in his calls for immediate emancipation. In fact, Minkema and Stout go so far as to say of both Hopkins and Lemuel Haynes that they were "so far ahead of their times that our own is barely catching up."[51] One might agree with this sentiment and still find objectionable details in Hopkins's own words as he described the promise of sending free African slaves, some of whom had been in America for generations, back to Africa: "This will gradually draw off all the blacks in New England, and even in the Middle and Southern States, as fast as they can be set free, by which this nation will be delivered from that which, in the view of every discerning man, is a great calamity, and inconsistent with the good of society, and is now really a great injury to most of the white inhabitants, especially in the Southern States."[52] The theologian's overriding concern for "a great injury to most of the white inhabitants" and the way in which he describes the desirability of removing Blacks from America serves as a sober reminder of how deeply embedded racial hierarchy was in his lifetime. Hopkins is careful to locate the cause of African inferiority in the "situation" and the "treatment" they have received in America. It is nevertheless the case that he saw Black and white interests as being opposed, or at the very least heading in different directions.

In a letter dated January 16, 1789, Hopkins wrote to Granville Sharp noting that Blacks would remain "unhappy, while they live here among the whites; the latter looking down upon them, and being disposed to treat them as underlings, and denying them the advantages of education and employment, &c., which tends to depress their minds and prevent their obtaining a comfortable living, etc."[53] In rich detail, Hopkins described racism in his town and likely also in his church community, where an unbridgeable chasm of division existed between Blacks and whites. At least for Hopkins, the problem was so deep that the solution of sending Blacks born in America back to Africa presented the more hopeful, feasible way forward. According to Conforti, "This new emphasis in his antislavery thought was a response to the realization that most whites were far from ready to view Africans as part of Being in general."[54] In addition to physical and social barriers, there were spiritual and metaphysical dividing lines that Blacks could not overcome. David Brion Davis remarked on the problematic nature of this new form of racial thought, "particularly the bedrock assumption that the blacks' degradation in America was irremediable and permanent."[55] This incipient racism was an unavoidable stain embedded in the colonization scheme. There was a concession and a compromise that Blacks could not fit into white society.

Even for devoted proponents of the antislavery cause like Hopkins, racial hierarchy was a deeply embedded, seemingly immovable force in social relations. As planning for colonization proceeded, Hopkins found himself in the unenviable position of making additional moral judgments about the worthiness of individuals for the overseas project. Organizers like Sharp and Zachary Macaulay emphasized the need for healthy and moral Africans, lest they discredit the work in Africa. There was also the problem of white backsliding: "Sharp notified Hopkins that many of the whites who had been sent to aid the settlement had become involved in the slave trade."[56] In all these ways, the spirit of evangelical abolition proved difficult to maintain in the post-Revolutionary era.

In conclusion, evangelicals' commitment to the antislavery cause came four decades after the dawn of evangelicalism. Once it did appear, their commitment to abolition was indebted to numerous social, economic, and political factors mainly having to do with Revolutionary fervor. And just as suddenly as it emerged, it faded in the years following the Revolution. Seymour Drescher's words about the removal of Jefferson's condemnation of slavery from the Declaration of Independence may also apply to the relationship between evangelicalism and abolition: "The deletion itself was a harbinger of the fate of the problem of slavery in America for half a century to come."[57] Far from being intrepid, pioneering activists, evangelical leaders struggled to articulate a clear antislavery position. More often than not, they elected to circumvent the problem of slavery. Despite auspicious beginnings in the Revolutionary era, efforts for abolition gave way to an uneasy accommodation of slavery. Evangelicals' halting steps led to ongoing theological rationalizations that contributed to a steady resurgence of proslavery arguments in the nineteenth century.

This essay's typological survey of evangelical responses to slavery makes it possible to discern a roughly chronological trajectory. Since its inception, American evangelicalism has contained forces supporting and constraining freedom. A movement toward intensifying resistance to slavery bogged down during the post-Revolutionary years in deep and abiding ambiguity. While rationalization and amelioration were proslavery positions that represented broad evangelical consensus, abolition and reparation reflected a partial transition among evangelical attitudes shifting toward antislavery that would eventually lead to equivocation and erupt in open conflict. That revolutionary fervor overcame early evangelical ambivalence shows the inherent resources within evangelicalism for social action and its dependence on external social factors to catalyze such latent potential. Showcasing a fleeting moment of possibility, the rise and fall of evangelical abolition in the Age of Revolution point to the ongoing contradictions in evangelical Protestantism that continued to reverberate well into the nineteenth century.

Notes

1. For the leading historian of slavery David Brion Davis, the relationship between evangelicals and slavery was complex and evolved over time. His earlier works emphasized the central role of evangelical religion in abolition, whereas in later works he offered more nuanced analysis of evangelical tendencies toward paternalism and racism. For examples of the former, see David Brion Davis, *The Problem of Slavery in Western Culture* (Ithaca, NY: Cornell University Press, 1966); and Davis, *The Problem of Slavery in the Age of Revolution, 1770–1823* (Ithaca, NY: Cornell University Press, 1975). For examples of the latter, see Davis, *Inhuman Bondage: The Rise and Fall of Slavery in the New World* (New York: Oxford University Press, 2006); and Davis, *The Problem of Slavery in the Age of Emancipation* (New York: Knopf, 2014). Works that more directly align evangelicals with abolition include Gilbert Hobbs Barnes, *The Antislavery Impulse: 1830–1844* (New York: Harcourt, Brace, 1933); Roger Anstey, *The Atlantic Slave Trade and British Abolition, 1760–1810* (London: Macmillan, 1975); Ann M. Burton, "British Evangelicals, Economic Warfare, and the Abolition of the Atlantic Slave Trade, 1794–1810," *Anglican and Episcopal History* 65, no. 2 (1996):

197–225; David Herbert Donald, "Toward a Reconsideration of Abolitionists," in *Lincoln Reconsidered: Essays on the Civil War Era* (New York: Random House, 1956), 19–36; Dwight Dumond, *Antislavery Origins of the Civil War* (Ann Arbor: University of Michigan Press, 1940); and Anne C. Loveland, "Evangelicalism and 'Immediate Emancipation' in American Antislavery Thought," *Journal of Southern History* 32, no. 2 (May 1966): 172–88. Interestingly and more recently, John Coffey's probing works on evangelicalism and abolition also appear to have shifted from a more humanitarian emphasis that highlighted evangelicals' "prophetic abolitionism" to a more ambiguous and guarded evaluation. In 2014, he focused "on how readers have used the liberation narrative of the Book of Exodus rather than the conquest narrative of the Book of Joshua." Coffey, *Exodus and Liberation: Deliverance Politics from John Calvin to Martin Luther King Jr.* (Oxford: Oxford University Press, 2014), 15. Ten years later, he appears more willing to acknowledge "ambiguities" in Wilberforce's legacy, at one point admitting, "Here we see the ambiguities of Christian abolitionism on full display." Coffey, "William Wilberforce and the Ambiguities of Christian Antislavery," in *Control, Coercion, and Constraint: The Role of Religion in Overcoming and Creating Structures of Dependency*, ed. Wolfram Kinzig and Barbara Loose (Berlin: Walter de Gruyter, 2024), 315. In addition to these academic works, a number of popular books have vigorously advanced the key role of heroic evangelical leaders in abolition, with the spotlight usually given to the Clapham Sect and heroic leaders like William Wilberforce. See Kevin Belmonte, *William Wilberforce: A Hero for Humanity* (Grand Rapids, MI: Zondervan, 2009); Eric Metaxas, *Amazing Grace: William Wilberforce and the Heroic Campaign to End Slavery* (Grand Rapids, MI: Zondervan, 2007); and John Piper, *The Roots of Endurance: Invincible Perseverance in the Lives of John Newton, Charles Simeon, and William Wilberforce* (Wheaton, IL: Crossway Books, 2006). This essay problematizes both the chronology and the credibility of the Clarkson Thesis; for more on the humanitarian argument, see Thomas Clarkson, *The History of the Rise, Progress, and Accomplishment of the Abolition of the African Slave-Trade by the British Parliament* (London: R. Taylor and Co., Shoe-Lane, 1808).

2. Padraic Scanlan's recent book challenges the Clarkson Thesis by showing how economic and military factors like the rise of Napoleon in France and rebellion and subsequent stabilization in Haiti animated British antislavery as a means of foiling external threats. He specifically identifies the ways evangelical religion both supported and constrained the cause of freedom: "British antislavery flowed in complicated ways from Evangelicalism, the Enlightenment and the rise of sensibility. It both rejected empire and imagined a new imperialism." His charge that "the campaign against the slave trade is too often remembered as a unique and exceptional achievement, as

evidence that for all its warts, the British empire wasn't all that bad," points to the need for a similar work of critical history with regard to American antislavery. Padraic X. Scanlan, *Slave Empire: How Slavery Built Modern Britain* (London: Little, Brown Book Group, 2020), 161, 186–87.

3. Katharine Gerbner, *Christian Slavery: Conversion and Race in the Protestant Atlantic World* (Philadelphia: University of Pennsylvania Press, 2018).
4. Theodore M. Vial, *Modern Religion, Modern Race* (Oxford: Oxford University Press, 2016), 1. On race as a historical construct, historians like Edmund Morgan and Theodore Allen have presented arguments for a "socio-economic approach." Theodore W. Allen, *The Invention of the White Race*, vols. 1 and 2 (London: Verso, 1994, 1997); Edmund S. Morgan, *American Slavery, American Freedom* (New York: Norton, 2003). Other scholars have presented theoretical frameworks for racial formation. See Michael Omi and Howard Winant, *Racial Formation in the United States* (New York: Routledge, 2014); and Gary Y. Okihiro, *Third World Studies: Theorizing Liberation* (Durham, NC: Duke University Press, 2016). This essay draws on both historical and theoretical approaches to trace links between evolving views of slavery and race.
5. Numerous works have noted evangelical retreat from short-lived abolitionist commitments. Donald Mathews observed: "The violent reaction of Carolinians and the inaction of ministers in the upper South revealed that antislavery activity in the South as early as 1800 was neither prudent nor easy. The revolutionary ideals of freedom, the enlightened belief in equality, and the Christian affirmation of suffering love were neither widespread nor powerful enough to command men to love or free a race which many believed unequal to their own." Mathews, *Methodism and Slavery* (Princeton, NJ: Princeton University Press, 1965), 22. Rachel Klein has argued that as backcountry farmers and low-country elites in South Carolina united around the cause of slaveholding, evangelicals largely followed suit: "Rather than challenging slavery, the evangelical churches that expanded with cotton and slaves though the backcountry mediated the uneasy relationship between planters and yeomen and did what they could to locate slaves in a broader network of unequal familial bonds." Klein, *Unification of a Slave State: The Rise of the Planter Class in the South Carolina Backcountry, 1760–1808* (Chapel Hill: University of North Carolina Press, 1990). Christine Heyrman has noted that "by 1784 the Methodists had given over any efforts to bar slaveholders from their fellowship." In her view, they abandoned abolition because "nothing meant more to them than reclaiming white souls and nearly any concession to the South's ruling race could be justified in the name of that end." Heyrman, *Southern Cross: The Beginnings of the Bible Belt* (New York: Knopf, 1997), 76, 92. In contrast to Heyrman, who detected a shift in evangelical attitudes toward antislavery, Jewel Spangler in her study

of Baptists in Virginia saw broad and sustained agreement between evangelicals and their contemporaries: "New Light Presbyterians were consistently protective of the institution of slavery, which was both a relation of the household and the fundamental labor relation of the colony." Spangler, *Virginians Reborn: Anglican Monopoly, Evangelical Dissent, and the Rise of the Baptists in the Late Eighteenth Century* (Charlottesville: University of Virginia Press, 2008). Other pertinent works that discuss evangelical support in the post-Revolutionary years through the antebellum period include David Bailey, *Shadow on the Church: Southwestern Evangelical Religion and the Issue of Slavery, 1783–1860* (Ithaca, NY: Cornell University Press, 1985); Charles F. Irons, *The Origins of Proslavery Christianity: White and Black Evangelicals in Colonial and Antebellum Virginia* (Chapel Hill: University of North Carolina Press, 2008); and Anne C. Loveland, *Southern Evangelicals and the Social Order, 1800–1860* (Baton Rouge: Louisiana State University Press, 1980).

6. Rebecca Anne Goetz, *The Baptism of Early Virginia: How Christianity Created Race* (Baltimore: John Hopkins University Press, 2016).
7. Irons, *Origins of Proslavery Christianity*, 18.
8. James D. Essig, *The Bonds of Wickedness: American Evangelicals Against Slavery, 1770–1808* (Philadelphia: Temple University Press, 1982), 5.
9. Goetz, *Baptism of Early Virginia*, 89.
10. Rebecca Goetz has written about incidents of cannibalism and the embrace of atheism among early settlers in Virginia: "To make matters worse, there was abundant evidence that the English themselves seemed to be sliding into heathenism." Goetz, *Baptism of Early Virginia*, 42.
11. Quoted in Stefan M. Wheelock, *Barbaric Culture and Black Critique: Black Antislavery Writers, Religion, and the Slaveholding Atlantic* (Charlottesville: University of Virginia Press, 2015), 37.
12. Gordon Turnbull, *An Apology for Negro Slavery: Or the West-India Planters Vindicated from the Charge of Inhumanity. By the author of Letters to a Young Planter* (London: J. Stevenson, Martlet-Court, 1786), 34–35.
13. George Whitefield, *A Letter to the Inhabitants of Maryland, Virginia, North and South-Carolina* (Philadelphia, 1740).
14. Samuel Davies, *A Sermon Preached in Hanover, January 8, 1757: The Duty of Christians to Propagate Their Religion Among Heathens.* (London: J. Oliver, 1758), 14.
15. Davies, *Duty of Christians*, 27.
16. Davies, *Duty of Christians*, 46.
17. Christopher Leslie Brown, *Moral Capital: Foundations of British Abolitionism* (Chapel Hill: Published for the Omohundro Institute of Early American History and Culture, Williamsburg, VA, by the University of North Carolina Press, 2006), 27.

18. Brown, *Moral Capital*, 28, 335.
19. Brown, *Moral Capital*, 339.
20. George Boulukos, *The Grateful Slave: The Emergence of Race in Eighteenth-Century British and American Culture* (Cambridge: Cambridge University Press, 2012), 10.
21. Ira Berlin, *Generations of Captivity: A History of African-American Slaves* (Cambridge, MA: Harvard University Press, 2009), 118.
22. Thomas Coke to Ezekiel Cooper, April 23, 1795, in *The Letters of Dr. Thomas Coke*, ed. John A. Vickers (Nashville: Abingdon, 2013), 200.
23. *The Journal and Letters of Francis Asbury*, ed. Elmer Clark, J. Manning Potts, and Jacob S. Payton (London: Epworth, 1958); 2:591, also quoted in Essig, *Bonds of Wickedness*, 125.
24. Bruce Gourley, "John Leland: Evolving Views of Slavery, 1789–1839: In 1789, the General Committee of Virginia Baptists Turned to Massachusetts Native John Leland to Craft a Statement concerning Slavery," *Baptist History and Heritage* 40, no. 1 (Winter 2005): 104.
25. Boulukos, *Grateful Slave*, 15.
26. For works that argue for strong causal connections between early evangelicalism and abolition, see Anstey, *Atlantic Slave Trade and British Abolition*; and Steven E. Woodworth, *Manifest Destinies: America's Westward Expansion and the Road to the Civil War* (2010; reprint, New York: Knopf Doubleday Publishing Group, 2011).
27. James Essig observed that "evangelicals began to lose interest in the slavery issue in the early nineteenth century" precisely for these reasons. Essig, *Bonds of Wickedness*, xii.
28. Eric Williams, *Capitalism and Slavery* (Chapel Hill: University of North Carolina Press, 1944). I am grateful to the anonymous reader for the University of Virginia Press who pointed me to H. Reuben Neptune, "Throwin' Scholarly Shade: Eric Williams in the New Histories of Capitalism and Slavery," *Journal of the Early Republic* 39, no. 2 (2019): 299–326. That article also cites Williams's seminal article "Laissez Faire, Sugar and Slavery," *Political Science Quarterly* 58, no. 1 (1943): 67–85. Neptune argues that where recent historical arguments cite Williams to emphasize the incompatibility between capitalism and slavery, Williams actually anticipated postcolonial arguments by elucidating the evolving, complex relationship between capitalism and slavery.
29. Williams, "Laissez Faire, Sugar and Slavery," 67.
30. David Brion Davis, *Inhuman Bondage: The Rise and Fall of Slavery in the New World* (Oxford: Oxford University Press, 2008), 379. For Davis's evolving interpretation of Eric Williams, see Neptune, "Throwin' Scholarly Shade," 307n15.
31. Brown, *Moral Capital*, 379.

32. Manisha Sinha, *The Slave's Cause: A History of Abolition* (New Haven, CT: Yale University Press, 2016), 41.
33. As Sinha aptly put it, "Not all Quakers were antislavery, but most abolitionists in the British colonies were Quakers." Sinha, *Slave's Cause*, 12.
34. *The Complete Antislavery Writings of Anthony Benezet, 1754–1783: An Annotated Critical Edition*, ed. David L. Crosby (Baton Rouge: Louisiana State University Press, 2014), 6.
35. Matthew Lockwood, *To Begin the World Over Again: How the American Revolution Devastated the Globe* (New Haven, CT: Yale University Press, 2019), 383.
36. Seymour Drescher, *Abolition: A History of Slavery and Antislavery* (Cambridge: Cambridge University Press, 2009), 124.
37. Quoted in Drescher, *Abolition*, 124.
38. Samuel Johnson, *Taxation No Tyranny: An Answer to the Resolutions and Address of the American Congress* (London: T. Cadell, 1775), 89.
39. Drescher, *Abolition*, 127.
40. John Wesley, *Thoughts upon Slavery* (London: R. Hawes, 1774), 20.
41. Samuel Hopkins, quoted in Joseph A. Conforti, *Samuel Hopkins and the New Divinity Movement: Calvinism and Reform in New England Between the Great Awakenings* (Eugene, OR: Wipf & Stock, 2008), 128. Kenneth Minkema and Harry Stout have argued that Hopkins's record challenges the idea that Revolutionary ideas and republican ideology influenced religious involvement in abolitionism. Instead, "disinterested benevolence" was the theological idea that led to what Bernard Bailyn called a political "contagion of liberty." Minkema and Stout, "The Edwardsean Tradition and the Antislavery Debate, 1740–1865," *Journal of American History* 92, no. 1 (2005): 47; Bailyn, *The Ideological Origins of the American Revolution* (Cambridge, MA: Harvard University Press, 1967).
42. Quoted in Conforti, *Samuel Hopkins and the New Divinity Movement*, 129.
43. Conforti, *Samuel Hopkins and the New Divinity Movement*, 128.
44. Minkema and Stout, "Edwardsean Tradition and the Antislavery Debate," 62.
45. Sinha, *Slave's Cause*, 72–74.
46. Sinha, *Slave's Cause*, 73.
47. Sinha, *Slave's Cause*; Wheelock, *Barbaric Culture and Black Critique.*
48. Sinha, *Slave's Cause*, 47.
49. Davis, *Inhuman Bondage*, 249.
50. Davis, *Inhuman Bondage*, 248.
51. Minkema and Stout, "Edwardsean Tradition and the Antislavery Debate," 72.
52. Samuel Hopkins, *The Works of Samuel Hopkins, D.D. . . .*, 3 vols. (Boston: Doctrinal Tract and Book Society, 1852–54), 2:611.

53. Samuel Hopkins to Granville Sharp, January 16, 1789, quoted in Conforti, *Samuel Hopkins and the New Divinity Movement*, 151.
54. Conforti, *Samuel Hopkins and the New Divinity Movement*, 148.
55. Davis, *Inhuman Bondage*, 258.
56. Conforti, *Samuel Hopkins and the New Divinity Movement*, 152.
57. Drescher, *Abolition*, 125.

"Every House a Church and State"

Piety, Authority, and the Problem of Family Governance in the Early Republic

SHELBY M. BALIK

★

To those who viewed the temporal world through spiritual lenses, the American victory over Great Britain carried many blessings. Citizens of the new nation generally agreed with a Presbyterian minister who wrote that "the acknowledged *independence* of *America* is an event that engages the eager attention of all *Christendom*," for it "secured those civil and religious liberties which are unknown in any other part of the globe."[1] But while the ideals of liberty seemed to have triumphed, independence was fraught with danger, and the euphoria of victory was tempered by caution. Perceived threats lurked everywhere, from the French Revolution's violent remains to bitter partisanship and corruption at home. Fragile church-state ties imperiled social order and appeared to nudge the republic toward anarchy. The task of building a nation was daunting, and its success was uncertain.

In this context, many Americans began to question whether victory and independence could, on their own, support a godly polity. Ministers—especially reformed Protestant clergy, who tended to see the nation's cosmic and political fates as intertwined—fretted about "the absurdities of irreligion" and mourned "the declension from the piety of our fathers."[2] God's will, they argued, would reveal itself only in a system built on virtue: a combination of wisdom, self-discipline, and disinterested benevolence that supported citizenship.[3] To promote virtue, the clergy employed a framework for a godly polity that intertwined providentialism, republicanism, and moral government. Urging Americans to welcome

God's interventions in human affairs, evangelical ministers connected the nation's spiritual destiny to its perceived political vulnerabilities. They argued that republicanism could fulfill divine will only if it acted against self-interest and supported God's preference for a benevolent polity.[4] Applying theories of virtue and vice to a nascent national self-image, ministers urged Americans to practice godliness for the greater good. They suggested that only a pious people could shoulder the burdens of independence, and they wondered about the republic's collective soul. What good was self-governance if the nation's spiritual core was rotten?

The republic's salvation, many Americans—and especially reformed Protestant ministers—were convinced, depended on the patriotic efforts of pious families. Accordingly, they called upon households to revive family worship to serve God and the republic. Family worship—including prayer, devotional reading, catechism, and godly discourse—fell within the realm of family governance, the means by which householders trained and disciplined subordinates.[5] The practice reinforced householders' supremacy; by leading their charges in devotion, they cultivated piety along with obedience.

After independence, the reformed Protestant clergy sought to reinforce family governance in a republic that many feared teetered toward collapse. They hoped to address two overlapping crises: one of the state, in which the fragile nation could succumb to disunion and democracy; and the other of families, in which liberty run amok could upend householders' authority. By promoting virtue among families, ministers hoped to reverse what they saw as a collapse of spiritual manhood: a decline in masters' piety that would sap their power over small domains, and by extension the nation. As the clergy grappled with how the body politic of the state intersected with the body politic of a family, they fixed their attention on family worship. If householders were entrusted with domestic religious supremacy, they might serve the state by restoring order.

The early republican evangelical clergy placed family prayer at the center of a new theory and practice of religion, which we may call republican Christianity—that is, a faith that promoted liberty and order by reinforcing citizens' patriarchal authority, as befit a godly polity.[6] A republic, ministers insisted, depended upon householders' stewardship of prayerful families. As miniature communities, families could train up citizens. As miniature churches, they could teach piety. In both capacities, they could teach self-restraint even as licentiousness threatened order. In the American Revolution's wake, the nation needed families to serve the public through prayer.

THE CLERGY'S idea that family worship would bolster both God and the state was based on an ideal of family governance that tied piety to patriotism. At its core lay two tensions that ministers sought to hold in balance: that between liberty and order and that between mastery and dependence. The republic needed to balance liberty with order to avoid excessive democracy or absolutism; it needed to balance mastery and dependence so that husbands and fathers could exercise authority while exhibiting good citizenship.[7] Householders' stewardship, then, was crucial to the nation's success.[8] Americans thought of families as building blocks of the polity, each "family a little community within itself; of which . . . states and kingdoms are composed."[9] Householders, modeling virtue, could employ family religion to contain excess and nurture a pious republic.

The clergy urged families to preserve godliness in a republic founded on liberty. With an underpinning in family prayer, they promised, "your sons will be good citizens of a free country [and] friends to the languishing church of God." Christian men could serve as "good jury-men," "good magistrates," and "discerning and faithful" voters.[10] The nation could trust pious servants to act with virtue, safeguarding "precious liberty and privilege for the soul."[11] Americans in the Calvinist tradition understood a virtuous citizenry in part through the lens of the theology of grace, which promised divine favor if Americans sacrificed personal gain for the greater good.[12] If the United States had a place in God's plan—if it was what one minister called "*our* Jerusalem"[13]—then citizens had to defend the nation's virtue along with their own liberties.

If godliness fostered liberty, so too did it secure order. The American Revolution had transformed the state, stripping away older constraints. But the household remained a pillar of authority. The *Piscataqua Evangelical Magazine* noted parallels between the family and the nation; in both, "we find those who are to govern, and those who are to be governed . . . those who are to make laws and regulations, and those who ought, when these are equitable and just, to yield obedience to them."[14] Family governance, accordingly, became instrumental to teaching republican habits of mind: self-discipline, civic-mindedness, and communal obligation.[15] Household by household, families could prepare a new generation to uphold social order.

Householders fostered order by exercising mastery—benevolent leadership that bolstered their supremacy. Citizenship and mastery were inherently masculine prerogatives; the republic required male citizens to carry out both with authority.[16] When voting rights hinged on property ownership, citizens acted as stewards—and stewardship began at home, where masters oversaw dependents' labor, worship, and conduct. Family prayer elevated masters' status, so they might apply a firm hand by directing prayer and encouraging pious obedience. They served as ministers by proxy; through masters, the clergy could reassert their authority as they guided the republic through spiritual trial.

Mastery and dependence were two sides of the same coin, for dependents accorded householders the authority that made them masters. Dependence had a long history in North America, where there were more servants, enslaved people, and (with higher fertility rates) children at home than in British households. After the American Revolution, slavery expanded, dower rights declined, women's Revolutionary political gains reversed, and children lived longer with their parents; these factors placed more people under householders' watch. State laws extended masters' control over dependents, who, despite using rhetoric of natural rights to petition for liberty, gained little traction.[17] Mastery continued as a matter of custom and law.

Perhaps because dependency was on the rise in an age of independence, the evangelical clergy fretted that masters were losing control. A prayerless house, they warned, was a "*synagogue of Satan*," in which children would bring shame upon their parents and inflict corruption on society.[18] Accordingly, members of households—fathers, mothers, children, servants, and enslaved people—needed to understand their place within the familial hierarchy. Exercising proper leadership, heads of families could reinforce piety along with discipline, self-restraint, and submission. Ministers, fearing the republic was vulnerable to corruption, appealed to householders to help order the republic through family prayer.

ALTHOUGH FAMILY worship converged with ideologies of republicanism and mastery, it was not an abstract political theory. It was also the foundation of practical religion: daily ritual to perform piety. It included religious education, which reinforced relationships that were both intimate and authoritarian. The clergy urged parents to strengthen these ties by directing family prayer.[19] They published a cascade of catechisms, hymnals, and sermons for household use, guides that buttressed mastery by making visible familial ties of authority and submission. Prayer and catechism supported the family hierarchy because they were inherently didactic, with one person instructing the others. Through daily practice, members of households acted out duty and mastery in tangible ways, befitting their assigned roles.

First among family members were husbands and fathers, whose duty it was to exercise benevolent and virtuous stewardship. Most family prayer books addressed them directly. Ministers insisted that a father's most important role was to lead by example. A Massachusetts minister reminded householders that "as a man," one should "maintain a strict Temperance and sobriety, by a wise Government of your Appetites and Passions."[20] Embracing self-discipline, householders might approach family prayer with the proper temperament. Thomas Clark, a New York Presbyterian, suggested that fathers exercise their duties patiently, for those with a "fiery temper" might act like "rigid petty tyrants," enraging children and servants, turning them against faith.[21] Better to lead with a kind but firm hand, so subordinates would comply.

After all, families' spiritual fate lay in fathers' hands. One minister implied that householders might "bring it upon themselves" when they faced "the disobedience, the unkindness, the unfaithfulness, or the wickedness of any in their families."[22] Another pointed out that family prayer would be "particularly advantageous to the Master of a Family himself," for it would preserve household order. "Promoting a Sense of Religion in his House," he insisted, would serve a master's "temporal Interest, it being observed that the more careful Persons are in discharging their Duty toward God, the more conscientious they are in discharging their Duty toward Man."[23] It followed that fathers should secure their charges' spiritual welfare.

Like fathers, mothers were to manage their children's and servants' spiritual lives. But they were not their husbands' equals; rather, they were junior partners who supported their spouses' authority. Descriptions of women's domestic duties reflected broader shifts in thinking about their roles. Whereas older customs had included women in the fray of Revolutionary politics, early republican culture placed civic-minded wives and mothers at home, nurturing citizens.[24] Ministers who prescribed family worship embraced the ideology of republican womanhood, using new ideals of women's virtues to define their duties. Ebenezer Thayer, who described husbands as "the head of the family as well as of the wife," insisted they should expect their wives' "love and respect" so that "nothing may occur to bring on . . . that bitterness and strife, which will greatly hurt the religious worship of the family."[25] It was incumbent on wives to smooth domestic conflicts so that their husbands' mastery would continue unabated.

Marriage conferred spiritual power on women. Wives were, in the terminology of Douglas Winiarski, the "chief providers" of the "household's religious economy," who safeguarded their families' spiritual welfare.[26] As Judith Sargent Murray observed, "The door of science [may be] barred to us," but "the path of truth . . . in the page of *revelation* lies open before us." Women, she suggested, were well equipped to devote "a sacred attention to those interests that are crowned with immortality."[27] The clergy, too, lauded republican women, praising their "national virtue and amazing industry." Godly women were "the powerful bond that binds the whole family together, with the golden chain of love."[28] Republican mothers could apply civic virtues, to their families' eternal benefit.

But ministers' rhetoric about women's virtues belied anxiety about their latent powers to corrupt. Alongside praise for godly helpmeets appeared warnings about the sinful woman, who was "a tigress," "grief to [her husband's] heart," "a tyrant to his servants," and "ruin to his children"; such women were "heathen mothers" who "never . . . pray" and were "no more than brutes."[29] Such language reflected visceral fear of women's sin. Whereas Americans viewed men's sin as a product of corrupt behavior, women's sin was rooted in a weak spiritual core, making them vulnerable to corruption that could tear down homes, churches, and a republic.[30] Christian women could serve as helpmeets, support family prayer, and educate children, but they needed masculine authority to contain their vile impulses.

Christian parents were expected to raise Christian children. Although church attendance likely figured into most children's experiences, religious education took place primarily at home, under parents' direction.[31] Ministers believed that threats to youthful piety lurked everywhere: the "evil of Sin," "irreligion and wickedness," and "profane language."[32] But householders who practiced family prayer "commonly live[d] in love and good agreement" with children who were "more obedient, submissive, and towardly in their behavior."[33] Using republican language, the Charleston (South Carolina) Baptist Association urged parents to nurture children's piety. "To govern by consent is the best method of exercising power in all kinds of government," they suggested, including in the home. Accordingly, parents should exercise "prudence . . . to lead [children] to the knowledge and practice of true religion" so they would become "useful members of society."[34] Family worship would have a happy effect on children and the polity.

Catechism, central to household religion, was designed to promote children's faith and obedience. Catechism instructed by teaching the Bible and doctrine through questions and answers, which parents asked and children recited. Early republican catechisms increasingly linked piety to citizenship. One edition urged "the rising generation" to "improve in piety and virtue" and sought to "induce [parents] to revive" family prayer. Another suggested that household religious training was essential to "a good operation of government." Yet another reinterpreted the Ten Commandments as directives "to honor and obey the Civil Authority, to submit [one]self to my governors, teachers, spiritual pastors, and masters."[35] Catechism, intended to teach devotion, could also foster civic virtue.

By exercising mastery in prayer, parents could ensure that piety would transcend generations. Older children might take their own "turn in family worship, so that when they go to begin housekeeping, they might not be so bashful about it in their own abodes."[36] The Connecticut minister Joseph Dana reminded parents that one day, "instead of the fathers there may be the children, to remember their Saviour . . . and shew forth his virtues." Children raised with family religion would pray for the "continuance of our important civil establishments" and "the preservation of our independence" and would be "faithful enough to elect" qualified leaders.[37] The Warren (Rhode Island) Baptist Association suggested that "we *cannot expect* [children] to become good citizens, or friendly to *good government in civil society*" if they are not reared in family prayer.[38] Children from well-governed households would learn to govern well.

Servants and enslaved people were unlikely to govern, but their inclusion in family worship was important nonetheless. Because they were conditional members of the household, masters often neglected their religious upbringing. But ministers counseled families to include dependents.[39] "MASTERS!" warned the Presbyterian William Arthur, "You have a solemn charge of the souls of your servants, such a charge as a minister has over his people." He added that "it matters not whether they be *black* or *white* men," for it would be "an eternal disgrace . . . for the head of a family to overlook the morals, and religious instruction of any under his roof."[40] Accordingly, the clergy advised householders that they needed to include the household's lowest subordinates in prayer.

To fail at Christianizing servants and enslaved people was to fail at mastery. So ministers warned "that the meanest servant may not be excluded," for those who participated in family prayer would be better Christians *and* better servants: "more faithful, honest, and diligent, *not seeking their own, but their masters' profit.*"[41] By inculcating servants in republican Christianity, masters might persuade them to dedicate themselves to the household's spiritual life; more importantly, they might cultivate obedience. For slaveholders, Christian mastery was especially important. The planter class had carefully constructed a self-image of genteel mastery.[42] Worship at home, adorned with sacred objects and social rituals, supported this facade.[43] It was difficult to see how enslaved people fit into settings of spiritual refinement. But ministers insisted that Christianity need not liberate. It could instead teach submission while promising heavenly rewards. Householders had no excuse but to pray with all their dependents.

Performances of plantation Christianity interwove a fiction of benevolence that recast slavery and freedom. According to this mythology, tyrannical slaveholders were of the past, and enslaved people were "well clothed, well fed," and given "a warm cabbin."[44] Henry Pattillo, a North Carolina Presbyterian, integrated elements of this fiction when he wrote in the voice of an enslaved worshiper who prayed that "I, a poor sinner, black in body, and still blacker in sin . . . heartily hate all my wicked ways" and asked God to "give me grace to love thee and make the land of my slavery, the place of my true freedom."[45] As the prayer implied, "true freedom" was not emancipation but Christian liberty, the freedom to seek salvation.[46] A similar prayer, also from the viewpoint of a fictional enslaved man, compared the "wretched state" of Africa with his new home, where he found "the way, the truth, the Life" of Christianity. In Africa, the narrator had been "A slave to sin [and] Satan, too," but now another sort of slavery liberated him "from sin and danger."[47] The opposite of spiritual slavery was not freedom but protection and salvation traded for obedience and submission. In this idyllic world, what master would choose *not* to welcome slaves into the family's circle of prayer?

Directions for family prayer were practical; they included specific texts, prayers, and instructions. But domestic piety also promoted a less tangible object: preserving ties of authority and subordination. Family worship would safeguard the household's hierarchy, and by extension the state's. Ministers called upon masters to exercise spiritual authority, explaining that "a husband, a father, a master, or . . . all these in one" could act as "one of the most useful members of our civil society." As one minister pointed out, "Out of your families are to arise the future citizens of these States."[48] With family prayer, households could secure the nation.

THE CLERGY who offered this advice tailored their counsel to a new American audience. The devotional literature they published provided, in Tracy Fessenden's terms, a "means to spiritual maturity," underscored by a "Protestant understanding" of American culture that interwove reformed Christian concepts of redemption and destiny with a sense of Revolutionary purpose.[49] A close look at linguistic shifts in these writings over the eighteenth century reveals efforts to link family prayer to republican virtue and the nation's collective fate. Writers offered both a religious education and a political one; they articulated a shared vision of American citizenship and civic authority through a Protestant lens.

Advice manuals, catechisms, prayer books, and sermons were written to appeal to broad audiences. Instead of engaging particulars of doctrine or regional religious cultures, authors spoke to a national Protestant identity, hoping to guide Americans as they adapted their religious culture to their newly independent status.[50] Ministers argued that the nation needed a distinctively American style of worship, including in the home. They pointed out that "under the new and independent form of government, the republican kind, particular attention [should] be paid to the religious education of youth." So, to introduce the rising generation to religion grounded in virtue, they streamlined texts to make them accessible to families. A book of psalms declared itself "carefully suited to the Christian Worship in the United States of America."[51] A catechism proclaimed itself "Adapted to the Liberal Spirit of the United States."[52] Others advertised their "plain and familiar manner," describing their contents as "useful," "practical," and "clearly intelligible."[53] These tracts suggested that simplicity would appeal to republican readers. Accessible to all, they might bolster the piety of a nation that had prized political and military victory at the expense of spiritual triumph.

Was this rhetoric mere window dressing, or did it reflect real changes in political and spiritual sensibilities? After all, before and after the American Revolution prescriptive literature promoted family prayer and supported both householders' mastery and dependents' obedience. Patriarchal order and family governance were well-worn concepts by the late eighteenth century, so to understand how the clergy linked republican and reformed Protestant theology, we must track how the discourse of family religion changed over time. Although there was no precise turn in language patterns and usage, there were clear trends in the vocabulary of family religion after independence that suggest efforts to connect household prayer to republican virtue.

Political language in religious tracts printed before and after independence reveal a changing civic identity. The words *king* and *kingdom* appear more often in colonial texts than they would later. Lewis Bayly praised God's "Everlasting *Kingdom*" and offered prayer for the "*Peace and Prosperity* of these *Churches* and *Kingdoms* wherein we live."[54] George Whitefield reminded householders to consider themselves as "a King to govern, direct, and provide" for their families, and Benjamin Colman argued that "Every Man is a *King* and *Priest* in his own house."[55] After independence, references to *kingdom* gave way to mentions of *nation* or *country* (as general terms or in reference to the United States). The Congregationalist Piscataqua Association advised households to "pray in particular for our nation" and "every branch of our civil magistracy." Alexander Proudfit, a New York Presbyterian, wrote that "if irreligion in a nation constitutes a heathenish nation . . . irreligion in a family . . . must constitute a heathenish family." A Massachusetts minister suggested that household worship would "promote union between the States, which is absolutely necessary." Henry Pattillo reminded householders that "to love your country, family, friends, and neighbors *is to love the Lord your God*."[56] The rhetorical shift from kingdom to nation reflected changing political contexts, but it carried yet more meaning when linked to family prayer. Whereas households had been the kingdom's spiritual outposts, now they were engines of the republic.

This shift is also evident in metaphors depicting households. Before independence, writers often described houses as little churches. Matthew Henry's *Church in the House* declared that "*our houses must be churches*" in which "Masters of families . . . must be as prophets, priests, and kings in their own families, and as such they must keep up family doctrine, family worship, and family discipline."[57] Benjamin Colman implored households to act as "little churches," and Joseph Sewall urged masters to emulate households of biblical patriarchs, whose "families were churches."[58] This language persisted into the late eighteenth century. But even as the metaphor of house as church remained, writers also portrayed families as little polities—not kingdoms, but commonwealths—suggesting that the household was a civil as well as religious body. Alexander Proudfit described families as "little societies . . . bound by obligations," which Ebenezer Thayer suggested were governed by "the revealed law of God" as well as by "*the law written on your hearts*." The *Piscataqua Evangelical Magazine* compared the family to a "community," "little society," and "commonwealth," noting that households depended on "due regulation, management, and good order."[59] Much like the shift from kingdom to nation, that from church to state (or to church *and* state) reflected a new political context for family prayer.

This reorientation of civic identity becomes clear when we locate political concepts in these texts. Once again, there is some continuity over time rather than a clear turn. Even so, the political vocabulary of family religion changed after independence. Colonial authors had encouraged family religion to promote good household government—at the time, *government* conveyed not just institutions but also discipline and restraint. That restraint could be internal, as in governing one's passions, or it could be external, as in governing subordinates. Either way, it implied restrictions on behavior.[60] George Whitefield suggested that "it is the Duty of every Governour of a Family to take care that those committed to his Charge should *serve the Lord*," and Benjamin Wadsworth encouraged parents to "*govern their Children well*" and to "*Restrain, Reprove, and Correct them*."[61] Another minister called upon the "*Head* of the family" to "Maintain his Authority [and] uphold due Government in his house."[62] Governance was authoritative; writers who imagined households as kingdoms imagined fathers as kings.

Early republican households were as authoritative as their colonial antecedents, but their political and religious roles changed along with the vocabulary of household religion. References to governance assumed added meanings as they interwove with the evolving language of virtue. Prior to independence, religious writers paired virtue with faith, as when Benjamin Wadsworth advised parents to "bring [their children] up vertuously and piously."[63] Early republican writers continued to use this connotation. But virtue also implied secular qualities like prudence and justice, and it increasingly suggested civic qualities like disinterested benevolence and independence of mind.[64] Accordingly, prayer books promised to "guide children into the path of truth and virtue."[65] Judith Sargent Murray urged Christians to "endeavor that Benevolence should guide their every Action" and "Virtue will be the Principle of their Life."[66] With this kind of virtue in mind, William Enfield encouraged families to thank God for the "establishment of civil society, the institution of wise and salutary laws, the progress of useful knowledge, . . . [and] the benefits of virtuous education."[67] Republican rhetoric and ideology accordingly interwove with prayer.

What would befall families who ignored these directives? Here, too, the language of family religion changed. Colonial authors had wanted impious families to face spiritual consequences; none would pay a greater price than the householder who neglected family worship. Cotton Mather castigated "prayerless Families" as "Nurseries of Ignorance and Wickedness" that "nourish . . . Dragons of Malignity against the Ways of God," and he predicted that "the prayerless Householder, who knows the Will of God, but refuses to do it" faced the "danger of eternal death."[68] George Whitefield warned errant householders against the "Damnation which Men must endure for their own Sins" along with "the additional Guilt of being accessary to the Damnation of others."[69] Others predicted that irreligious masters would preside over "*infidel* house[s]" that would face "the outpouring of God's fury." They unquestionably bore responsibility for this spiritual calamity. "Can you pretend that you love your Family," Benjamin Colman asked, "without a religious and Godly care for their Souls?"[70] This language of hell and damnation had long roots in American Calvinism, which persuaded believers that most people were irrevocably damned. Even though the Great Awakening offered a wider road to heaven, and the Enlightenment suggested rational alternatives to damnation, anxieties about moral and spiritual declension revived fears of hell.[71]

After the Revolutionary War, these spiritual hazards conflated with another peril: political corruption. The stakes were higher now; not only did prayerless families risk individual damnation but they also endangered the nation. Pious families offered a bulwark against this menace. So believed Joseph Dana, who urged parents to "guard [children] (by an early impression of the spirit and glory of the gospel)" against "every danger for the maintenance of those precious liberties which we have received."[72] Thomas Clark insisted that "neglect of family religion is one great hindrance to . . . the languishing church of God and to your late bleeding country."[73] Families must be vigilant, argued John Lathrop, for "the enemies of religion, and the enemies of our Government, are uncommonly busy," leaving "the patriot and the Christian . . . called to uncommon exertion."[74] Henry Pattillo warned that moral decay would seep from households to the nation. "*O my countrymen,*" he exclaimed, "we have arrived at an awful resemblance to those nations whose vices and luxury" brought them "into final ruin."[75] Vigilance must begin at home, under the watch of virtuous parents, so that the republic might avoid this fate. As Enos Hitchcock asked, "What Parent does not see the necessity of balancing the young mind with good principles against the dangerous delusions of vice?"[76] Family religion could safeguard the republic from the rot of corruption.

We must exercise caution when interpreting the evolving language of family religion. Did later references to the civil functions of household prayer mean that families had not been important to the state before independence? Of course not. Colonial families supported both church and state; they enforced social order on the empire's periphery, where the state was fragile. But families' spiritual and civil roles changed. The changing rhetoric of family worship pointed both to the household's increasing political importance and to families' new responsibilities to teach republican habits through religious means. If early Americans were to think of their families as states in miniature, then it makes sense that ministers looked to households to foster religious sensibilities that encouraged good citizenship.

FAMILY WORSHIP was both practical religion and practical politics; it prepared each member of the household to uphold the republic. Protestants generally agreed that religion bound any society: only widespread faith and attentive worship could ensure that families, economies, and governments would function ethically and morally. Most reformed Protestants took this idea a step further, tying the republic's political success to its spiritual state and cosmic fate. Without religion to undergird secular institutions, one Vermont minister predicted, society would witness "courts of justice converted into dens of thieves, . . . [and] all parental authority lost." In short, a godly society held in check "the violence of the passions" that might otherwise destroy religious and political pillars.[77] The waning strength of those pillars, however, gave Americans pause. Churches were losing their footing as state-supported bodies. Many Americans welcomed this change, but others worried that disestablishment might create a moral vacuum. The secular state inspired little confidence. The Confederation had collapsed, the federal republic was untested, and the nation seemed to wither under partisan rivalry.

What pillar remained but the family? The ways families interpreted their spiritual duties reveal much about changing religious practice and the perceived crisis of authority in the new nation. Family worship took on new significance as households promised to train citizens. Domestic prayer and mastery offered householders the means to stave off revolt and channel corrupt impulses into religious devotion that served the public good. Homes, as little states and little churches, became settings for controlling a populace in a nation where few other measures seemed to work. Through family prayer, householders could discipline minds, bodies, and spirits in the service of a fragile nation.

Notes

The author is grateful to those who offered feedback on versions of this essay: the 2013–15 cohort of Young Scholars in American Religion, the attendees of the 2015 meeting of the Front Range Early American Consortium, the attendees of the 2021 Annual Meeting of the Sons of the American Revolution, Katherine Carté, Christopher Grasso, Meg Frisbee, Kim Klimek, Janet Moore Lindman, Jonathan Sassi, Brian Weiser, Christine Sheikh, and the anonymous reviewers for this volume.

1. Henry Pattillo, *The Plain Planter's Family Assistant, Containing an Address to Husbands and Wives, Children and Servants, with Some Help for Instruction by Catechism; and Examples of Devotions for Families, with a Brief Paraphrase on the Lord's Prayer* (Wilmington, NC: James Adams, 1787), 7.
2. Joseph Dana, *The Duty and Reward of Loving Our Country, and Seeking Its Prosperity: A Discourse Delivered in Two Parts, at the National Fast, April 25th, 1799* (Boston: Manning & Loring, 1799), 27, 19.
3. Ruth Bloch, "The Gendered Meanings of Virtue in Revolutionary America," *Signs* 13, no. 1 (Autumn 1987): 37–58; Richard Dagger, *Rights, Citizenship, and Republican Liberalism* (New York: Oxford University Press, 1997), chap. 1.
4. Others shared the concerns that reformed Protestants expressed, and household religion played an important role in a range of Protestant, Catholic, and other faiths. But the clergy discussed in this essay—including Congregationalist, Presbyterian, and Baptist ministers—used a shared evangelical language to implore families to support the republic through prayer. Michael Winship, *Seers of God: Puritan Providentialism in the Restoration and Early Enlightenment* (Baltimore: Johns Hopkins University Press, 1996); Alexandra Walsham, *Providence in Early Modern England* (New York: Oxford University Press, 2001), intro., chap. 1; Nicholas Guyatt, *Providence and the Invention of the United States, 1607–1876* (Cambridge: Cambridge University Press, 2007), 3–4, 82–90, 96–104; Douglas L. Winiarski, *Darkness Falls on the Land of Light: Experiencing Religious Awakenings in Eighteenth-Century New England* (Chapel Hill: University of North Carolina Press, 2017), 62–64, 66n; Katherine Carté, *Religion and the American Revolution: An Imperial History* (Chapel Hill: University of North Carolina Press, 2019); Philippa Koch, *The Course of God's*

Providence: Religion, Health, and the Body in Early America (New York: New York University Press, 2021), intro., chap. 5.

5. Writers referred to family worship by various terms, including *family religion* and *family prayer*, which encompassed rituals and practices beyond formal prayer. Andrew Cambers and Michael Wolfe, "Reading, Family Religion, and Evangelical Identity in Late Stuart England," *Historical Journal* 47, no. 4 (December 2004): 875–96; Nancy Christie, "'He is the master of his house': Families and Political Authority in Counterrevolutionary Montreal," *William and Mary Quarterly*, 3e ser., 70, no. 2 (April 2013): 341; Kathleen Wilson, "Rethinking the Colonial State: Family, Gender, and Governmentality in Eighteenth-Century British Frontiers," *American Historical Review* 116, no. 5 (December 2011): 1295–97.
6. Mark A. Noll, *America's God: From Jonathan Edwards to Abraham Lincoln* (New York: Oxford University Press, 2002), 14, 57–92; Richard Kyle, *Evangelicalism: An Americanized Christianity* (New Brunswick, NJ: Transaction, 2006), 28; Ruth Bloch, *Visionary Republic: Millennial Themes in American Thought, 1756–1800* (Cambridge: Cambridge University Press, 1985); Nathan O. Hatch, *The Sacred Cause of Liberty: Republican Thought and the Millennium in Revolutionary New England* (New Haven, CT: Yale University Press, 1977).
7. Christie, "'He is the master of his house,'" 346–47, 62; Carole Shammas, *A History of Household Government in America* (Charlottesville: University of Virginia Press, 2002), chap. 1; Kenneth A. Lockridge, "Colonial Self-Fashioning: Paradoxes and Pathologies in the Construction of Genteel Identity in Eighteenth-Century America," in *Through a Glass Darkly: Reflections on Personal Identity in Early America*, ed. Ronald Hoffman, Mechal Sobel, and Frederika J. Teute (Chapel Hill: University of North Carolina Press, 1997), 274–339; Sarah M. S. Pearsall, *Atlantic Families: Lives and Letters in the Later Eighteenth Century* (New York: Oxford University Press, 2008), 111–12, 77–78, 243; Wilson, "Rethinking the Colonial State," 1300; Paul B. Moyer, *The Public Universal Friend: Jemima Wilkinson and Religious Enthusiasm in Revolutionary America* (Ithaca, NY: Cornell University Press, 2015).
8. Wilson, "Rethinking the Colonial State," 1298.
9. Pattillo, *Plain Planter's Family Assistant*, 7. On families as polities, see John Demos, *A Little Commonwealth: Family Life in Plymouth Colony*, 2d ed. (New York: Oxford University Press, 2000).
10. Thomas Clark, *Plain Reasons* (Albany: Balentine & Webster, 1783), 32; Dana, *Duty and Reward of Loving Our Country*, 6.
11. Dana, *Duty and Reward of Loving Our Country*, 4.
12. Bloch, "Gendered Meanings of Virtue in Revolutionary America"; Robert Bellah, "Civil Religion in America," *Daedalus* 96, no. 1 (Winter 1967):

1–21; Amanda Porterfield, Phillip E. Hammond, James G. Moseley, and Jonathan Sarna, "Forum: American Civil Religion Revisited," *Religion and American Culture: A Journal of Interpretation* 4, no. 1 (Winter 1994): 1–23.

13. Dana, *Duty and Reward of Loving Our Country*, 4.
14. Paulinus [pseud.], "Family Order and Government, or the Pious and Exemplary Household, Num. I," *Piscataqua Evangelical Magazine*, January 1, 1805, 23.
15. Wilson, "Rethinking the Colonial State," 1298.
16. Rhys Isaac, *The Transformation of Virginia, 1740–1790* (New York: Norton, 1982); Christine Leigh Heyrman, *Southern Cross: The Beginnings of the Bible Belt* (Chapel Hill: University of North Carolina Press, 1997), chap. 5.
17. Shammas, *History of Household Government in America*, 61–65; Rosemarie Zagarri, *Revolutionary Backlash: Women and the Politics of the Early American Republic* (Philadelphia: University of Pennsylvania Press, 2008), chap. 1; Zagarri, "The Rights of Man and Woman in Post-Revolutionary America," *William and Mary Quarterly*, 3d ser., 55 (1998): 203–30; Jack P. Greene, *Understanding the American Revolution: Issues and Actors* (Charlottesville: University of Virginia Press, 1995), chap. 15.
18. Clark, *Plain Reasons*, 27.
19. E. Brooks Holifield, "Let the Children Come: The Religion of the Protestant Child in Early America," *Church History* 76, no. 4 (2007): 775–76.
20. Thomas Stephens, Religious Manuscript, 1772–1784, SER 85, Phillips Library, Peabody Essex Museum, Rowley, MA.
21. Clark, *Plain Reasons*, 29.
22. Ebenezer Thayer, *Family Worship: Two Sermons of the Late Rev. Ebenezer Thayer, A.M., Pastor of the Church in Hampton* (Newburyport, MA: Edmund M. Blunt, 1799), 25.
23. Uzal Ogden, *The Theological Preceptor; or Youth's Religious Instructor* (New York: John Holt, 1772), 163.
24. Linda K. Kerber, *Women of the Republic: Intellect and Ideology in Revolutionary America* (Chapel Hill: University of North Carolina Press, 1980); Jan Lewis, "The Republican Wife: Virtue and Seduction in the Early Republic," *William and Mary Quarterly*, 3d ser., 44 (1987): 689–721; Kerber, "Making Republicanism Useful," *Yale Law Journal* 97 (July 1988): 1663–72; Kerber, "Separate Spheres, Female Worlds, Woman's Place: The Rhetoric of Women's History," *Journal of American History* 75 (1988): 9–39; Cynthia A. Kierner, "Genteel Balls and Republican Parades: Gender and Early Southern Civic Rituals, 1677–1826," *Virginia Magazine of History and Biography* 104 (1996): 185–210; Zagarri, *Revolutionary Backlash*, 5, 74–75.
25. Thayer, *Family Worship*, 9.
26. Winiarski, *Darkness Falls on the Land of Light*, 104–8.

27. Judith Sargent Stevens Murray, *Some Deductions from the System Promulgated in the Page of Divine Revelation, Ranged in the Order and Form of a Catechism, Intended as an Assistant to the Christian Parent or Teacher* (Norwich, CT: John Tumbull, 1782).
28. Pattillo, *Plain Planter's Family Assistant*, 14, 17.
29. Pattillo, *Plain Planter's Family Assistant*, 14; Clark, *Plain Reasons*, 31.
30. Susan Juster, "'In a Different Voice': Male and Female Narratives of Religious Conversion in Post-Revolutionary America," *American Quarterly* 41 (1989): 34–62; Juster, *Disorderly Women: Sexual Politics and Evangelicalism in Revolutionary New England* (Ithaca, NY: Cornell University Press, 1994); Elizabeth Reis, *Damned Women: Sinners and Witches in Puritan New England* (Ithaca, NY: Cornell University Press, 1997).
31. Patricia U. Bonomi and Peter R. Eisenstadt, "Church Adherence in the Eighteenth-Century British American Colonies," *William and Mary Quarterly*, 3d ser., 39 (1982): 245–86; Jon Butler, *Awash in a Sea of Faith: Christianizing the American People* (Cambridge, MA: Harvard University Press, 1990), 4–5, 191–93, 206–7; Roger Finke and Rodney Stark, *The Churching of America, 1776–1990: Winners and Losers in Our Religious Economy* (New Brunswick, NJ: Rutgers University Press, 1992); Shelby M. Balik, *Rally the Scattered Believers: Northern New England's Religious Geography* (Bloomington: Indiana University Press, 2014), 235n32; Holifield, "Let the Children Come," 765–66.
32. Clark, *Plain Reasons*, 26; *The American Independent Catechism, Adapted to the Liberal Spirit of the United States* (Boston: Edes, 1789), preface; Ogden, *Theological Preceptor*, 164; Thayer, *Family Worship*, 25; Pattillo, *Plain Planter's Family Assistant*, 20.
33. Thayer, *Family Worship*, 33.
34. Charleston Association (SC), *Minutes of the Charleston Association, Held at Coosawhatchie, the 3rd of November, 1792* (Charleston, 1792), 10; *A Prayer Book for the Use of Families, Prepared by the Association of Ministers on Piscataqua River and Recommended by Them as an Assistant to the Social Devotions of Families* (Portsmouth, NH: Charles Pierce, 1799), viii–ix.
35. Daniel Shute, *A Compendious and Plain Catechism, Designed for the Benefit of the Rising Generation and Recommended to the Attentive Use of Heads of Families in the Education of Their Children as Adapted to Improve Them in Piety and Virtue* (Boston: Samuel Hall, 1794), 3–4; *American Independent Catechism*, 3; *The Parent's Best Gift: Containing the Church Catechism with Many Questions and Answers out of the Holy Scriptures* (New York: J. Harrisson, 1796), 9.
36. Clark, *Plain Reasons*, 29.
37. Dana, *Duty and Reward of Loving Our Country*, 5–6.

38. Warren Association (RI), *Minutes of the Warren Association, at their Annual Convention, held at Mr. Wiliams's Meeting-House, in Wrentham, 1785* (Boston: Adams and Nourse's Office, Court-Street, 1785).
39. Wilson, "Rethinking the Colonial State," 1298.
40. William Arthur, *Family Religion Recommended: A Sermon Preached from Joshua XXIV 15* (Philadelphia: Stewart & Cochran, 1794), 22.
41. Thayer, *Family Worship*, 16, 23.
42. Butler, *Awash in a Sea of Faith*, chaps. 5–6; Donald G. Mathews, *Religion in the Old South* (Chicago: University of Chicago Press, 1977); Sylvia Frey, *Water from the Rock: Black Resistance in a Revolutionary Age* (Princeton, NJ: Princeton University Press, 1992), chaps. 1–2; Heyrman, *Southern Cross*, chap. 1; Cynthia Lynn Lyerly, *Methodism and the Southern Mind, 1770–1810* (New York: Oxford University Press, 1998); Albert J. Raboteau, *Slave Religion: The "Invisible Institution" in the Antebellum South*, updated ed. (New York: Oxford University Press, 2004), chap. 3; Trevor Glasson, *Mastering Christianity: Missionary Anglicanism and Slavery in the Atlantic World* (New York: Oxford University Press, 2017), chap. 4; Katharine Gerbner, *Christian Slavery: Conversion and Race in the Protestant Atlantic World* (Philadelphia: University of Pennsylvania Press, 2018).
43. Lauren F. Winner, *A Cheerful and Comfortable Faith: Anglican Religious Practice in the Elite Households of Eighteenth-Century Virginia* (New Haven, CT: Yale University Press, 2010); Nicholas M. Beasley, "Domestic Rituals: Marriage and Baptism in the British Plantation Colonies, 1650–1780," *Anglican and Episcopal History* 76, no. 3 (September 2007): 353–54.
44. Pattillo, *Plain Planter's Family Assistant*, 22.
45. "Prayer for a Negroe," in Pattillo, *Plain Planter's Family Assistant*, 51–52.
46. Scholars cite Luther's *On Christian Liberty* (1520) and Locke's *Letter Concerning Religious Toleration* (1689) when distinguishing between Christian and legal liberty. E. Brooks Holifield, *Theology in America: Christian Thought from the Age of the Puritans to the Civil War* (New Haven, CT: Yale University Press, 2003), 397; Christopher S. Grenda, "Faith, Reason, and Enlightenment: The Cultural Sources of Toleration in Early America," in *The First Prejudice: Religious Tolerance and Intolerance in Early America*, ed. Chris Beneke and Christopher S. Grenda (Philadelphia: University of Pennsylvania Press, 2010), 23–52; Jakob De Roover and S. N. Balagangadhara, "John Locke, Christian Liberty, and the Predicament of Liberal Toleration," *Political Theory* 36, no. 40 (2008): 529–33.
47. "The Negro's Prayer," ca. 1800, MS VFF, Maryland Historical Society, Baltimore, Maryland.
48. Pattillo, *Plain Planter's Family Assistant*, 7.
49. Tracy Fessenden, *Culture and Redemption: Religion, the Secular, and American Literature* (Princeton, NJ: Princeton University Press, 2007), 7–8, chap. 2.

50. William J. Gilmore, *Reading Becomes a Necessity of Life: Material and Cultural Life in Rural New England, 1780–1835* (Knoxville: University of Tennessee Press, 1989), pt. 2; T. J. Tomlin, *A Divinity for All Persuasions: Almanacs and Early American Religious Life* (New York: Oxford University Press, 2014); David Paul Nord, *Faith in Reading: Religious Publishing and the Birth of Mass Media in America* (New York: Oxford University Press, 2004).
51. *Psalms Carefully Suited to the Christian Worship in the United States of America, Being an Improvement of the Old Versions of the Psalms of David* (Philadelphia: Francis Bailey, 1787).
52. *American Independent Catechism.*
53. Daniel Read, *The American Singing-Book; Or a New and Easy Guide to the Art of Psalmody, Designed for the Use of Singing Schools in America* (New Haven, CT, 1785), preface; Shute, *Compendious and Plain Catechism,* 3–4; John Willison, *The Mother's Catechism, Containing Short and Easy Questions, Designed as an Introduction to Understand the Assembly's Shorter Catechism,* 6th ed. (Trenton, NJ: Matthias Day, 1795).
54. Lewis Bayly, *Meditations and Prayers for Household Piety: Taken out of the Practice of Piety, to Which is Added, The Drunkard's Looking-Glass, Or, A Short View of their Present Shame, and Future Misery* (Boston: Alford Butler, 1728), 15. The content from this pamphlet was taken from a longer work by Bayly, *The Practice of Piety,* published in 1611 and reprinted widely.
55. George Whitefield, *The Great Duty of Family Religion* (Boston: Fleet for Harrison, 1739), 8; Benjamin Colman, *An Argument for and Persuasive unto the Great and Important Duty of Family Worship: With Rules and Directions for the Due Performance of It* (Boston: Gamaliel Rogers, 1728), 14.
56. *Prayer Book for the Use of Families,* 21–22; Alexander Moncrief Proudfit, *The Importance of Family Religion: A Sermon* (Salem, NY: Henry Dodd, 1799), 6; *New Year's Discourse on Recommending the Necessity of a Union in the Churches and States* (Springfield, MA: Ashley & Brewer, 1800), 5; Pattillo, *Plain Planter's Family Assistant,* 12.
57. Matthew Henry, *A Church in the House: A Sermon Concerning Family-Religion* (London: Tho. Parkhurst, 1704), 8, 13–14.
58. Colman, *Great and Important Duty of Family Worship,* 17; Joseph Sewall, *Desires that Joshua's Resolution May Be Revived, or, Excitations to the Constant and Diligent Exercise of Family Religion* (Boston: B. Green, 1716), 312.
59. Proudfit, *Importance of Family Religion,* 7; Thayer, *Family Worship,* 20; Paulinus, "Family Order and Government."
60. Raymond Williams, *Culture and Society: 1780–1950,* 2d ed. (New York: Columbia University Press, 1983), 8; Michael Meranze, "Culture and Governance: Reflections on the Cultural History of Eighteenth-Century British America," *William and Mary Quarterly,* 3d series, 65, no. 4 (2008): 714–15;

Christie, "'He is the master of his house,'" 341–50; Shammas, *History of Household Government in America*, chap. 2.

61. George Whitefield, *Great Duty of Family Religion*, 7; Benjamin Wadsworth, *The Well-Ordered Family: Or, Relative Duties* (Boston: B. Green, 1712), 55.
62. James Parker, *Family-Religion Revived: Or, an Attempt to Promote True Religion and Virtue in Families* (New Haven, CT, 1755), 13.
63. Wadsworth, *Well-Ordered Family*, 43.
64. J. G. A. Pocock, *The Machiavellian Moment: Florentine Political Thought and the Atlantic Republican Tradition*, rev. ed. (Princeton, NJ: Princeton University Press, 2016), chap. IIB; Philip Gould, "Virtue, Ideology, and the American Revolution," *American Literary History* 5, no. 3 (Autumn 1993): 564–77; Bloch, "Gendered Meanings of Virtue in Revolutionary America," 42–43.
65. Shute, *Compendious and Plain Catechism*, 3.
66. Murray, *Some Deductions from the System*, 35.
67. William Enfield, *Prayers for the Use of Families*, 4th ed. (Philadelphia: William Spottswood, 1788), 9.
68. Cotton Mather, *Family Religion Urged, or, Some serious Considerations Offered to the Reason and Conscience Of Every Prayerless Householder*, 3d ed. (Boston: D. Henchman, 1747), 5, 7.
69. Whitefield, *Great Duty of Family Religion*, 22.
70. Wadsworth, *Well-Ordered Family*, 15; Colman, *Great and Important Duty of Family Worship*, 34.
71. Kathryn Gin Lum, *Damned Nation: Hell in America from the Revolution to Reconstruction* (Oxford: Oxford University Press, 2014), intro. and chap. 1.
72. Dana, *Duty and Reward of Loving Our Country*, 28.
73. Clark, *Plain Reasons*, 32.
74. John Lathrop, *Patriotism and Religion: A Sermon, Preached on the 25th of April, 1799, the Day Recommended by the President of the United States, to Be Observed as a National Fast* (Boston: John Russell, 1799), 24.
75. Pattillo, *Plain Planter's Family Assistant*, iii–iv.
76. Enos Hitchcock, *The Parent's Assistant: A Short, Practical Catechism, Compiled for the Instruction of Children in the Principles and Practice of Virtue and Piety* (Providence, RI: B. Wheeler, 1788), 2.
77. Samuel Sumner, "The Importance of Religion" (undated manuscript of sermon delivered several times in Vermont and Massachusetts, 1790–1806), Vermont Historical Society, Barre.

The Religious Appropriation of Revolutionary Rhetoric in the Early Republic

SETH PERRY

★

HOW THE IDEOLOGIES and energies of the American Revolution relate to the subsequent vibrancy of Protestant Christianity in the nation it birthed is likely the single most frequently asked question in the study of religion in the early national period. There was a time when many historians downplayed the irony implicit in the question, attempting to draw a line between colonial religiosity and the Revolution itself, but since the late 1980s, at least, that has mostly been out of fashion.[1] As Dee Andrews put it twenty-five years ago, "For historians of the American Revolution, there can be few more compelling questions than how a republic forged in the image of enlightened rationalism and shaped by the rejection of state-sponsored church coercion should come to be marked by a powerful and widely accepted religiosity."[2]

The best historiographical answers to this question have emphasized that the early republic's embrace of "a powerful and widely accepted religiosity" was the intentional creation of religious partisans. That is to say, a group of Protestants who feared for their own loss of power in the early national period campaigned to have their religious commitments woven into the fabric of the new nation. This essay joins earlier attempts to chart that campaign by tracking how one of those partisans—Lorenzo Dow, the most famous preacher in America for thirty years—co-opted familiar Revolutionary rhetoric to support an imbrication of religion and the state that it was never intended to endorse. One of Dow's most famous publications was a rewriting of Thomas Paine's *Rights of Man,* in which he transformed the archrationalist's republican argument for human rights into a frankly monarchical plea for a Protestant God's central role in good government. Needless to say, this took a lot of work. For that reason, it is an ideal site for viewing the strategies religious partisans like Dow used when laboring to carve out a place of power for themselves in the wake of the Revolution.

As a case study, Dow's deliberate co-opting of Paine is evidence against arguments about religious growth in the early national period that script that growth as the passive outcome of consonant forces coming together. Nathan Hatch's answer to the question of early national religious expansion is probably the most widely known and accepted, even though it's not really an answer. Hatch argued that the populism unleashed by the Revolution remade American Protestantism in its own image. His focus was on what the democratic impulses of the Revolution did to religion, rather than the other way around. "American Protestantism has been skewed away from central ecclesiastical institutions and high culture; it has been pushed and pulled into its present shape by a democratic or populist orientation," Hatch wrote.[3] How religion managed to hang around at all wasn't really a question for Hatch, because he took for granted the consonance between revivalist Protestantism and republicanism: for Hatch, once the two met, they were bound to get along. Many subsequent scholars have internalized this assumption and used Hatch's "democratization" thesis to suggest that the hybridization of revivalist Protestantism and Revolutionary principles allowed both to flourish.[4]

Mark Noll, focusing on the elites who, among other things, founded and orchestrated early national religious voluntary societies, positioned the post-Revolutionary period within the development of a "surprising intellectual synthesis" that he argues has defined Protestant theology in America. This melding of "evangelical Protestant religion, republican political ideology, and commonsense moral reasoning" works sort of like Hatch's democratization—a hybridization that facilitated the expansion of religion by melding Protestant commitments and the rationalist assumptions of republican political ideology—but has the singular advantage of being couched in the active voice.[5] While Hatch downplayed the active intentionality of religious partisans—suggesting, for example, that religious populists found themselves making use of "a rhetoric of liberty that would not have occurred to them were it not for the

Revolution"—Noll carefully documented the academic labor required to create the synthesis.[6]

Going a controversial step further, Amanda Porterfield's answer to the question of how the nation became so religious in the decades after its not so religious founding is the most explicit with respect to the actors involved, their methods, and their intentions. In *Conceived in Doubt*, she amplified the irony implicit in the question and flipped Hatch's focus, asking what religion did to the democratic potential of the Revolutionary era. Further, she expanded the set of actors who worked to make religion central to the American polity beyond Noll's ivory tower, focusing on a range of religious partisans who exploited post-Revolutionary uncertainties in order to resuscitate and grow religion's place in American political life. Revivalist preachers and the organizers of voluntary societies, she argued, had deliberately cultivated a "blinding mistrust of secular politics" in public life as a means of suppressing rationalism, creating a void of uncertainty for religion to fill.[7]

Noll and Porterfield, crucially, pushed beyond Hatch to demonstrate that the synthesis with which we are concerned was made, not found. Porterfield rightly took Hatch to task for failing "to pierce the evangelical cloaking and exploitation of doubt"—that is, for not looking at the deliberate obfuscation required to supplant Revolutionary rationalism with revivalist religiosity. The case study explored here shows a populist preacher twisting Revolutionary rhetoric to evangelical ends. Dow's use of Paine is evidence, I argue, for expanding the range of agents and methods involved in creating the early republican mash-up of Revolutionary and evangelical ideologies, both beyond Noll's focus on academic theology and Porterfield's attention to doubt.

The move from rationalist Revolution to de facto Protestant establishment was the work of religious partisans, men and women who set out to push their religious commitments to the center of national life and succeeded. Their tools were not limited to academic theology and the cultivation of doubt, as important as those elements were. One of their key strategies consisted in co-opting the rhetoric of the Revolution. Deliberately, strategically, religious partisans of the early national period took the familiar republican language of the Revolutionary era and gave that language religious meaning. Dow's treatment of Paine is an unusually stark and legible example of this type of work.

Dow published *An Essay on the Rights of Man* in 1812. It is a populist diatribe against religious establishments and the presumptions of status and wealth. Dow's statement of his primary argument in the *Essay* is a direct appropriation of Revolutionary rhetoric: "It is a self-evident truth, that all men are born *equal* and *independent*, and endowed by their Creator with certain unalienable rights—among which are Life, Liberty, the use of property, the pursuit of Happiness, with the privilege of *private judgment*."[8] He employs the terms of Enlightenment rationalism throughout, insisting that he is making an argument for the "head," while at the same time deploying familiar evangelistic modes aimed at the heart. The piece ends in a paroxysm of biblical prophecy, millennialist predictions about the coming end times, and exhortations to repentance.

Here, then, is a display in writing of that convergence of Revolutionary and evangelical thought on what Porterfield identifies as a "passion for liberty."[9] What makes Dow's *Rights of Man* singularly interesting, though, is that far beyond merely sharing a title, upon examination the piece turns out to be a redacted and heavily supplemented version of *Rights of Man*, Thomas Paine's 1791 treatise on human dignity. Dow lifted about a third of his pamphlet's material more or less verbatim from Paine. This is surprising, to say the least, because by 1812 the once-vaunted reputation of the man who wrote *Common Sense* had been wrecked by the fallout from two of his pamphlets of the early 1790s: *Age of Reason*, Paine's two-part deistical assault on biblical authority and the very notion of revealed religion; and *Rights of Man*, in which Paine defended the revolution in France while agitating for one in England. Dow abhorred both deism and everything French (which to his mind encompassed both radical skepticism and Catholicism). However, when he wrote to valorize the authority and dignity of common people, assert the greatness of American democracy, and abjure religious establishments on the way to a synthesis of evangelical and republican ideals, he did not just write *like* Thomas Paine: he conscripted the words of Paine himself.

Untangling Dow's use of Paine's *Rights of Man* shows the deliberate work that was required to turn radical egalitarianism to the purposes of early national evangelicalism. Dow's contortion of Paine exemplifies how the evangelical-Revolutionary synthesis was made in the popular press. Dow's synthesis hinges on (1) the soldering of what he called "moral rights" onto the framework of individual and civil rights posited by Paine; (2) a notion of religious toleration that parroted that of revolutionaries like Paine and Thomas Jefferson but was in fact much more conservative; and (3) the openings that Paine himself—deist though he was—left in his rhetoric for its exploitation by Christian thinkers. In the first decades of the early nineteenth century, politically attuned Protestants—including anti-formalists like Dow, not only the theologians of Noll's synthesis—deliberately co-opted the ideals of the Revolution by using its ideas and its words to rearticulate their religious prerogatives.[10]

This example of the appropriation of even the most rationalist, most radical democratic rhetoric by ultimately conservative religious thought is distinct from the exploitation of doubt examined by Porterfield. However, it had similar effects, and I share Porterfield's orientation toward the consequences of early national evangelical rhetoric. The first audience for Dow's *Rights of Man* underscores the stakes of his appropriation of Paine. In the 1790s Thomas Paine was burned in effigy by the slaveholding classes of the Caribbean because they believed *Rights of Man*'s radical argument for human dignity had helped incite the revolt of the enslaved in Saint Domingue.[11] Dow, by contrast, first published his *Rights of Man* twenty years later in Lynchburg, Virginia, for an audience of slaveholders. This is not a generalization about the South. Because he printed a subscriber list with the first edition, it is possible to know that most of the first readers of his *Rights of Man* owned other human beings. Dow, that is, eased Paine's radicalism into an evangelical framework in order to explain the "rights of man" to those Americans most oblivious to them.

Rights of Man (1791–1792)

Thomas Paine wrote *Rights of Man* to respond, most immediately, to Edmund Burke's criticism of the French Revolution, in which Paine was directly involved. Paine positioned the revolutions in France and America as victories for human dignity over inherited, presumptuous, irrational constraints on it and mocked Burke's royalist disdain for political agitation by the laboring classes in England. From the publication of part 1 in 1791 (part 2 appeared in 1792), *Rights of Man* was immediately popular on both sides of the Atlantic—Seth Cotlar calls it "the Atlantic World's most widely read pamphlet of the 1790s"—and Paine's American supporters initially saw it as of a piece with his writings on behalf of the American Revolution.[12] Defenses of the French Revolution written before 1793 looked dated after the onset of the Terror that year, however, and by the end of the decade Paine's *Rights of Man* had taken on dangerous associations for many Americans. This was owing not only to the plain facts of the Terror—which nearly claimed Paine himself—but also to deliberate efforts by Federalists to use those facts to yoke, in the minds of the public, Jeffersonian democracy to frightening violence.[13]

Inseparable from the political insecurities made exploitable by the French Revolution was its association with religious infidelity. Even after he found himself caught in the churn of the Terror, Paine endorsed the French Revolution's rejection of traditional forms of religion and exulted in his own brand of "infidelity," writing the first part of *Age of Reason* from a Republic prison. That pamphlet—part 1 appeared in the United States in 1794, part 2 in 1795—was a frank assault on revealed religion. Paine, a deist, left room for the God of the Creation but mocked any notion that such a being revealed himself to humanity in any other way. "It is a contradiction in terms and ideas to call any thing a revelation that comes to us at second hand, either verbally or in writing," he wrote.[14] In part 2, Paine went book by book through the Christian Bible, mocking basically all of it. Religious responses to *Age of Reason* proliferated in the 1790s, and by the end of the decade the political and religious vitriol aimed at Paine knew no limits.[15] In 1800 one anonymous writer, addressing Paine directly, wished that every town would set up effigies of him so that decent Americans might "as nature requires . . . have a convenient opportunity to piss in your face."[16]

An Essay on the Rights of Man (1812)

Twenty years after the publication of *Rights of Man*, Lorenzo Dow stole Paine's words for the Lord. By 1812 Dow had been traveling in the United States and the United Kingdom for fifteen years convicting audiences of their sinfulness and their urgent need to repent and serve God. Although he declined (after at first being denied) Methodist ordination out of a refusal to confine himself to a circuit or submit to the Methodist hierarchy, Dow was devoted to Wesleyan theology and personified the revivalist strain of American Protestantism that early national Methodism came to represent.[17]

Dow is remembered today primarily for his eccentric, populist preaching style, but from early in his career he was an accomplished author and editor. By 1812, under his own name he had published three ever-expanding editions of his own journal and multiple editions of several polemical tracts. He had also edited a collection of Methodist preachers' letters, several hymnals, a treatise on women's health written by a (male) doctor friend of his, and at least two "miscellany" volumes of magazine material picked up during his trips to the United Kingdom. For these books Dow acted as editor and publisher only, and this is clearly indicated. What separates his *Rights of Man* from his other editorial work is that Paine's name appears nowhere on it, in any edition, and Paine's words are folded into Dow's own. It first appeared as a "preface" to another of Dow's works, *A Journey from Babylon to Jerusalem, or The Road to Peace and True Happiness*, printed in Lynchburg, Virginia, in 1812. For a second edition, printed in Alexandria, Virginia, a few months after the first, Dow separated *Rights* out as a freestanding pamphlet and renamed it *Analects*. Shortly after that, in March 1813, he carried it to John Totten in New York, a major printer of Methodist texts, for a revised third edition. There were other freestanding editions, and beginning in 1814 *Analects* became a standard part of Dow's ubiquitous omnibus collection, which was in print through the 1880s.

On analysis, Dow's original title performs a dual role: the piece is both a meditation on the "rights of man" in a general sense and a collection of passages from Paine's *Rights of Man*. It is very likely, however, that much of Dow's audience—both the original subscribers and the text's many subsequent readers—might not have realized the connection to Paine at all.[18] Paine's name appears nowhere on any edition, and the revised title—*Analects, or Reflections upon Natural, Moral, and Political Philosophy: Including the Rights, Interests, and Duties of Man*—further obscures the connection to Paine's title and to Paine. The first edition has some scattered quotation marks on a few of the passages lifted from Paine, but these are not consistent and disappear in subsequent printings. Paine's infamy, particularly among the slaveholders who were Dow's first audience for the piece, may partly explain why his name appears nowhere in Dow's text.[19] Because Paine's incendiary writings from the 1790s were effectively banned in the Anglophone world by the first decade of the nineteenth century, Dow's 1812 version of *Rights of Man* was actually the first one put to press anywhere for almost fifteen years.[20]

Beginning especially with *Age of Reason*, Paine's work had long been a challenge to religious partisans.[21] Dow himself had been grappling with and making use of Paine's writing for some time before working on his own *Rights of Man*. As a young man he was affected by Paine's deistical arguments, a test of his faith that he chronicled in *The Chain of Lorenzo*

(1804), an early polemical tract. There and in many of his other works, Dow takes a sort of inoculating approach to Paine's arguments, allowing shades of them into his own writing as a way of protecting against them. Dow records that he had developed a sermon in which he drew in unsuspecting crowds by announcing that he was going to take his text from *Age of Reason*, only to flip the script partway through.[22] His autobiographical and polemical writings show the influence of Paine's brand of Jeffersonian egalitarianism. Dow was surely drawn to Paine's style as much as to his radical individualism: *accessible*, *plain*, and *sarcastic* accurately describe both authors. However, in its wholesale copying of Paine's words, Dow's *Rights of Man* sticks out from the rest of his publications, and not least because by any reasonable measure Thomas Paine was a much better writer than Lorenzo Dow. The devil has all the best tunes.

Appropriating Revolutionary Rhetoric for Evangelicalism

Dow could not, however, take on Paine's words and positions without some work. In his version of *Rights of Man* he does lean into some of Paine's most radical statements about individual rights. "Society grants us nothing," Dow writes, in a passage that is nearly verbatim from Paine. Rather, "we exchange a part of our 'personal rights' for 'social rights,' by casting a part into the common stock by delegation," and "we draw on the capital as matter of right."[23] However, he can only do this after conscripting Paine's Revolutionary egalitarianism into a framework of human sinfulness and responsibility to God. Dow begins and ends his version of *Rights of Man* by flipping on its head Paine's defense of the French Revolution—the primary rationale behind Paine's *Rights of Man* to start with. In 1791 Paine had dedicated his work to George Washington, a gesture Dow neutralizes with a religiously inflected 1798 quote from Washington condemning the Terror: "But this seems to be the age of wonders. And it is reserved for intoxicated and lawless France, *for purposes of Providence far beyond the reach of human ken*, to slaughter her own citizens, and disturb the repose of all the world besides."[24] Dow then uses the example of France to advance the "self evident" assertion "that there is such a thing in the world as 'Natural Evil,'" itself a consequence of "Moral Evil," and by the end of *Rights of Man* he has used the French Revolution itself as a harbinger of the millennium to spackle a full-blown call for global evangelism onto Paine's deistic, rationalist elaboration of human rights.[25] He gets there over the course of the essay by adding a third type of rights to Paine's two; applying Paine's description of religious toleration to a version of toleration Paine explicitly rejected; and making full use of Paine's own occasional use of Christian scripture. These three moves will be explored in turn.

Dow's first move is to amend Paine's categorization of human rights by establishing freedom of conscience specifically in religious matters as a distinct category of rights separate from and equivalent to the two categories of rights identified by Paine. The "rights of man" in Paine's analysis are divided into natural rights, "those which appertain to man in right of his existence," and civil rights, "those which appertain to man in right of his being a member of society." The former encompasses "all the intellectual rights, or rights of the mind," and to Paine it is obvious that "religion is one of those rights."[26] Dow copies Paine's language more or less exactly on these categories of rights, though he renames them "Personal" and "Social" rights. However, even though he mentions "Religious Liberty" under personal/natural rights, he adds "Moral Rights" as a third category: these, Dow writes, are the "rights of man" "considered as he stands in relation to his Creator."[27] At first blush, Dow's moral rights are something like the "rights of conscience" that Paine placed under natural rights. "'Moral Rights' are the personal privilege to think, and judge, and act for one's self in point of moral duty," Dow writes.[28] For Paine, however, human beings have natural rights, including the rights of conscience, just by virtue of existing, in and of themselves, not in relation to some posited other. They are the result of creation. Dow's moral rights, on the other hand, are held in relation to God; they require not just creation but a creator. While as a deist Paine himself acknowledged a creator, none of the "rights of man" he posited required one. Paine was concerned with earthly, human rights and relationships. By contrast, Dow defined this third type of rights with elements of both natural and social rights as defined by Paine: they are individually held (like the former) but exist only in relation to some other (like the latter). The problem, as defined from the standpoint of Paine's radical republicanism and rejection of religious establishments, is that in the tradition out of which Dow came, the tradition that he and his coreligionists have bequeathed to American political thought, at the end of the day there can be only one type of human relationship to God, and it is the same as the relationship of a subject to a king. "*Moral Rights,*" Dow writes, "are the result of *moral law*[.] And as a Creature dependent on the supreme governor of the world, who enjoins the obligation, and prescribes the Law, and rule of practice, man has a *right to obey*, by attending to the law, and by keeping the *rule*."[29]

Moral rights are the right to obey. By placing this third type of rights on par with the others, scripting it as "self-evident" in the same way that Paine scripts natural and civil rights, Dow crashed Christian theism in its most monarchical form into Paine's radical republican egalitarianism. As Porterfield writes, "The language of divine monarchy was rooted in scripture and tradition, and anyone who turned to the Bible for guidance would encounter it. As deistical attempts to divest God of royalist authority failed [in the early republic], and growing numbers of people turned to the language of divine kingship for solace and courage, ministers exploited nostalgia for monarchy with as much zeal as they responded to popular demands for political representation."[30] Dow's *Rights of Man* is, in part, a moment in that exploitation, one carried out in the very language of radical republicanism. Swaddled in the natural-rights language of the Revolution, laid in a manger of Jeffersonian disestablishment, a divine king is reborn.

Dow's integration of monarchical moral rights into Paine's *Rights of Man* facilitated, or required, a coordinating move regarding religious toleration. Paine identified toleration as yet another imposition of government. "Toleration is not the *opposite* of Intoleration, but is the *counterfeit* of it. Both are despotisms. The one assumes to itself the right of withholding liberty of conscience, and the other of granting it."[31] For Paine, a government's pretense to bestow upon its citizens freedoms they had naturally, by virtue of their existence, was a dangerous usurpation of authority. Throughout his career Dow was a vociferous opponent of religious establishments, classing them as what he called "Law Religion," and in his *Rights of Man* he parrots Paine's view of toleration, copying his critique almost word for word.[32] In the same passage, Dow even paraphrases the famous line from Jefferson's *Notes on the State of Virginia* regarding the civil state's proper indifference to matters of religious belief: "Suppose that one man believes in one God, another believes in *ten*, what is that to the *first*: 'It neither picks his pocket nor breaks his leg,'" Dow writes, here (for once) using quotation marks to indicate his debt to Jefferson.[33] Careful readers will note significant elisions in Dow's use of Jefferson's line, however. The original reads, "But it does me no injury for my neighbor to say there are twenty Gods, or no God. It neither picks my pocket nor breaks my leg."[34] It is hard to say why Dow limited the hypothetical polytheist to ten gods only, but his erasure of the possibility of tolerable atheism is explainable. Dow could not actually abide the Paine/Jefferson brand of indifference to, rather than toleration of, variation in religious belief, because the edifice of moral rights that he constructed introduced the necessity of error and judgment: refusals of the right to obey must be, in Dow's view, subject to consequences. In the text of Dow's *Rights of Man*, the civil implications of Dow's version of toleration are made most apparent, perhaps, in an analogous absence. Despite paraphrasing much of the surrounding material, Dow leaves out Paine's most radical statement of the salutary effects of voiding religious establishments: "In America, a catholic priest is a good citizen, a good character, and a good neighbour; an episcopalian minister is of the same description: And this proceeds, independent of men, from there being no law-establishment in America."[35] Dow—who would spend the last years of his career railing about Jesuit conspiracies—could not be so generous regarding the relationship of proper religious belief to good citizenship.

To be sure, Dow was unequivocal in his belief that the civil state could not punish religious belief with force. However, his notion of toleration was defined ultimately by the moral right to obey God, not the natural right of conscience. God may choose to punish dissent or not (that is, to permit by his grace people to be wrong—exactly the sort of "toleration" Paine abhorred); however, he cannot be indifferent to dissent, because dissent with respect to the moral right to obey God amounts to *sin*. And for Dow and those like him, sin is a problem that cannot be tolerated with the indifference of Paine or Jefferson.

Reframed as the "freedom to sin," the "freedom to be wrong"—bestowed by God, performed civilly by the state's abjuring of religious establishments—comes with the possibility of correction. Dow's simultaneous embrace of Paine's rejection of coercion in religious matters and injection of a monarchical notion of sin into Paine's argument renders evangelism into the public sphere as a necessity: "Persecution is contrary to *Natural Justice*, inasmuch as it *assumes* a power which no mortal can claim, it being the *Divine right* only, to *judge* in such cases. But nevertheless *moral duty*, from pity, and a concern for his welfare, may excite a man to strive to *convince* another for his good, to shun the *error* and find the *happy road*."[36] Dow makes this clearer as he proceeds into the latter half of his *Rights of Man*, in which Paine's language recedes in a tide of biblical prophecy. Having established "universal liberty of conscience," Dow writes, "nothing further is wanting, but the 'Moral Law' of Love, should be wrote in every heart."[37] This writing on the heart is the work of evangelism, religious work made necessary precisely by the success of disestablishment.

Here, in the context of Dow's biblical proof texting and his appeal to "writing on the heart," it is important to note the ways in which his parroting of Paine's radical reliance on reason does and does not reflect what Paine meant. Rhetorically, Dow preserves a distinction between reason and affect: "A man must be *convinced* in his *Judgment*, by evidence to his understanding, before he is converted in his heart."[38] However, what Dow considered "evidence to the understanding" of his audiences were essentially their affective reactions to his emotional appeals. Conviction of sin—the fundamental goal of his homiletic style—might be helped along by appeal to commonsense evidences, but it was ultimately a matter of conscience. "There is a *moral duty—and a moral obligation* to the man to perform that duty. If he does not perform it he falls under condemnation; which he is conscience of, for not acting as well as he knew how."[39] In spinning all his appeals to reason into biblical proof texting, moreover, Dow exemplifies what Porterfield characterizes as the evangelical effort to associate reason with revelation and "drive a wedge" between reason and skepticism like Paine's, even as he directly cribbed *Paine's exact words* on the importance of rational inquiry.[40]

From here, Dow builds upon his early assertion, based on the observation of sin in the world, that "something isn't right with the human family," working ultimately toward a millennial vision of future perfection that crashes, again, Paine's version of natural rights into his own notion of moral rights. "Before all things can be right in the Human family, the 'Moral Law' must reign in all parts. Before that can exist universally, the 'Law of Nature' must be revived and restored, to reign among all nations," Dow writes. "But all things are not right yet, nor can they be, until the 'Personal, Social and Moral Rights' of mankind are restored."[41] Humanity's full rights will be restored, that is, only when evangelism like Dow's is successful.

Finally, as in many of his writings, Dow arrives at an apocalyptic crescendo through dense analysis of biblical prophecy, all of it still presented as following the path of commonsense reasoning and springing from the realization of republican ideals. "The Almighty hath long borne with the nations of the Earth, but now this controversy has begun and happy will it be for those who are prepared for the storm," he writes.[42] In what one might regard as a final insult to Paine, he circles back to the George Washington quote about France with which he opened, placing the Terror firmly within his prophetic chronology. Having established that freedom of conscience was a necessary precursor of the millennium—that is, that people had to be freed from state abuse of their moral right to obey God so that they could be convinced of it by the likes of Dow—he rests his case, looking forward to Christ's return.

The aperture of revelation that Dow welded onto Paine's egalitarianism was, by any measure, directly antithetical to Paine's religious, epistemological, and political commitments. However, it is important to note that Paine left ample room in his own arguments for this type of co-opting to happen. The republican-evangelical mash-up was created by evangelicals, but even Paine helped it along by leaning on Christian aesthetics in his own writing. He sprinkled just enough biblical language throughout *Rights of Man* for Dow to grab ahold of, making reference, for example, to the creation story of Genesis in order to talk about the ultimate origins of human rights and using the historical books of the Bible to suggest that monarchy originated in human error. In all cases Paine employed framing phrases to hold those citations at arm's length from his own arguments, but these were easily removed by an opportunistic editor like Dow. "Though I mean not to touch upon any sectarian principle of religion," Paine wrote, "yet it may be worth observing, that the genealogy of Christ is traced to Adam. Why then not trace the rights of man to the creation of man?"[43] Dow simply removed the rhetorical brackets and made use of the biblical precedent. "The genealogy of Christ is traced to Adam. Why not trace the rights of man up to his creation?"[44]

Paine had no regard for the Bible as revelation, but he knew what it took to make a persuasive argument in the late eighteenth century. He had used biblical evidence similarly in *Common Sense,* something critics pointed to as evidence of his personal lack of sincerity after the publication of *Age of Reason*. By drawing on the conventional religious idioms of his day, even obliquely, Paine unintentionally gave purchase to evangelical appropriation of his arguments. Noll (in this case following Hatch) has sharply observed the ways in which Enlightenment-informed Revolutionary rhetoric, because it was useful and persuasive, became a resource for early national theology and thereby exerted an unforeseen influence on it: "Since ideologies embedded in cultures have a historical logic of their own, there is scant surprise that as theologians embraced the language of commonsense republican democracy, commonsense republican democracy transformed the expressions of theology."[45] In the same way, Paine's strategic recourse to biblical idioms had the unplanned effect of suiting it to evangelical appropriation.

These openings, and their exploitation, had consequences for the usefulness and the uses of radical democratic thought into the nineteenth century. Among all Dow's publications, the Lynchburg edition of *Journey from Babylon to Jerusalem, or The Road to Peace and True Happiness, Prefaced with an Essay on the Rights of Man*—the first printing of Dow's appropriation of Paine's writing—was the only one for which he solicited subscribers, printing their names in the book. Dow itinerated more or less constantly until the late 1820s, rarely residing in any one place for very long. However, he and his wife, Peggy, were in residency in Lynchburg for much of 1812 and 1813. Dow's signature line at the end of *An Essay on the Rights of Man* indicates that he finished writing it near Lynchburg on August 21, 1812.[46] Dow and his associates would have canvassed for subscribers in the area during the spring and summer of 1812, asking locals to pay a portion of the book's purchase price in advance in order to finance the cost of printing.[47] The list of subscribers printed in the resulting volume consists of 543 names along with their places of residence. They are mostly from Virginia, with a handful located in neighboring Tennessee and North Carolina.[48] Census analysis reveals that most of them were, or would be, slaveholders. Nearly half (237) reported owning slaves in the 1810 census; an additional 132 were confirmed slaveholders as of 1820.[49] The vast majority of these subscribers owned fewer than ten slaves—they were not, that is, landed Southern planters but (relatively speaking) the common people Dow was always saying he was trying to reach.

This subscriber list provides important perspective on the consequences of the incorporation of republican rights rhetoric into monarchically governed religious frameworks. As the planters who had burned Paine in effigy nearly two decades earlier had recognized, his arguments had obvious relevance for an audience of slaveholders. By subsuming Paine's egalitarian rhetoric into a moral universe governed by a divine monarch, Dow continued to draw on the language of commonsense reasoning and natural equality while assuring his audience that the slave system had been providentially ordained and, in God's own time, was on a liberatory trajectory.

Like Paine, Dow was consistently antislavery. In *Journey from Babylon to Jerusalem* he argues clearly that abolition is the only fitting end to the problems caused by slavery, albeit in ways that are disturbing to contemporary readers. It is not possible to be both a successful slaveholder and a kind one, Dow writes. "The mind of Man is ever aspiring for a more exalted station; the consequence is, the better Slaves are used, the more saucy and impertinent they become; of course the practice must be wholly abolished or the slaves must be governed with *absolute* sway."[50] Since the latter made monsters of the master class, giving up slavery was the only desirable outcome, Dow reasons. Beyond that, he directly judges the depredations of Europeans against Indigenous Americans and enslaved Africans, citing "the love of money" as the human motivation that has "led the Nations of Europe to enslave, and destroy the poor *Blacks* of *Africa:* And the miserable *Indians* of *America.*" Continuing to work within Paine's framework of natural rights, Dow endorses the notion of human equality, suggesting that "the *Natural Abilities* of the *Europeans* and the *Africans,* perhaps admit of improvement equally *alike*" and lamenting, as he does in many places in his writing, the condition of the latter.[51]

However, Dow also makes it perfectly plain that he is not an abolitionist. He bows to the God of Providence regarding slavery's origins and purposes. "Doubtless it is the providence of God," he writes, that the natural ability of the European "is now rising to its highest *excellence,*" while that of the African "is *justly* visited with the entailment of ignorance, stupidity, and sloth, whilst moral evil fills their hearts and governs all their actions." Dow tells his audience that most of their enslaved laborers are content with their situation: "Most of those unhappy wretches, after being in slavery a term of time, will be affronted at the idea of being sent back to their native shores; and many are rejoiced at their situation, miserable as it is, and express gratitude that by this means they have found the *faith of Abraham* in the Gospel of God's dear son." Distinguishing, in a common strategy, between the Atlantic slave trade and the system of forced labor itself, he commends the fact that "the dirty *slave trade* . . . is now forever at an end." Finally, he assures his readership that their treatment of the enslaved has improved over time, plotting them on the liberatory trajectory of Providence: "In those countries where slavery exists they are used more *humanely* than formerly—and instead of *death* for mere trifles, the *penitentiary* system is adopted." He hints that the depredations of slavery, decreed by Providence, are in service of the advance of the natural, social, and moral rights of Africans, inasmuch as through the currently enslaved "one day the Gospel shall return to their native shores."[52]

Dow replaced Paine's enthusiasm for revolution, that is, with a faith in Providence. Dow took his virulent opposition to unjust constraints on human freedom and his enthusiasm for the dignity and individuality of human beings straight from Paine. By integrating that language of radical republicanism into a providential framework overseen by a monarchical God, however, Dow domesticated Paine's formerly incendiary rhetoric into a discourse of American liberty that suited an audience of slaveholders.

In the final analysis, though, the Revolutionary orientation of Paine's egalitarian rhetoric was not entirely lost on Dow. His appeal to Providence's oversight of the evils of slavery left room for a corollary assurance of punishment. On rare occasions in his writings he was surprisingly explicit about this coming punishment, such as in a later edition of *Rights of Man* that recouped some of Paine's Revolutionary fervor by granting the Haitian Revolution providential validation: "As *Hayti* was the first place where slavery began in the 'New World,'" he wrote in 1813, "so the *first* Visit in the Just retaliation began there likewise; thus the Hand of Justice will not always sleep."[53] Paine's Revolutionary idealism, though strained and contorted, did not lose its power to affect the monarchical frame into which Dow forced it.

Notes

1. See, e.g., Harry S. Stout, "Religion, Communications, and the Ideological Origins of the American Revolution," *William and Mary Quarterly*, 3d ser., 34, no. 4 (1977): 519–41.
2. Dee Andrews, *The Methodists and Revolutionary America, 1760–1800: The Shaping of an Evangelical Culture* (Princeton, NJ: Princeton University Press, 2000), xi.
3. Nathan Hatch, *The Democratization of American Christianity* (New Haven, CT: Yale University Press, 1989), 5.
4. Dee Andrews's own answer to the question operates along these lines. See also, e.g., Sam Haselby, *The Origins of American Religious Nationalism* (New York: Oxford University Press, 2015); and Shelby M. Balik, *Rally the Scattered Believers: Northern New England's Religious Geography* (Bloomington: Indiana University Press, 2014).
5. Mark Noll, *America's God: From Jonathan Edwards to Abraham Lincoln* (Oxford: Oxford University Press, 2002), 9.
6. Hatch, *Democratization of American Christianity*, 6.
7. Amanda Porterfield, *Conceived in Doubt: Religion and Politics in the New American Nation* (Chicago: University of Chicago Press, 2012), 11.

8. Lorenzo Dow, *A Journey from Babylon to Jerusalem . . . Prefaced with an Essay on the Rights of Man* (Lynchburg, Virginia: Haas & Lamb, 1812), 6. Throughout these notes, I cite Dow's *Rights of Man* and *Journey from Babylon to Jerusalem* individually, though they are published together in the 1812 edition, with which I am primarily working. Within that edition, the two works have separate pagination.
9. Porterfield, *Conceived in Doubt*, 171.
10. I use the word *evangelical* lightly here to denote those Protestants most bent on active evangelism in the early national period; this encompasses both revivalists like Dow and the social and cultural elites primarily responsible for founding voluntary societies. *Formalist* and *anti-formalist* are Curtis D. Johnson's very useful terms for distinguishing these sorts of evangelicals in *Redeeming America: Evangelicals and the Road to Civil War* (Chicago: I. R. Dee, 1993). For detailed reflection on the history and historiographical stakes of *evangelical* as a term, see Linford D. Fisher, "Evangelicals and Unevangelicals: The Contested History of a Word, 1500–1950," *Religion and American Culture* 26, no. 2 (Summer 2016): 184–226; and, most recently, Matthew Avery Sutton, "Redefining the History and Historiography on American Evangelicalism in the Era of the Religious Right," *Journal of the American Academy of Religion* 92, no. 1 (2024): 37–60.
11. See Julius S. Scott, *The Common Wind: Afro-American Currents in the Age of the Haitian Revolution* (New York: Verso, 2018), 155–57.
12. Seth Cotlar, *Tom Paine's America: The Rise and Fall of Transatlantic Radicalism in the Early Republic* (Charlottesville: University of Virginia Press, 2011), 2.
13. See Cotlar, *Tom Paine's America*, esp. chap. 1; and Porterfield, *Conceived in Doubt*.
14. Thomas Paine, *The Age of Reason: Being an Investigation of True and of Fabulous Theology* (Philadelphia: Folwell, 1795), 5–6.
15. See Porterfield, *Conceived in Doubt*. See also Eric Schlereth, *An Age of Infidels: The Politics of Religious Controversy in the Early United States* (Philadelphia: University of Pennsylvania Press, 2013); and Christopher Grasso, *Skepticism and American Faith: From the Revolution to the Civil War* (New York: Oxford University Press, 2018).
16. A Delaware Waggoner [David Nelson], *An Investigation of That False, Fabulous and Blasphemous Misrepresentation of Truth, Set Forth by Thomas Paine . . . Dedicated to the Protection of the United States of America . . .* ([Lancaster, PA: W. & R. Dickson, 1800]), 26.
17. Personified for his contemporaries and for subsequent historians, that is. Dow plays a large role in Hatch's *Democratization of American Christianity* and a smaller one in Noll's *America's God*. For further background on Dow,

see Seth Perry, *American Preacher: The Life and Times of the Eccentric Lorenzo Dow* (Philadelphia: University of Pennsylvania Press, 2026).

18. Hatch actually quotes a good deal from Dow's *Rights of Man* to illustrate Dow's "vigorous Jeffersonian rhetoric" without making the connection to Paine's *Rights of Man*. See Hatch, *Democratization of American Christianity*, 37.
19. Legal concerns may have been a factor, but Paine had died in 1809, making things easier for Dow in that respect.
20. Prior to Dow's, the last edition printed in America was from 1797.
21. See Perry, "*Paine Detected* in Mississippi: Slavery, Print Culture, and the Threat of Deism in the Early Republic," *William and Mary Quarterly*, 3d ser., 78, no. 2 (April 2021): 313–38.
22. Lorenzo Dow, *The Life and Travels of Lorenzo Dow* (Hartford, CT: Lincoln & Gleason, 1804), 301.
23. Lorenzo Dow, *An Essay on the Rights of Man* (Lynchburg, VA: Haas & Lamb, 1812), 43. Cf. Paine, *Rights of Man*, pt. 1, in *The Works of Thomas Paine* (Philadelphia: James Carey, 1797), 63.
24. Dow, *Essay*, 3. The quote is from a July 4, 1798, letter from Washington to John Adams; see *Founders Online*, National Archives, https://founders.archives.gov/documents/Washington/06-02-02-0290. Dow would have known it in published form from John Marshall's biography of Washington, *The Life of George Washington*, vol. 5 (Philadelphia: C. P. Wayne, 1807), 750. The italics are Dow's, emphasizing (it would appear) Washington's gesture toward providential thinking.
25. Dow, *Essay*, 3.
26. Paine, *Rights of Man*, 62–63.
27. Dow, *Essay*, 6.
28. Dow, *Essay*, 12.
29. Dow, *Essay*, 79.
30. Porterfield, *Conceived in Doubt*, 115.
31. Paine, *Rights of Man*, 77–78.
32. Dow, *Essay*, 14.
33. Dow, *Essay*, 13.
34. Thomas Jefferson, *Notes on the State of Virginia* (Boston: H. Sprague, 1802), 218–19.
35. Paine, *Rights of Man*, 79.
36. Dow, *Essay*, 14.
37. Dow, *Essay*, 37.
38. Dow, *Essay*, 13.
39. Dow, *Essay*, 16.
40. Porterfield, *Conceived in Doubt*, 23.
41. Dow, *Essay*, 37–38.

42. Dow, *Essay*, 38.
43. Paine, *Rights of Man*, 61.
44. Dow, *Essay*, 20.
45. Noll, *America's God*, 229.
46. Dow, *Essay*, 96.
47. It is interesting that Dow sold subscriptions for this book and printed the subscribers' names. Subscription sales and the publication of subscribers' names were common enough practices at various points in American book publishing. However, such practices were often employed to raise advance money for printing large books of particular note, such as bibles, and even that had waned by the second decade of the nineteenth century, as more publishers were capitalized enough to undertake large projects without advance sales. In any case, subscriptions were never that common for smaller books such as *Journey from Babylon to Jerusalem*. This incidence of subscription sales was probably a consequence of the environment of print in Lynchburg at this time but also of Dow's knowledge of his receptive public. For Dow at this moment, printing his subscribers' names in the book did as much for him as it did for them; he appreciated every opportunity to show off the number of people interested in and willing to vouch for his work. It is also worth noting that this was the first of Dow's publications to include an engraving of the author, suggesting that he had enough subscription money left over from printing to have such a likeness made and included in the book.
48. The subscriber list appears on the last eight pages of the *Journey* volume; these pages are unnumbered.
49. For this research, I am deeply indebted to my research assistant, Michael Fording.
50. Dow, *Journey from Babylon to Jerusalem*, 72.
51. Dow, *Essay*, 71–72.
52. Dow, *Essay*, 71–73.
53. Dow, *Analects, or Reflections upon Natural, Moral, and Political Philosophy: Including the Rights, Interests, and Duties of Man* (New York: John C. Totten, 1813), 101. Here again Dow paraphrases Jefferson's *Notes on the State of Virginia*: "Indeed I tremble for my country when I reflect that God is just; that his justice cannot sleep for ever" (224). Dow refers to "Jefferson's predictions" on this point elsewhere; see *The Yankee Spy*, yet another edition of his *Rights of Man* (Nashville: Thomas G. Bradford, 1813), xi–xii.

CONTRIBUTORS

Shelby M. Balik is professor of history at Metropolitan State University of Denver. She is the author of *Rally the Scattered Believers: Northern New England's Religious Geography* (Indiana University Press, 2014), which won the 2014 Best First Book Award from the Phi Alpha Theta history honor society. Her work has appeared in *Church History*, the *Journal of Social History*, the *Massachusetts Historical Review*, the *New England Quarterly*, and the *Journal of Church and State*, along with the *Washington Post* and *Religion Dispatches*. Her second book project (in progress) explores the social, emotional, and political dimensions of household religious practice in the long eighteenth century.

Michael Baysa, a postdoctoral fellow in the Department of Religion at the University of Vermont, is a scholar of religion, history, and media. His current book project, titled "Unpublishing Religion: Race, Heterodoxy, and the Printing Press in Early America"—under contract with NYU Press—examines the mechanical constraints and networks of influence on media production to facilitate religious expression, dialogue, and debate in early America. He has published research articles in journals like *Religion and American Culture: A Journal of Interpretation*, *Religion Compass*, and *Church History: Studies in Christianity and Culture*.

Katherine Carté is professor of history at Southern Methodist University. She is the author of *Religion and the American Revolution: An Imperial History* (UNC Press for the Omohundro Institute, 2021), which received the 2023 Outler Prize from the American Society of Church History; and *Religion and Profit: Moravians in Early America* (University of Pennsylvania Press, 2009, paper 2011), which was awarded the 2010 Dale W. Brown Award for Outstanding Scholarship in Anabaptist and Pietist Studies. Her articles have appeared in the *William and Mary Quarterly*, *Church History*, and *Early American Studies*.

Peter Y. Choi is a historian, educator, and public theologian. He serves on the core doctoral faculty at the Graduate Theological Union in Berkeley, California, where his teaching and research explore the intersections of religion, history, and public life. He is also the executive director of the Center for Faith and Justice in San Francisco and author of *George Whitefield: Evangelist for God and Empire* (Eerdmans, 2018). His research has been funded by the Andrew Mellon Foundation, the Historical Society of Pennsylvania, the Huntington Library, and the Library Company of Philadelphia.

Christopher Cannon Jones is assistant professor of history at Brigham Young University and the editor of the *Journal of Mormon History*. He is a coeditor (with David Golding) of *Missionary Interests: Protestant and Mormon Missions in the Nineteenth and Twentieth Centuries* (Cornell University Press, 2024) and is currently completing a book manuscript on the making of American Methodism in the Revolutionary Atlantic world. His articles have appeared in *Religion and American Culture: A Journal of Interpretation*, the *Journal of Mormon History*, and *Mormon Historical Studies*. At BYU he teaches courses on missionaries in American history, slavery and the slave trade, the American Revolution, and family history.

Adam Jortner is the Goodwin-Philpott Professor of Religion in the Department of History at Auburn University. He is the author of several books on religious freedom and religious conflict in the United States, including *A Promised Land: Jews, the American Revolution, and the Genesis of Religious Freedom* (Oxford University Press, 2024). He is the host of Wondrium's series *Ten Great What-Ifs in American History* and the Audible series *American Monsters* and a former member of the script team on the PBS show *Where in Time Is Carmen Sandiego?*

Spencer W. McBride is the associate managing historian of the Joseph Smith Papers. In addition to working as coeditor of three volumes of the Joseph Smith Papers, he is the creator, writer, and host of the project's critically acclaimed podcast series. McBride has published multiple books on the history of religion and American political culture, including *Pulpit and Nation* (University of Virginia Press, 2016), *Contingent Citizens* (Cornell University Press, 2020), *Joseph Smith for President* (Oxford University Press, 2021), and *New York's Burned-Over District* (Cornell University Press, 2023). His writing has also been published in the *Deseret News* and the *Washington Post*.

Jessica Lauren Nelson is a public historian and assistant visiting professor at the University of Wisconsin–Milwaukee, where she teaches courses in public history, early US history, and Latin American history. Previously, she was the director of religion and cultural initiatives at the Eiteljorg Museum of Native Americans and Western Art. She is editor of the book *Religion and the American West: Belief, Violence, and Resilience from 1800 to Today* (University of New Mexico Press, 2023). Her research focuses on the experiences of Native women in Christian spaces in Mexico and the United States in the eighteenth and nineteenth centuries.

Alyssa Penick is a senior fellow at the Jefferson Scholars Foundation at the University of Virginia and a JD candidate at Yale Law School. Her dissertation was awarded the William Nelson Cromwell Foundation Dissertation Prize by the American Society for Legal History, and she is the author of *A Great Revolution in Church and State: Religion, Government, and Property in the Chesapeake, 1700–1830* (University of Virginia Press, 2026).

Seth Perry is associate professor of religion in America at Princeton University. His first book, *Bible Culture and Authority in the Early United States* (Princeton University Press, 2018), explores the performative, rhetorical, and material aspects of Bible-based authority in early national America. His work has appeared in *Church History*, *Early American Studies*, the *Journal of the American Academy of Religion*, the *William and Mary Quarterly*, *Slate*, and many other outlets. He teaches courses on religion in early America, theory and method in the study of religion, scripture as a genre, and Satan. His second book, *American Preacher* (University of Pennsylvania Press, 2026) is a biography of Lorenzo Dow, the early national period's most famous and most eccentric itinerant preacher.

Peter W. Walker is assistant professor of history at the University of Wyoming. He is working on a book manuscript titled "The Power of Suffering: Loyalism and the Church of England in the Age of the American Revolution." The project has been supported by a Summer Stipend award from the National Endowment for the Humanities, the Whitehill Prize from the Colonial Society of Massachusetts, the Prichard Prize from the Historical Society of the Episcopal Church, and a Mellon-ACLS Dissertation Completion Fellowship.

INDEX

abolition: and accrual of "moral capital," 180; African Americans in fight for, 188–89; in Britain, 193n2; and capitalism, 184; diminishment of calls for, after Revolution, 186; and Dow, 232–33; and New Divinity movement, 187; in Northern states, 188; and Protestant security, 183; and Quakers, 184–85, 190; in states with the smallest number of slaves, 186. *See also* evangelical abolition
Adams, John: on ability of United States to maintain moral citizenry without religion, 4; correspondence with Jedidiah Morse, 5–6, 24n15; fast day called by, 4; on fast day declared by Continental Congresses, 34, 36, 94; and Illuminati, 4; on print debate among Boston clergy, 109
Adams, John Quincy, 120
Adams, Samuel, 111
Adventures of Jack Ramble, the Methodist Preacher, The (Bailey), 158
African Americans, 15, 91, 188–89. *See also* Black Methodists; slaves/slavery
African Methodist Episcopal Church, 167
African Methodist Episcopal Zion Church, 167
Age of Democratic Revolution, The (Palmer), 13
Age of Reason (Paine), 222, 224
Albert, Peter, 12
Algonquian Christian communities, 80
Allen, Richard, 167
Allison, Patrick, 139, 143, 144
All Men Will Not Be Saved Forever (Mather), 118
American Board of Commissioners for Foreign Missions, 72
American Episcopal Church, 39
American Revolution: as civic, moral issue, 94–95; as civil war, 44; as comparatively unrevolutionary, 13; and "contagion of liberty," 197n41; disestablishment and rhetoric of, 142–44; disestablishment as climax to, 11; disestablishment as key part of, 8; and divisions among Methodists, 153, 167; and establishment of Brothertown, 77–78; and evangelical abolition, 175, 187–88; evangelicals' co-option of ideals of, 222–23; freedom for Virginia slaves joining British army, 155–56; and Great Awakening, 9, 25n23; migrations of Methodists during, 154–55; and Proclamation Line of 1763, 68; as "profoundly secular event," 3, 16, 30n48; Protestantism as doing essential national work for, 10; as providential event, 16; reliance of London publishers for religious printing due to, 110; religion's importance to Americans of era of, 3–4; religious diversity of America compared to English religious tyranny as cause of, 6; religious freedom as fundamental to, 131, 132–33; remaking of American Protestantism as unleashed by, 220–21; rhetoric of, as resource for early national theology, 231–32; rhetoric of, repurposed by Dow, 219–20; as "unfavorable" for religion, 7
Amory, Hugh, 125n13, 127n28
Amos, Joseph, 74
Analects, or Reflections upon Natural, Moral, and Political Philosophy: Including the Rights, Interests, and Duties of Man (Dow), 225, 237n53

Anderson, Virginia DeJohn, 14
Andrews, Dee, 219
Andrews, Edward E., 70
Andrews, William, 43
Anglicanism. *See* Church of England
Annals of the American Revolution (J. Morse), 5
Apess, William, 70, 73–74, 80
Apology for Negro Slavery (Turnbull), 178
Arthur, William, 205
Asbury, Francis, 151–52, 157, 166, 182
Ashpo, Samuel, 73
Aupaumut, Hendrick, 78–79, 83n22
Awash in a Sea of Faith (Butler), 3

Backus, Isaac, 109, 110, 117, 120, 128n43
Bailey, Jacob, 37, 157–58
Bailyn, Bernard, 9, 10, 197n41
Baird, Robert, 6–8, 11
Baltimore Gazette, 141
Bangs, Nathan, 159
Baptists, 138, 142–43
Barry, Robert, 155
Barton, Esther Rittenhouse, 48, 60
Barton, Thomas, 48–49, 52, 55, 57–60
Bass, Edward, 42
Batwell, Daniel, 65n44
Bavarian Illuminati panic (1790s), 4
Bayly, Lewis, 208
Belknap, John, 116, 128n37, 128n47
Bellamy. Joseph, 120
Benezet, Anthony, 184–85, 186
Berlin, Ira, 181
Black, William, 156, 158–59
Blackfeet belief systems, 70
Black Methodists: in Canada, 155–57, 160–61; exodus of, from MEC, 167; lay preachers, 156; in Northwest Territory, 165–66; partnership with white Methodists in Nova Scotia, 156–57; in Sierra Leone, 161–63, 166–67; and white church leaders, 154
Bloch, Ruth, 10
Bonner, Frederick, 164, 165
Bonomi, Patricia, 9, 10
Book of Common Prayer (Church of England), 40, 51, 52, 53, 54, 64n31
Boston: British occupation of, 113–14; change in Anglican liturgy in, 42; Congregationalist domination of, 42; exodus of printers from, 114; leading patriots in, 110–11; resurgence of printing after Revolution, 117; subjecting of Congregationalist ministers to regional Anglican bishops in, 113
Boulukos, George, 181, 183
Bradford, Andrew, 128n41
Brady, N., 114
Brainerd, John, 79
Brannon, Rebecca, 49
Brekus, Catherine, 15
Brice, John, 43
Bridenbaugh, Carl, 9
Britain: antislavery movement in, 193n2; Catholicism as treason after Glorious Revolution in, 133; Methodism as threat to sovereignty of, 157–58; religious printing in, 119–20; scaffolding of Protestantism in, 92; toleration as religious freedom after Glorious Revolution in, 133; tradition of fast days in, 34; war with U.S. and Methodists, 166; Williamite oaths, 54–55, 56, 61
Brooks, Lisa, 70
Brotherton, New Jersey, 79, 86n60
Brothertown (now Brothertown Indian Nation): adoption of citizenship by, 80; ethnogenesis of, 69, 75–78, 82n3; and Johnson, 69, 76–77, 78, 85n40; as under pastoral care of Occom, 73; Stockbridge connections, 78, 79–80
Brown, Christopher, 180–81, 184
Burke, Edmund, 223
Bush, Solomon, 96
Butler, Jon, 3, 16

Calumet & Cross Society, 81
Calvert, Jane E., 38
Calvin, Bartholomew, 79
Calvin, Hezekiah, 71, 79

Canada: Black Methodists in, 154–57, 160–61; English preachers under umbrella of British Wesleyan Methodist Church, 159; indenture of Blacks to whites in, 161; lay Methodist preachers in, 160; MEC and established church in, 157; segregated Methodist worship services in, 161; slaves brought to, 160; US-based Methodist preachers sent to, 157; war between U.S. and Britain and Methodists, 166; Wesley's refusal to send English preachers to, 158; white Methodists in, 154–55, 156–57
capitalism, relationship with slavery of, 184, 196n28
Capitalism and Slavery (Williams), 184
Caribbean, 91–93, 100, 157
Carp, Benjamin, 37
Carr, Ryan, 70, 77
Carroll, Charles (barrister), 147n11
Carroll, Charles (of Carrollton), 147n11
Carroll, John, 135–36, 137–38, 141–42, 143–44
Carté, Katherine, 92, 95
Carter, John, 120
Catholics/Catholicism: discrimination against, in Virginia, 91; and Maryland's Clergy Bill (1783) and general assessment, 145; restrictions on, in Maryland, 134, 135; in Revolutionary Maryland, 137–38; as treason after Glorious Revolution in England, 133
Chain of Lorenzo, The (Dow), 225–26
Chandler, Thomas, 39, 113
Charleston (South Carolina) Baptist Association, 204
Chase, Samuel, 147n11
Chauncy, Charles: attacks against Anglican episcopacy by, 113; and Backus, 117, 128n43; on British occupation of Boston, 113–14; as colonial author, 109–10, 123n6; distraction theory explaining publication gap of, during Revolution, 111, 123n8; and John Murray, 117; and New Divinity movement, 120; patriotic publications by, 112–13; as "patriot preacher," 110; and Price, 119, 130n53; public appearances by, 114; as public defender of New England orthodoxy, 109–10; published in England, 119–20; responses to *Salvation of All Men*, 118–19; use of conversations, correspondences, conversations, correspondences to circulate views, 114–16, 128n38
Christian nation, 1–2, 6–7
Christians/Christianity: in *Age of Reason*, 224; authenticity of conversion to, 69; compatibility of slavery with, 176; conversion of slaves as moral duty of slaveholders, 179–80; education of children to nurture piety, 204, 205; and "hereditary heathenism," 175; and intertribal relationships among Indigenous Americans, 68; in Maryland and Virginia 1776 constitutions, 135; and morality of citizenry, 4–5; penalties and restrictions placed on non-Anglicans in Maryland and Virginia, 133–34; republican, 200; rhetoric of, as language of diplomacy, 76–77; as system of knowledge about the world, 70; test oath for holding office requiring belief in, 99–100. *See also* Native Christians/Christianity; Protestants/Protestantism; *and specific denominations*
"Christian slavery," 174
Church in the House (Henry), 208
Church of England: disestablishment of, and formation of MEC, 153; as essential bodies of local government in Maryland and Virginia, 133; as established religion in Maryland and Virginia, 133; loyalists and conservative, hierarchical Anglicanism, 10; in Maryland constitution (1776), 136; Methodism as threat to hegemony of, 157–58; preservation of, in America, 42; and regulation of marriage in Maryland and Virginia, 137; reorganization of, as Protestant

Church of England (*continued*)
Episcopal Church in Maryland, 139; as state church, 52; subjecting Congregationalist ministers to regional, bishops in Boston, 113
Church of England clergy: active versus passive, as loyalists, 55; Anglican liturgy changes during Revolution, 33, 39–42, 52–53, 54, 64n31; Declaration of Independence and liturgy, 39–42; as disproportionately loyalist, 52; neutrality as tactic by, 55; nonjurors to Williamite monarchy, 54; oaths taken upon ordination, 51, 53–55; and Thirty-Nine Articles of Religion, 53
cities, fast day participation in, 37–38
citizenship: Brothertown adoption of, 80; and family worship, 205, 211; as inherently masculine prerogative, 201–2; of Jews, 99, 107n73; and piety, 205; and race, 107n73; and synagogues as institutions of choice for Jews, 19; and universality of moral virtue, 95
Clark, Thomas, 203, 210
Clark, William, 53
Clarkson, John, 161
Clarkson, Thomas, 173
Clarkson Thesis, 173
clergy: coopting pulpits of, with declarations of fast days, 17, 34–35, 94; education of, 35; as exempt from test oath, 58; influence of Chauncy on New England, 116, 128n38; loyalist, and fast days, 36–37, 38–39; political activism of, 35; and social class, 43; subjecting Congregationalist ministers to regional Anglican bishops in Boston, 113; as unconcerned with civil affairs, 58. *See also* Church of England clergy
Coffey, John, 193n1
Cohen, Jacob Raphael, 101
Coke, Thomas, 151, 152, 157, 182
Colley, Linda, 12
Colman, Benjamin, 208, 210
colonization in Africa, 161–63, 166–67, 190–91
Come Shouting to Zion (Wood and Frey), 15
Common Cause: Creating Race and Nation in the American Revolution, The (Parkinson), 13
Common Sense (Paine), 38, 231
Company for the Propagation of the Gospel in New England, 71
Conceived in Doubt (Porterfield), 221
Conforti, Joseph, 187, 191
Congregationalists, 42, 113
Connecticut, 188
conscientious objection and oaths, 50, 54
Continental Congresses, declaration of fast day by, 34–35, 36, 94
Coombé, Thomas, 41–42
Cooper, Myles, 39
Cotlar, Seth, 223
Crabtree, Sarah, 15
Cranch, Mary, 120
Crises, The (Paine), 38
Cromwell, James, 156
Cugoano, Ottobah, 188

Dana, Joseph, 205, 210
Davies, Samuel, 177, 179–80
Davis, David Brion, 184, 189, 191, 192n1
Declaration of Independence: and Anglican liturgy, 39–42; Jefferson credited with authorship of, 46n3; removal of condemnation of slavery from, 186, 191; and slavery, 185–86
deists/deism: and Dow, 225–26; Paine as, 224; and Seixas's approach to religion, 93–94
Delaware (tribe), 78–79
Democratization of American Christianity, The (Hatch), 20, 121, 130n60
Dialogue Concerning the Slavery of the Africans, A (Hopkins), 187, 197n41
Dickdook Leshon Gnebreet (*Grammar of the Hebrew Tongue, A*, Monis), 129n48
disestablishment: and ability of free government to continue, 8; of Church

of England and formation of MEC, 153; as climax to Revolution, 11; as ending "ecclesiastical tyranny," 142–43; fear of moral vacuum as result of, 211; histories of, 11; historiography of religiosity in U.S. after, 219–21, 222, 223, 228, 230; and historiography of Revolution, 11; as integral part of Revolution, 131; as key result of Revolution, 8; losses of "blood and treasure" as reason for equality provided by, 144; and Maryland 1776 constitution, 136; movement use of language of Revolution, 142–44; non-Christians often not included in equality arguments for, 144; process in Virginia of, 11; and *Rights of Man*, 228; and Virginia 1776 constitution, 135

"disinterested benevolence," 197n41

Doctrine of Final Universal Salvation Examined and Shewn to Be Unscriptural (William), 118

doctrine of "fortunate fall," 176–77, 179

Doctrine of Sovereign Grace, The (Backus), 120

Doctrine of Universal Salvation Examined and Refuted, The (Backus), 109, 117, 120, 128n43

Dodd, William, 114

Dooley, Joe, 21

Dow, Lorenzo: basic facts about, 224–25, 232; and Paine's deistical arguments, radical individualism, and writing style, 225–26; purpose of co-opting of rhetoric of American Revolution by, 219–20. See also *Essay on the Rights of Man, An* (Dow)

Dow, Peggy, 232

Drescher, Seymour, 185–86, 191

Duché, Jacob, 40–42

Dulmage, John, 154

"The Duty of Christians to Propagate Their Religion Among Heathens" (Davies), 179–80

Dwight, Timothy, 4

Dwight, Timothy, IV, 110, 121

education: Christian, to nurture piety of children, 204, 205; of clergy, 35; Foreign Mission School, 72; of Indigenous Americans, 71, 74, 79; Native Christians as teachers, 72–73, 74, 79

Edwards, Jonathan, 109–10, 120, 122n3

Edwards, Jonathan, Jr., 120–21, 186

Eeyamquittoowauconnuck/Eeyawquittoowauconnuck. *See* Brothertown (now Brothertown Indian Nation)

Eisenhower, Dwight D., 6–7

Eleff, Zev, 103n6, 104n13

Eliot, John, 116, 118, 128n37, 129n47

Embury, Margaret, 155

Embury, Philip, 154

Embury, Samuel, 155

Enfield, William, 209

England. *See* Britain

Epistle of Caution and Advice Concerning the Buying and Keeping of Slaves, An (Benezet), 185

Equiano, Olaudah, 188

Essay on the Rights of Man, An (Dow): basic facts about, 221–22; Christian theism of, 227–28; dual role of title, 225; first appearance of, 225, 232; first audience for, 21, 223, 225, 232, 234, 237nn47–48; foundational ideas allowing exploitation of Paine's language, 222; France as example of "Natural Evil" as consequence of "Moral Evil" in, 226; individual rights in, 226; integration of monarchical moral rights, 228; Paine's categorization of human rights as amended in, 220, 227; purpose of, 222; purpose of Dow's co-opting of rhetoric of *Rights of Man*, 219–20; as redacted and heavily supplemented version of *Rights of Man*, 221–22; sin in, 229; toleration in, 228–29; use of Paine's use of biblical language, 231

Essig, James, 196n27

evangelical abolition: amelioration as stepping stone to, 179, 181; arc of, 174, 181–82, 186, 187–88, 191, 192, 194n5;

evangelical abolition (*continued*)
and Clarkson Thesis, 173; colonization in Africa, 190–91; effectiveness of, 184; historiography of, 192n1; and idea of racial hierarchy, 188; at peak during Revolutionary period, 175; reparation, 189–90; role of heroic evangelical leaders, 193n1; slave trade as focus of, 184; Wesley, 186–87

evangelicals/evangelicalism: acquiescence to economic, social, and political exigency in complicity with slavery of, 183, 192, 196n27; amelioration response to slavery, 178–83; association of reason with revelation by, 230; changing positions toward slavery of, 174; co-option of ideals of Revolution by, 222–23; as defined by Perry, 235n10; elements necessary for U.S. to fulfill divine will, 200; and Maryland's Clergy Bill (1783) and general assessment, 145; in public sphere as necessary, 229–30; racism of, 185, 187, 188, 190–91; rationalization response to slavery, 175–77; restoration of full human rights only after success of, 230; separation of spiritual needs from physical needs of slaves, 176, 177, 179, 181; and Virginia's general assessment, 145. *See also* Methodists/Methodism

Ewer, John, 113

family worship: catechisms for, 202, 205; elements of, 200; as elevating master's status, 202; family governance as tying piety to patriotism, 201; as foundation of practical religion, 202–3; inclusion of servants and enslaved people in, 205–6; mother's role in, 203–4; as necessary for good government, 205, 211; as necessary for new U.S.'s salvation, 200; and need to balance patriarchal mastery and dependence, 201; political vocabulary of, 208–11; as preserving patriarchal authority, 203; publication of guides for, 202, 207–8; as safeguarding patriarchal authority, 206

Farrelly, Maura, 15

fast days: as battlefields for public opinion, 38–39; called by John Adams, 4; as civic, moral issue, 94–95; in colonial America, 34; as effort by Revolutionary leadership "to forge a political alliance" with clergy, 94; English tradition of, 34; First Continental Congress's declaration of, 34–35, 36; first national, 17–18; participation in cities, 37–38; political consequences of, 17; as public rituals to nurture common identity, 35–36; as signals of allegiance during Revolution, 33, 36–37; and tenable political middle ground, 44–45

Federalists, 4–5, 224

felix culpa doctrine, 176–77, 179

Fessenden, Tracy, 207

First Continental Congress, 34–35, 36

Fisher, Linford, 15

Fleet, John, 117–18, 129n44

Fleet, Thomas, 117–18, 129n44

Foreign Mission School, 72

founders: colonists' unfamiliarity with, 35, 45n3; as deists, 224; as Protestant Christians, 6–7; and public opinion about United States as Christian nation, 2; religion of, 30n48. *See also specific individuals*

Fowler, David, 69, 71, 79

Fowler, Hannah, 72

Fowler, Jacob, 74

Freeman, Elizabeth, 188

French Revolution, 223–24, 226

Frey, Sylvia, 15

Garrettson, Freeborn, 156, 157, 158, 161

Gatch, Elizabeth, 164

Gatch, Philip, 163–65

Gin Lum, Kathryn, 15

Godbeer, Richard, 15

Goetz, Rebecca, 177, 195n10

Gordon, William, 118

Gospel Comfort, Under Heavy Tidings (Backus), 120
grace, theology of, 201
Grammar of the Hebrew Tongue, A (*Dick-dook Leshon Gnebreet*, Monis), 129n48
Grasso, Christopher, 139n59
Great Awakening: growth of dissenting denominations in Maryland and Virginia, 134; and new Native congregations, 75, 76; as unifier of American people against tyranny, 9, 25n23
Green, Thomas, 121
Greene, Nathaniel, 127n29
Greenleaf, James, 114, 126n24
Gregerson, Linda, 14

Haitian Revolution, 234
Hall, David D., 14, 127n28
Hammon, Jupiter, 188
Hancock, John, 111
Hannit family, 71
Hanson, Peter, 188–89
Harrison, William, 43
Hart, Levi, 187
Hastings, Selina, 185
Hatch, Nathan O., 10, 20, 121, 130n60, 220–21
Haudenosaunee, 69, 71, 74
Haynes, Lemuel, 190
Hays, Barack, 92, 96
Hays, Solomon, 92
Hazlitt, William, 119
Heck, Barbara, 154–55
Heck, Paul, 154–55
Heimert, Alan, 9
Henry, Matthew, 208
Henry, Patrick, 140
"hereditary heathenism," 175
Heyrman, Christine, 194n5
historiography of American Revolution: conflation of religion with Protestant churches in, 8; and differences in Maryland's and Virginia's constitutions, wartime laws, and postwar reforms, 132; and disestablishment, 11; fears of slave revolt and Indigenous attack as unifier for, 13; Great Awakening's role, 9, 25n23; Indigenous Americans in, 80–81; political ideology in 1760s and 1770s as proxy for much of Revolutionary War in, 10; Protestantism as doing essential national work for Revolution, 10; Protestants' investment of Americans in Britain's empire just before Revolution, 12–13, 27n36; recent trends in, 15–16, 30n48; religion as essential if nonspecific influence, 11–12; religion as largely peripheral to causes of, 14; religions beyond dominant Protestantism, 15; religiosity after disestablishment, 219–21, 222, 223, 228, 230; and studies of transatlantic Age of Revolutions, 13
History of Jamaica in Three Volumes (Long), 178
Hitchcock, Enos, 210–11
Hoffman, Peter, 12
Hofstadter, Richard, 130n60
Hopkins, Samuel, 118, 187, 190–91
Hutcherson, James, 162

Illuminati, 4
Independent Gazetteer, 100
Indigenous Americans: advantages of identifying as Christian in Anglo-American society, 73–74; authenticity of conversion to Christianity questioned, 69; belief systems of, 70; Christianity and intertribal relationships, 68; education in English literacy as strategy for defending lands, 71; fears of attacks by, in historiography of Revolution, 13; Great Awakening and new congregations, 75; Jacksonian removal policies (1820s and 1830s), 80; and oath-taking, 57; place of, in historiography of American history, 80–81; and Proclamation Line of 1763, 68. *See also* Brothertown (now Brothertown Indian Nation); Native Christians/Christianity

Inquiry Concerning the Future State of Those Who Die in Their Sins (Hopkins), 118
Irons, Charles, 176
Isaac, Rhys, 9, 10–11

Jefferson, Thomas: credit for authorship of Declaration of Independence, 46n3; on just God, 237n53; knowledge of, in New England, 45n3; state's proper indifference to matters of religious belief, 228
Jews/Judaism: in Caribbean, 91–93, 104n21; and citizenship, 19, 99, 107n73; deist approach to, 93–94; discrimination against, in Virginia, 91; first in America, 91; historiography of American, 89; as loyalists, 95, 96, 206n48; and Maryland's 1776 constitution, 144–45, 150n56; as patriots, 90, 92, 93, 94, 95–96, 97–99, 100; as percent of white population of U.S., 92; post-Revolution approach to religious institutional life of, 88–89, 100, 103n6; post-Revolution political rights of, 89; Revolution and democratization of, 89–90, 104n13; and Revolution as civic, moral issue, 94, 95; status in Europe of, at time of Revolution, 91; synagogues as institutions of choice, 19; and test oaths, 101
Jick, Leon, 104n13
Johnson, Joseph: and Brothertown, 69, 76–77, 78, 85n40; death of, 78; diplomatic peace mission of, 74; at Moor's Indian Charity School, 79
Johnson, Samuel, 186
Johnson, Sylvester, 14
Jordan, Luke, 156, 161, 162
Josephson, Manuel, 88–89, 92, 96
Journey from Babylon to Jerusalem, A (Dow), 225, 232–33
Judah sisters, 101
Juster, Susan, 12–13, 14, 15

Keane, Webb, 69
Kidd, Thomas, 9
King, Boston, 156, 161
Kirkland, Samuel, 79
Klein, Rachel, 194n5
Kneeland, Thomas, 113, 120, 126nn20–21

LaPier, Rosalyn, 70
Lathrop, John, 210
Lawrence, John, 155
Lawson, Kim, 81
Lee, Jesse, 166
Leland, John, 182
Letter to a Friend, Containing Remarks on Certain Passages in a Sermon Preached by the Right Reverend Father in God, John Lord Bishop of Landaff, A (Chauncy), 113
Letter to a Friend, Giving a Concise, but Just, Representation of the Hardships and Sufferings the Town of Boston Is Exposed to, A (Chauncy), 113–14
Leverett, Thomas, 113, 114, 126nn20–21
Levy, Hayman, 97
Lewis, David, 166, 171n44
Liaster, James, 162
lived religion, 14
Lockwood, Matthew, 185
Long, Edward, 178
Losee, William, 159
Love, Harold, 127n28
loyalists/loyalism: Barton as martyr, 58–59; Black, 155–57, 160–61; and Church of England clergy, 52, 55; and conservative, hierarchical Anglicanism, 10; familial ties of, 43; Jews of Shearith Israel, 95, 96, 206n48; and martyrdom, 61; Methodist, 154; and SPG, 52. *See also specific individuals*
loyalty oaths: allegiance to king as void because of actions of George III, 56–57; as oath against king, 18; Pennsylvania Test Act, 55–56, 57–60, 61, 65n44; and political allegiance, 50, 51; refusal to take, as religious persecution, 48–49, 51; religious dimensions of, 60–61; and SPG missionaries, 48, 52;

as transforming Revolution into civil war, 44; Williamite, 54–55, 56, 61
Lunsford, Isaac, 159
Lyell, Thomas, 172n44

Macaulay, Zachary, 161–62, 163, 191
Madison, James, 140
Mann, John, 155, 156
Marcus, Jacob Rader, 95
marriage laws, 136–37
Mars, James, 188
Martin, Joel W., 69, 70
martyrdom, 58–60, 61
Maryland: ambiguous position of established religion in (1776–1783), 132; Church of England as bodies of local government in, 133; Church of England as established religion in, 133; Clergy Bill (1783, Maryland), 139, 145; constitution (1776), 144–45, 150n56; Declaration of Rights in 1776 constitution, 134, 135–36, 138–39, 142, 147n11; established church as "ecclesiastical tyranny" in, 143; established church as "religious slavery," 143; and Great Awakening, 134; marriage law changes during Revolution, 137; penalties and restrictions placed on non-Anglicans in, 133–34; proposed general assessment for religion in (1785), 141–42; reorganization of Church of England as Protestant Episcopal Church in, 139; toleration for Catholics in Revolutionary, 137–38
Mather, Cotton, 210
Mather, Samuel, 118
Mathews, Donald, 194n5
Mayhew, Jonathan, 110
McBride, Spencer W., 17, 94
McConville, Brendan, 12
Mears, Samson, 97
Memorial and Remonstrance (Madison), 140
Methodist Episcopal Church (MEC): and American preachers in Canada, 158; Black Methodists exodus from, 167; decisions to send US-based preachers to British Caribbean and Canada, 157; and disestablishment of Church of England, 153; ending of Canadian ties with, 159; growth of, 152–53, 167; jurisdiction of, 153–54; in Northwest Territory, 165–66; organization of, 151–52, 154, 156; proslavery compromises in, 168; transnational nature of, abandoned, 168; and Wesley, 151, 152, 153
Methodists/Methodism: abandonment of abolition by, 182, 194n5; American Revolution and divisions among, 153; antislavery, emigration from Virginia to Northwest Territory, 163–66; Independent Methodist Church of Freetown, 162–63; lay preachers in Canada, 160; loyalist, 154; migrations of, during Revolution, 154; as religious threat to Anglican hegemony and political threat to British sovereignty, 157–58; segregated worship services in Canada, 161; slaves owned by, 160; and war between U.S. and Britain, 166; white, in Canada, 154–55, 156–57. *See also* Black Methodists; Dow, Lorenzo; *Essay on the Rights of Man, An* (Dow); Methodist Episcopal Church (MEC)
Mickvé Israel (Curacao), 91–92
Mikveh Israel (Philadelphia), 90, 97–100, 102
Miller, Perry, 11
Minkema, Kenneth, 188, 190, 197n41
missionaries: authenticity of, 69–70; Native Christians as, 71, 72; SPG, 48, 52, 58; SSPCK, 71, 74
Mitre and Sceptre (Bridenbaugh), 9
Monis, Judah, 118, 129n48
Moor's Indian Charity School, 71, 74, 79
Moral Capital (Brown), 184
moral establishment, 5, 6
moral virtue: as beginning with family worship, 201; characteristics of women's, 204; and Christianity, 4–5; and disestablishment, 211; fast days for, 94–95;

moral virtue (*continued*)
as increasingly suggesting civic qualities after Revolution, 209; moral government as necessary to promote, 199; as needed to balance liberty with order, 201; and need for Revolution, 94–95; rather than creedal statements determination of membership in body politic, 99; as universal and required for a republic, 95
Mordecai, Esther Whitlock, 101
Morgan, Edward, 9
Morse, Abel, 121
Morse, Jedidiah: on ability to maintain moral citizenry without religion, 5; and Bavarian Illuminati panic (1790s), 4; building of "moral establishment" by, 5; correspondence with John Adams, 5–6, 24n15; and creation of story of U.S. as Christian nation, 6; "frontier" Methodist and Baptist preachers and post-Revolutionary religious culture, 11; Revolution as providential event, 16
Moses (former slave), 155, 156
Murphy, Kevin, 51
Murray, James, 112
Murray, John, 109, 115, 117, 118–19
Murray, Judith Sargent, 204, 209
Murray, Moses, 162
Murrin, John, 9, 10
Mystery Hid from Ages and Generations (Chauncy), 117, 120

Narragansetts, 74, 75
Nathan, Simon, 97
nationalism and fast days, 94
Native Christians/Christianity: Algonquian communities, 80; authenticity of conversion questioned, 69; diplomatic missions by, 74; increase in number of, 71; as missionaries, 71, 72; ordination of, 73–74, 84n24; practice as part of minutiae of daily life, 70; as schoolteachers, 71–73, 74, 79; as solidifying connections among different tribes, 69, 75–78, 79–80, 82n3; white racial prejudice against, 74. *See also* Brothertown (now Brothertown Indian Nation)
Neptune, H. Reuben, 196n28
neutralists: Anglican clergy as necessarily apolitical by virtue of status as clergymen, 58; and Barton as martyr, 60; failure to choose side during Revolution, 43–44; persecution of, under banner of liberty and providentialism, 37–38; and public rituals, 44–45
New Divinity movement, 120, 187, 188
New England, preaching of universal salvation in, 109, 116, 128n38
New Light congregations, 71
New Version of the Psalm of David, A (Brady and Tate), 114
Nicholas, Mark A., 69, 70
Niles, Samuel, 74, 75
Noll, Mark, 220, 221, 231–32
Northwest Territory, antislavery Methodists emigration to, 163–66
Notes on the State of Virginia (Jefferson), 228, 237n53

oaths: of allegiance to the Crown prior to Revolution, 51; clerical exemption, 58; and conscientious objection, 50, 54; as contract with God, 18, 49, 50; justifications for renouncing obsolete, 50–51; moral capacity to take, 57, 60; and Puritans, 50; and Quakers, 50, 56; religious requirement as part of holding office, 99–100; taken upon ordination of Anglican clergy, 51, 53–55; test, in South, 101. *See also* loyalty oaths
Observations on Universal Salvation: Teach Not for Doctrine the Vain Traditions of Men (anon), 121
Occom, Samson: on authenticity of missionaries, 69–70; and Brothertown, 77, 79; and formation of Brothertown, 69; fundraising campaigns by, 74; God as on side of patriots, 67; as minister Stockbridge, 79; as missionary, 71;

ordination of, 73; promotion of Moor's Indian Charity School by, 74
Occum, Sarah, 71
Oneida, 75–77, 78
Orsi, Robert, 14

Paine, Thomas, 219–20; Christian aesthetics in writings by, 231; and Dow's *An Essay on the Rights of Man*, 220, 221–22, 225, 227, 231; foundational ideas of writings of, 222–23; and Quakers, 38; and religion, 224; reputation of, 222; slavery and writings of, 232. See also *Rights of Man* (Paine)
Palmer, R. R., 13
Park, Joseph, 75
Parkinson, Robert, 13
patriarchal authority: change in language of, after revolution, 209; exercised through benevolent leadership, 201, 202; exercised through example, 203; and family governance, 201; family worship as elevating, 202; family worship as preserving, 203, 206; and genteel mastery of slaves, 206; as matter of custom and law, 202; and need to balance mastery and dependence, 201; as part of citizenship, 201–2; promotion of godliness to reverse collapse of, 200; women's role in maintaining, 203–4
patriots: antislavery Methodists emigration to Northwest Territory, 163–66; Chauncy, 110, 112–13; Jews as, 90, 92, 93, 94, 95–96, 97–99, 100; leading, in Boston, 110–11; John Murray, 115
Pattillo, Henry, 206, 208, 210
Pearsall, Sarah, 80
Pelham, Peter, 165
Pennsylvania: loyalty oaths and SPG missionaries in, 48, 52; Test Act, 55–56, 57–60, 61, 65n44; test oath for holding office requiring belief in Christianity, 99–100. *See also* Philadelphia
Pestana, Carla, 12
Peters, Mary Doxtator, 72
Philadelphia: change in Anglican liturgy in, 40–42; fast day participation in, 37–38; loyalty oaths and Anglican clergy, 52; Mikveh Israel synagogue community, 90, 97–99
Phillips, Jonas, 88, 97
Pinto, Rachel, 96
Piscataqua Evangelical Magazine, 201, 208–9
political allegiance: expansion of, into religious structure, 90, 97; fast days as signals of, 33, 36–37; and fealty of preexisting oaths, 51; moral virtue rather than creedal statements determination of, 99; oaths as effective guarantees of, 50; religious implications of, 60–61; and synagogue divisions, 95, 96–97, 206n48
politics: clergy as active in, 35; of declaring fast days, 17, 34–35, 94; factors in choosing side during Revolution, 42–43; failure to choose side during Revolution, 43–44; public rituals and tenable middle ground, 44–45; and Quakers in Philadelphia, 38
Porterfield, Amanda, 221, 222, 223, 228, 230
"Port Jews," 91, 104n21
Presbyterians/Presbyterian Church, 73, 195n5
Preston, Thomas, 112
Price, Richard, 115, 119, 128n47, 130n53
Price, Thomas, 43
Prince, Thomas, 120
Proclamation Line of 1763, 68
Protestant Episcopal Church, 139, 142
Protestants/Protestantism: "Christian slavery," 174; conflation of religion with, in histories of Revolution, 8; as doing essential national work for revolution, 10; founders as, 6–7; investment of Americans in Britain's, empire just before Revolution, 12–13, 27n36; New Divinity movement, 120, 187, 188; remaking of American, as unleashed by Revolution, 220–21; restrictions on

Protestants/Protestantism (*continued*)
dissenting, in Virginia, 134; revelation of God's will in polity built on virtue, 199; scaffolding of, in Britain, 92; sincerity in conversion to, 69; and slave manumission versus security, 183; as way populace explained world, 10; worship as necessary for ethical, moral families and state, 211. *See also* missionaries; Native Christians/Christianity
Proudfit, Alexander, 208
public rituals, 44–45. *See also* fast days; loyalty oaths
Puritans, 50, 69

Quakers: and abolition, 184–85, 190; and Bradford, 128n41; and fast day participation in Philadelphia, 37–38; and incorporation of freed slaves in American life, 190; and oaths, 50, 56; and Paine, 38; in Virginia, 134
Quinney, Electa, 72

Rabin, Shari, 103n6, 107n73
race/racism: and citizenship, 107n73; of evangelicals, 185, 187, 188, 190–91; against Native Christians, 74
"Recentering Indian Women in the American Revolution" (Pearsall), 80
Reflections on Death (Dodd), 114
religion(s): and ability to maintain moral citizenry, 4–5, 95; American population as unified in, 10; colonial America as period of decline of, 7; "common cause" rhetoric as vilifying dissenters, 38; conflation with Protestant churches in histories of Revolution, 8; conflict in late colonial, as cause of social changes necessary for revolution, 10–11; discrimination in Virginia, 91; family worship as foundation of practical, 202–3; of founders, 30n48; and French Revolution, 224; God as having covenant with American people, 7; God as on side of patriots, 67; importance of, in era of Revolution, 3–4, 11–12, 16, 30n48; as largely peripheral to causes of Revolution, 14; need for distinctively American style of worship, 207; ongoing, dynamic relationship with realities of everyday life of, 14; persecution of dissenters under banner of liberty and providentialism, 37–38; and political allegiance, 60–61, 99; and post-Revolution political rights, 89; revealed, 93; Revolution as "unfavorable" for, 7; rhetoric of Revolution as resource for early national, 231–32; rift between American and English, as cause of Revolution, 6; role in public policy of, 1; taking oaths as acts of, 18, 49, 50
Religion and the American Mind (Heimert), 9
Religion in a Revolutionary Age (Hoffman and Albert), 12
religious freedom: and Barton, 48–49, 58–60; Declaration of Rights in 1776 Maryland and Virginia constitutions as decrees for, 138–39; as dependent on goodwill of state, 137–38; freedom of conscience distinguished from free exercise, 135; as fundamental to Revolution, 131, 132–33; Madison's *Memorial and Remonstrance*, 140; refusal to take loyalty oaths as persecution, 48–49, 51; toleration as, after Glorious Revolution in England, 133; toleration as, in Revolutionary Maryland, 137–38; use of term "dissenting" faiths in laws, 137. *See also* disestablishment
religious printing: booksellers' role in, 113; by Chauncy, 109, 110; without conventional print intermediaries, 115, 127n28; in England, 110, 119–20; and exodus of printers from Boston, 114; guides for family worship, 202, 207–8; Hebrew and Greek typefaces, 118, 129n48; and increasing availability of printers, 121, 130n60; independent of urban printers,

112, 125n13; manuscript publication defined, 127n28; publication gap of Universalists during Revolution, 111; resurgence of, in Boston after Revolution, 109, 117; and secularization of printing press, 139n59; and shifting relationship between religious communities and printers, 111–12, 124n11
Relly, James, 129n43
republican Christianity, 200
republican womanhood, ideology of, 203–4
revivalism: Chauncy's opposition to, 109–10; and doctrine of "fortunate fall," 177; and Dow, 224; Great Awakening, 9, 25n23, 75, 76, 134; and persecution, 57
Rezneck, Marcus, 96
Rhode Island, 188
Rights of Man (Paine): dedication to Washington, 226; as defense of French Revolution, 223, 226; and disestablishment, 228; fallout from, 223; natural rights of man in, 227; popularity of, 223; purpose of Dow's co-opting of rhetoric of, 219–20; toleration as form of despotism in, 228; use of biblical language in, 231. See also *Essay on the Rights of Man, An* (Dow)
Rodeph Shalom, 102
Rush, Benjamin, 96

Salvation for All Men Strictly Examined (Chauncy), 109, 117, 118–19, 128n43
Salvation of All Men Strictly, The (Edwards, Jr.), 120–21
Samuel, Rebecca, 88, 89
Sargent, Judith, 115, 117
Sarna, Jonathan, 104n13
Sassamon, John, 71
scaffolding, 92
Scanlon, Padraic, 193n2
schoolteachers, Native Christians as, 72–73, 74, 79
Scott, James C., 69
Seabury, Samuel, 36–37, 39
Seasonable Thoughts on the State of Religion in New England (Chauncy), 109–10
secular, use of term, 22n2
Sehat, David, 5
Seixas, Benjamin, 97
Seixas, Gershom: and American Judaism, 100, 103n6; basic facts about, 93; deist approach to religion of, 93–94; and fast days, 94; and full Jewish rights, 90; and Jews and citizenship, 99; as patriot, 93, 94, 95; and Pennsylvania's test oath for holding office requiring belief in Christianity, 99–100
Seixas, Rachel, 97
Semple, Robert, 131
Sergeant, John, 69
Sewall, Joseph, 208
Sharp, Granville, 184, 191
Shearith Israel (New York), 92, 93, 95, 96–97, 100, 206n48
Sierra Leone, 161–63, 166–67
Silverman, David, 15
Simon, Daniel, 79, 96
Simson, Joseph, 92
Sinha, Manisha, 184, 188
slaves/slavery: and audience for first publication of *An Essay on the Rights of Man*, 21, 223, 225, 232, 234, 237nn47–48; brought to Canada, 160; compatibility of Christianity with, 176; conversion of, as moral duty of slaveholders, 179–80; Declaration of Independence as subversive to institution of, 185–86; as decreed by Providence, 233; and disestablishment, 143; as distinct from trade in, 233; and Dow, 232–33; emigration of Virginia Methodists opposed to, 163–66; evangelicals' acquiescence to economic, social, and political exigency in complicity with, 183, 192, 196n27; evangelicals' amelioration response to, 178–83; evangelicals' rationalization response to, 175–77;

slaves/slavery (*continued*)
evangelicals' separation of spiritual needs from physical needs of, 176, 177, 179, 181, 206; fears of revolt by, in historiography of Revolution, 13; freedom for, in Virginia joining British army during Revolution, 155–56; genteel mastery of, 206; Haitian Revolution, 234; and heathenism, 175, 178; inclusion in family worship of, 205–6; and MEC, 154, 168; as necessary for cultural advancement, 178; and New Light Presbyterians, 195n5; owned by Methodists, 160; and Paine's writings, 232; relationship with capitalism of, 184, 196n28; removal of condemnation of, from Declaration of Independence, 186, 191; spiritual salvation as justifying, 176, 182; trade in, as focus of evangelical abolition, 184; trope of grateful, 183. *See also* abolition; evangelical abolition
Snowball, Nathaniel, 162
Society for the Propagation of the Gospel (SPG), 48, 52, 58
Society in Scotland for Propagating Christian Knowledge (SSPCK), 71, 74
Society of Friends. *See* Quakers
Solomon, Haym, 89
Some Considerations on the Keeping of Negroes (Woolman), 185
Some Deductions from the System Promulgated in the Page of Divine Revelations (Sargent), 115, 117
Some Remarks on a Pamphlet Intituled All Men Will Not Be Saved for Ever (Townsend), 118
Sons of the American Revolution (SAR), 21
Spangler, Jewel, 194n5
Stanwood, Owen, 12
Statute for Religious Freedom (1786, Virginia), 141
Stevens, John, 115
Stiles, Ezra, 38–39, 115
Stockbridge (now Stockbridge-Munsee Band of Mohicans): Brothertown connections, 78, 79–80; founding of, 69; Native women schoolteachers, 72–73; and Oneida, 78; production of cloth by women of, 72, 83n22; westward migration of, 69; white settlers in, 78
Story, Joseph, 8
Stout, Harry, 9, 188, 190, 197n41
Strauch, Tara, 61
Stuyvesant, Peter, 91
Sullivan, Aaron, 56
survivance strategies, 68, 80
synagogue(s): in Caribbean, 91–93, 100; and Jews' post-Revolution approach to religious institutional life, 88–89, 100, 103n6; leadership in hands of congregation, 101–2, 108n92; Mikveh Israel (Philadelphia), 90, 97–100, 102; number of, during Revolution, 92; political divisions in, 95, 96–97, 206n48; post-Revolution splits in, 102; power of, 91–92; Rodeph Shalom, 102; Shearith Israel (New York), 92, 93, 95, 96–97, 100, 206n48; as totally religious institutions, 102; as vehicle of religious choice, 90

Tate, N., 114
Tawler, James, 165
Test Act (Pennsylvania, 1777), 55–56, 57–60, 61, 65n44
Thayer, Ebenezer, 203, 204, 208
Thoughts upon Slavery (Wesley), 186
Tiffin, Edward, 165
Tillotson, John, 50
Totten, John, 225
Touro, Isaac, 206n48
Townsend, Shippie, 118
Transformation of Virginia (Isaac), 10–11
Triumph of Infidelity, The (T. Dwight, IV), 121
Trumbull, John, 117, 128n42
Trust in God, The Duty of a People in a Day of Trouble (Chauncy), 112–13
Turnbull, Gordon, 178

United States: creation of story of, as Christian nation, 6; family as building block of, 201, 202, 206, 210–11; family worship as necessary for salvation of new, 200; godly polity intertwining providentialism, republicanism, and moral government as necessary to promote virtue, 199; need to balance liberty with order, 201; patriarchal authority as necessary for success of, 200; political language changes after Revolution in religious tracts, 208–11; public opinion about, as Christian nation, 1–2; threats perceived upon independence to, 199
Universalists/Universalism: earliest publications of, 115; first convention of, 115; gospel of salvation of all, 109; growth of, 117; publication gap of, during Revolution, 111; publication of views of, without conventional print intermediaries, 115, 127n28; spread of gospel of salvation of all, 116, 117–21, 128n38, 129n44, 129n47

Vasey, Thomas, 151
Vermont, 188
vinig yidishkayt, 89, 91
Virginia: ambiguous position of established religion in (1776–1783), 132; Baptists in Revolutionary, 138; change in Anglican liturgy in, 40; Church of England as essential bodies of local government in, 133; Church of England as established religion in, 133; Declaration of Rights in 1776 constitution, 134–35, 138–40, 141; disestablishment process in, 11; established church as "ecclesiastical tyranny" in, 142–43; freedom for slaves in, joining British army during Revolution, 155–56; and Great Awakening, 134; heathenism among whites in, 195n10; "hereditary heathenism" in, 175; marriage law changes during Revolution, 137; penalties and restrictions placed on non-Anglicans in, 133–34; proposed tax to support of teachers of Christian religion in, 140–41, 145; religious discrimination in, 91; Statute for Religious Freedom, 141
virtue. *See* moral virtue
Vizenor, Gerald, 68

Wadsworth, Benjamin, 209
Wampy, Elijah, 72
Warren (Rhode Island) Baptist Association, 205
Washington, George, 4
Wesley, John: and antislavery movement, 186–87; and Black Methodists, 156; Coke and Asbury's version of *Discipline* by, 157; on MEC and established church in Canada, 157; opposition to Revolution of, 151; and organization of MEC, 151, 152, 153; refusal of to send English preachers to Canada, 158; and slavery, 174–75
West African Methodist Society, 167
Whatcoat, Richard, 151
Wheatley, Phillis, 188
Wheeler, Rachel, 15
Wheelock, Eleazar, 69, 70, 71, 73
Wheelock, John, 70
White, William, 42
Whitefield, George: and doctrine of "fortunate fall," 179; and family worship rhetoric, 208, 209, 210; opposition to, 109–10, 122n3; and Quaker anti-slavery arguments, 185; and rationalization of slavery, 177
Wilberforce, William, 184
Wilkinson, Moses, 161
Williams, Eleazar, 73
Williams, Eric, 184, 196n28
Winchester, Elhanan, 109, 119
Witherspoon, John, 94–95
women: and adoption of citizenship by Brothertown, 80; ideology of republican womanhood, 203–4; Jewish, 101; moral Christian, versus sinful, 204;

women (*continued*)
mother's role in family worship, 203–4; Native, as schoolteachers, 72–73; and oath-taking, 57; and religious revivalism, 57; role of, in maintaining patriarchal authority, 203–4; of Stockbridge, 72, 83n22
Wood, Betty, 15
Wood, Gordon, 10
Wooley, Joseph, 71
Woolman, John, 184–85

Zubly, John, 44
Zuntz, Alexander, 96, 101

www.ingramcontent.com/pod-product-compliance
Ingram Content Group UK Ltd.
Pitfield, Milton Keynes, MK11 3LW, UK
UKHW041026070826
474165UK00005B/508